Grey Skies Black Birds

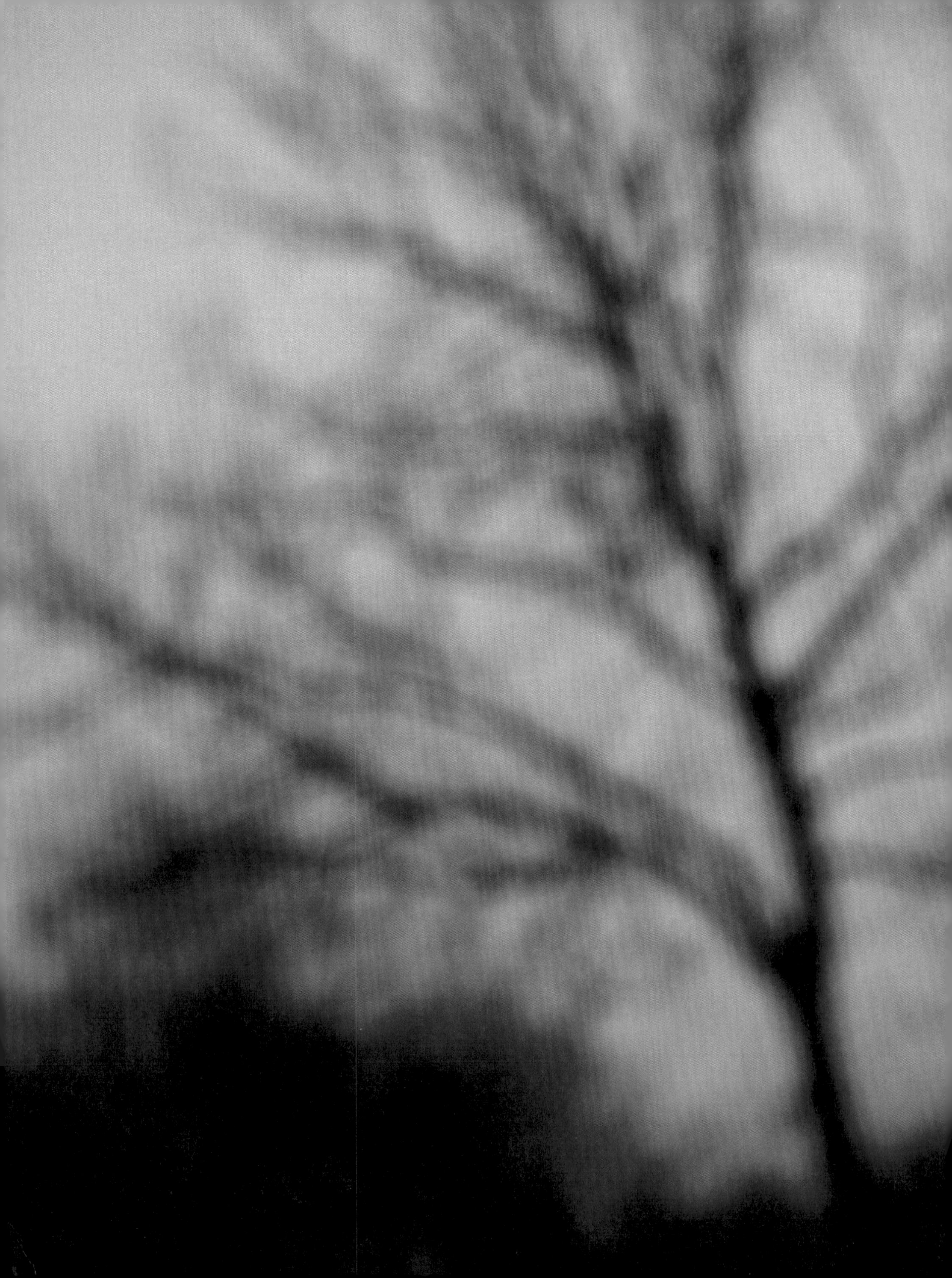

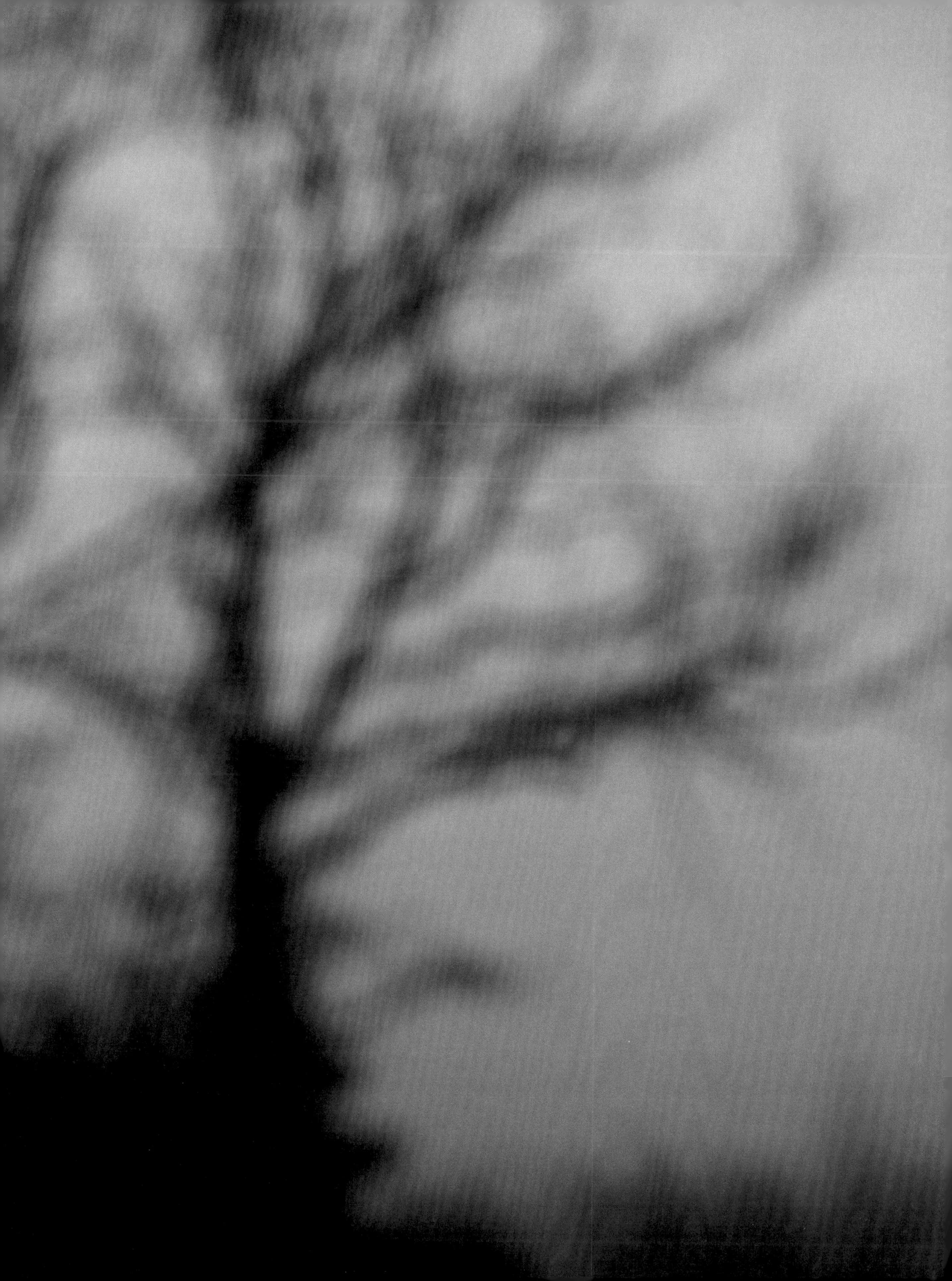

Stéphanie Borcard
Nicolas Métraux

Saša Stanišić
Srećko Latal
Christian Caujolle

Grey Skies Black Birds

GOST

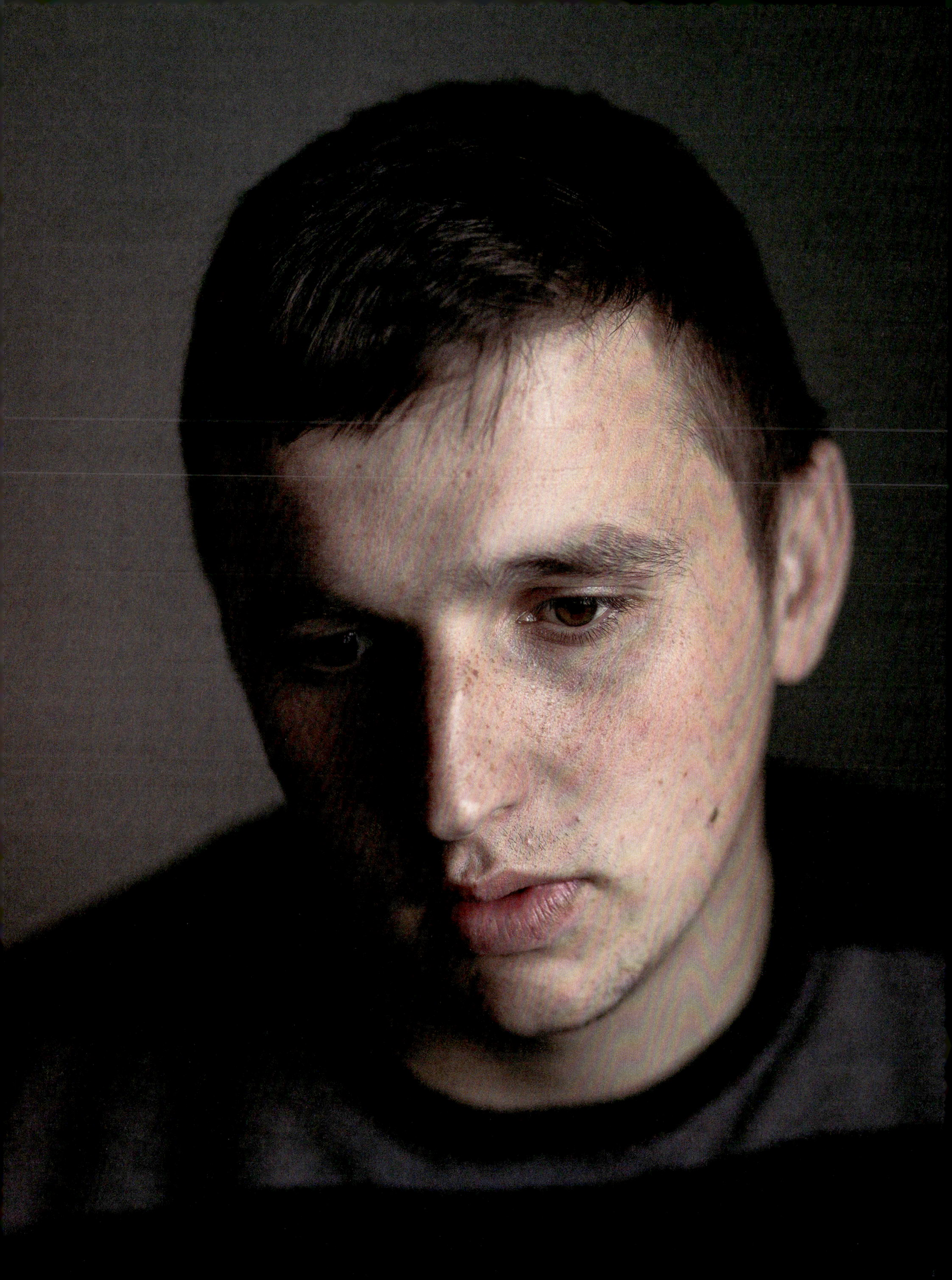

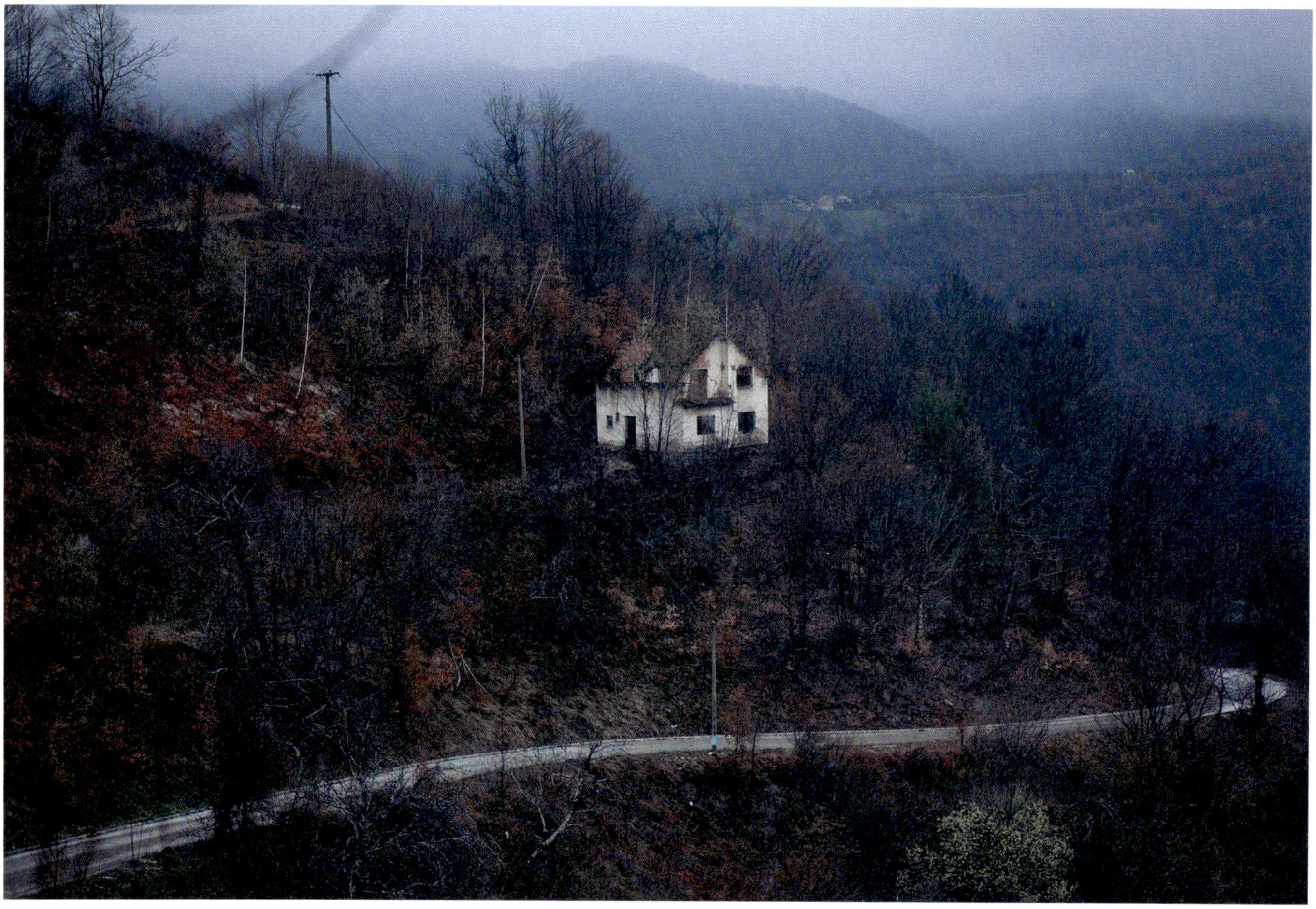

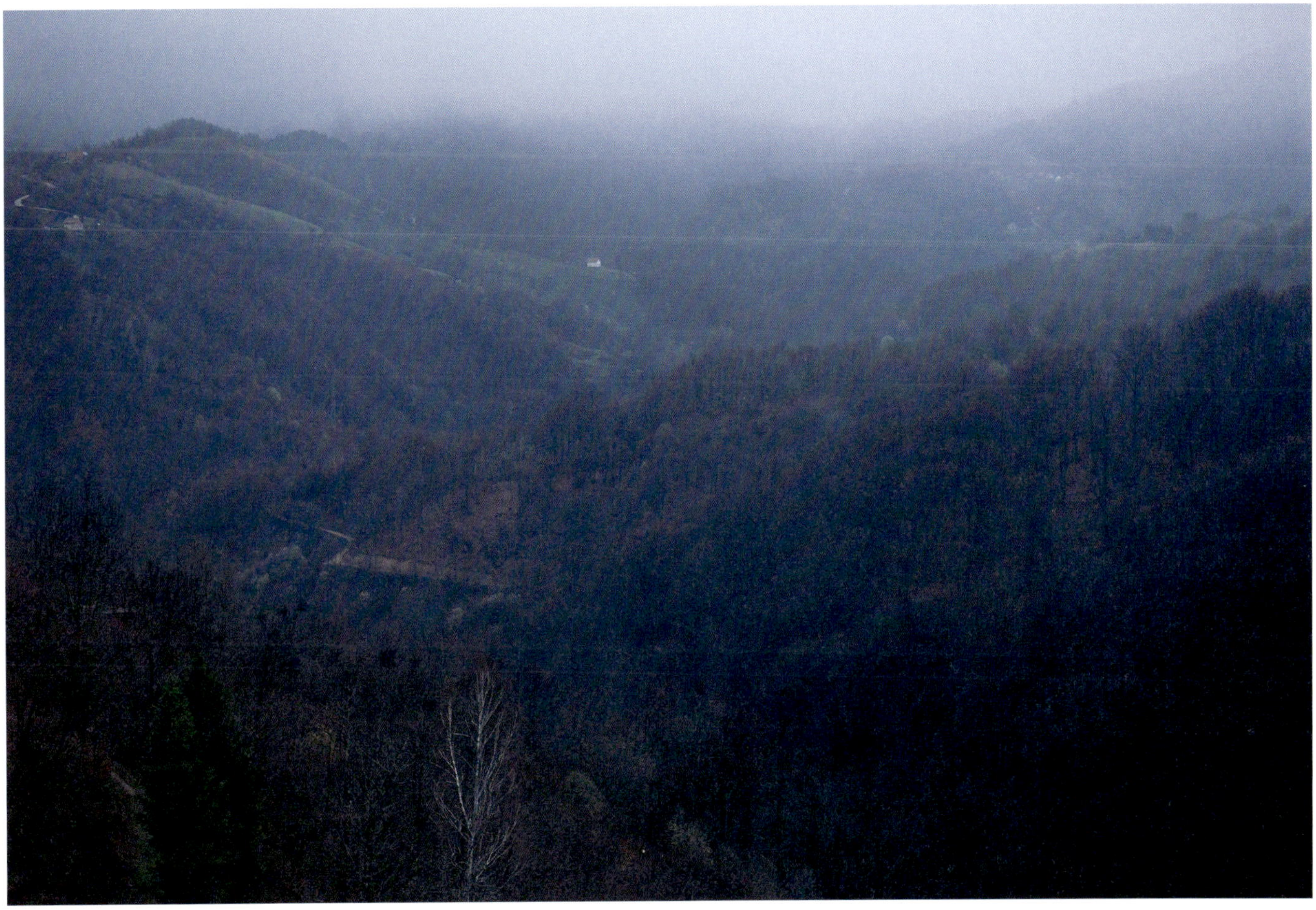

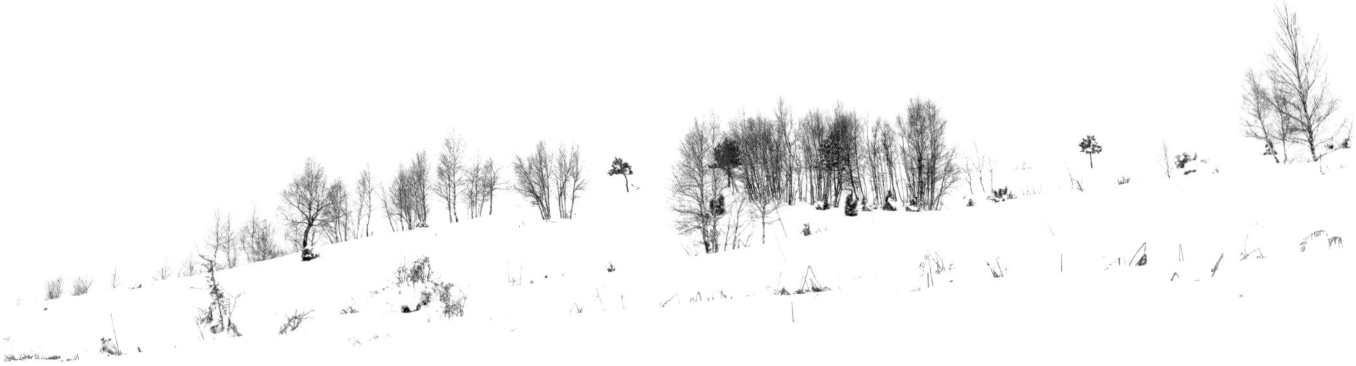

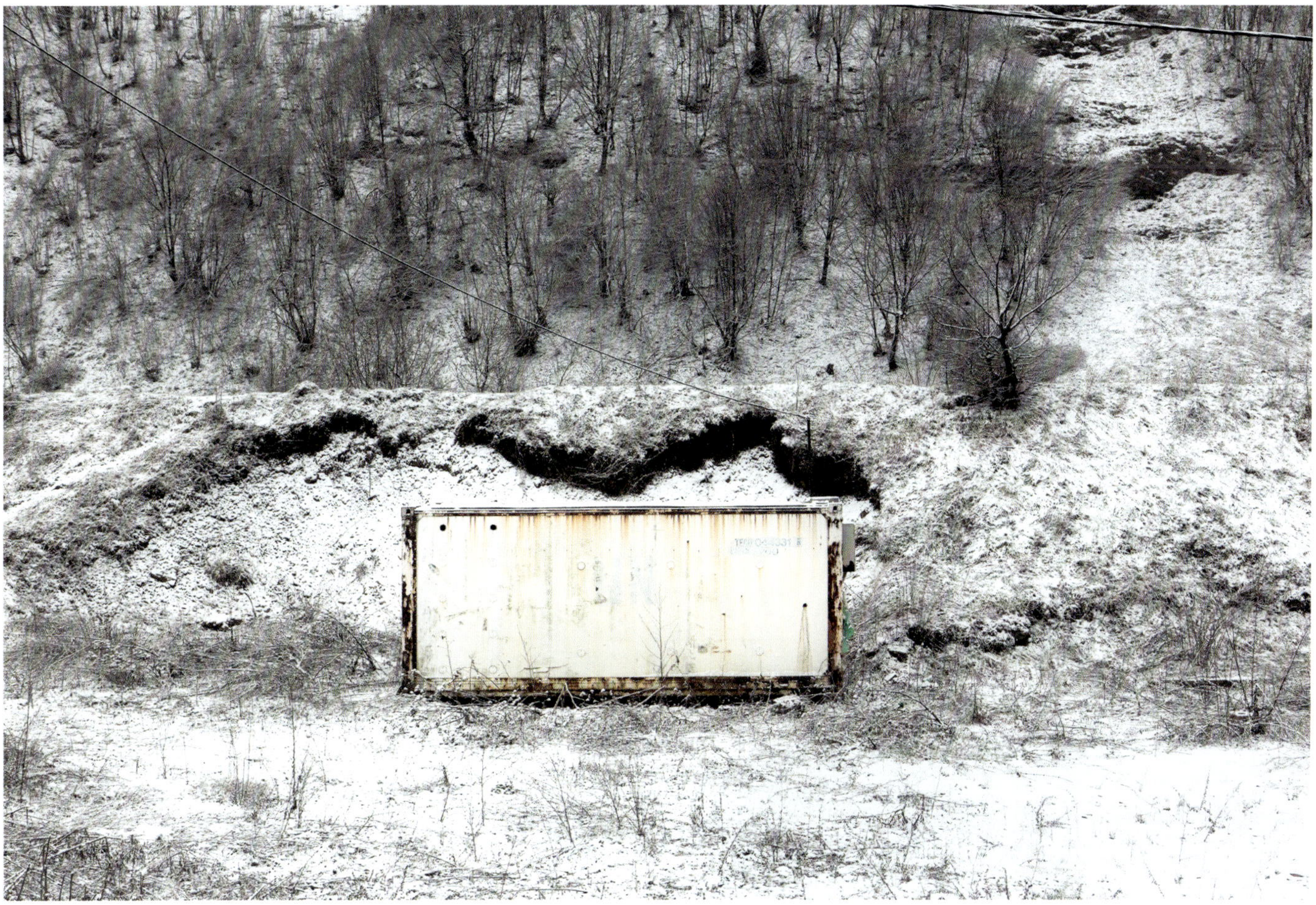

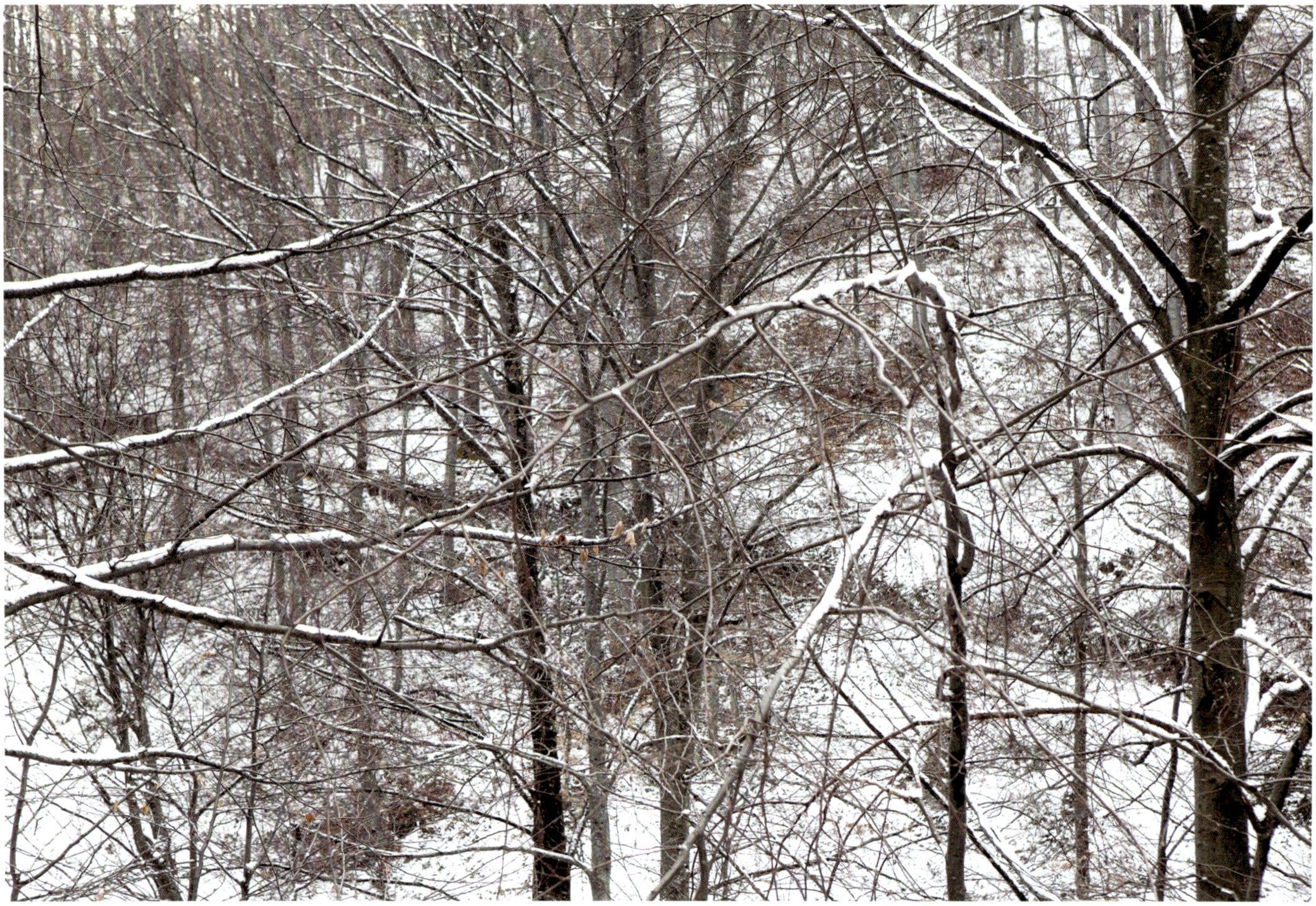

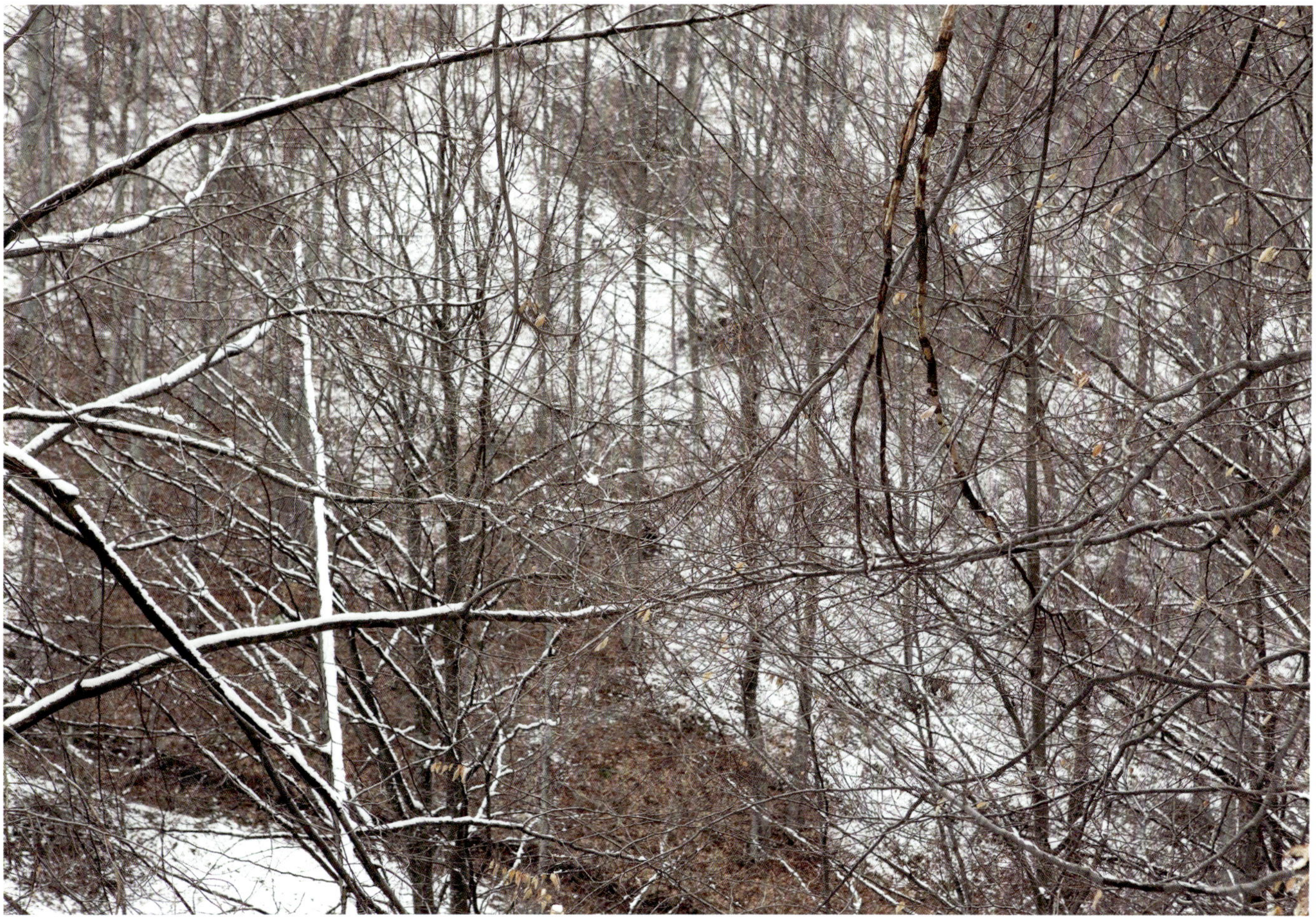

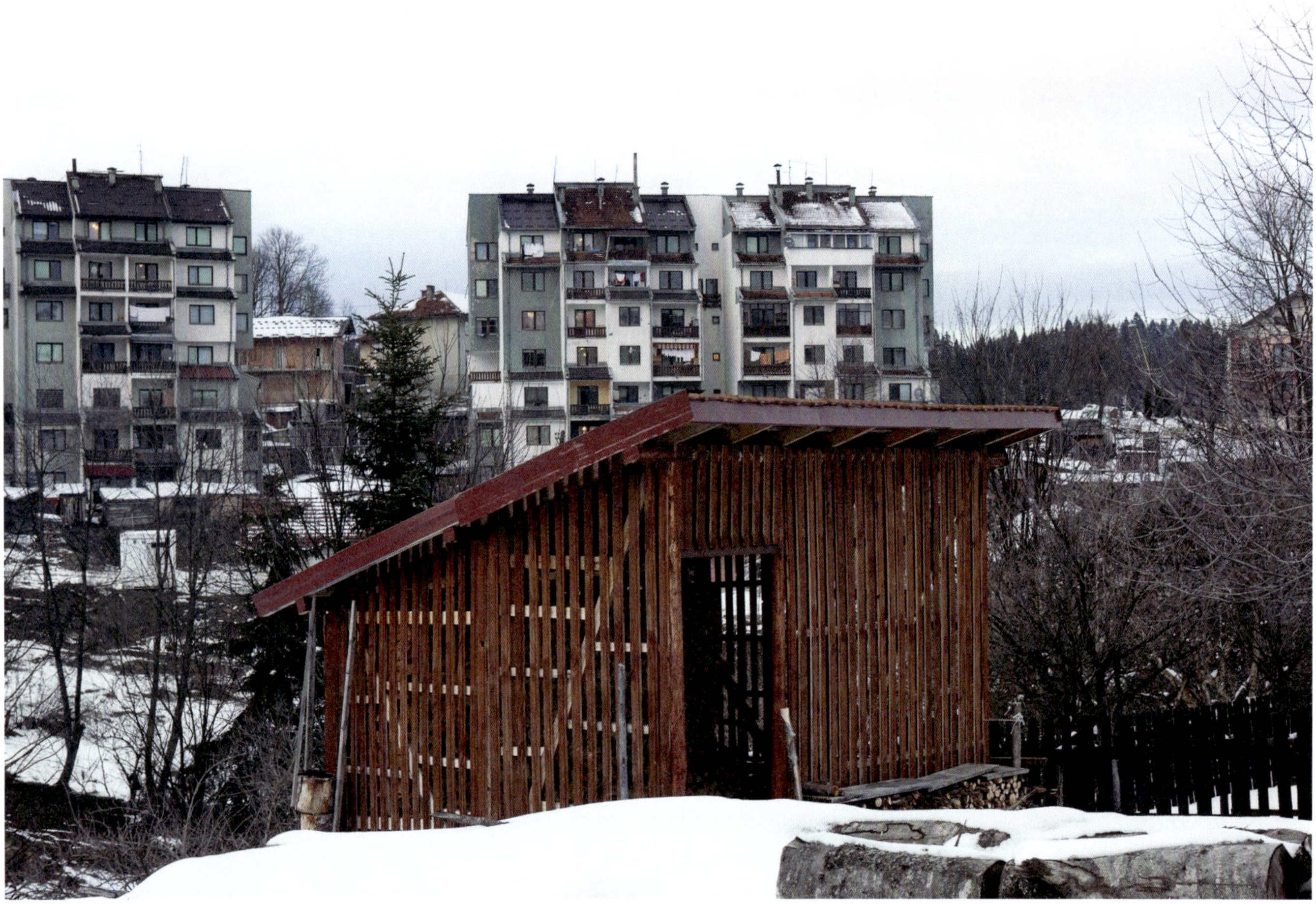

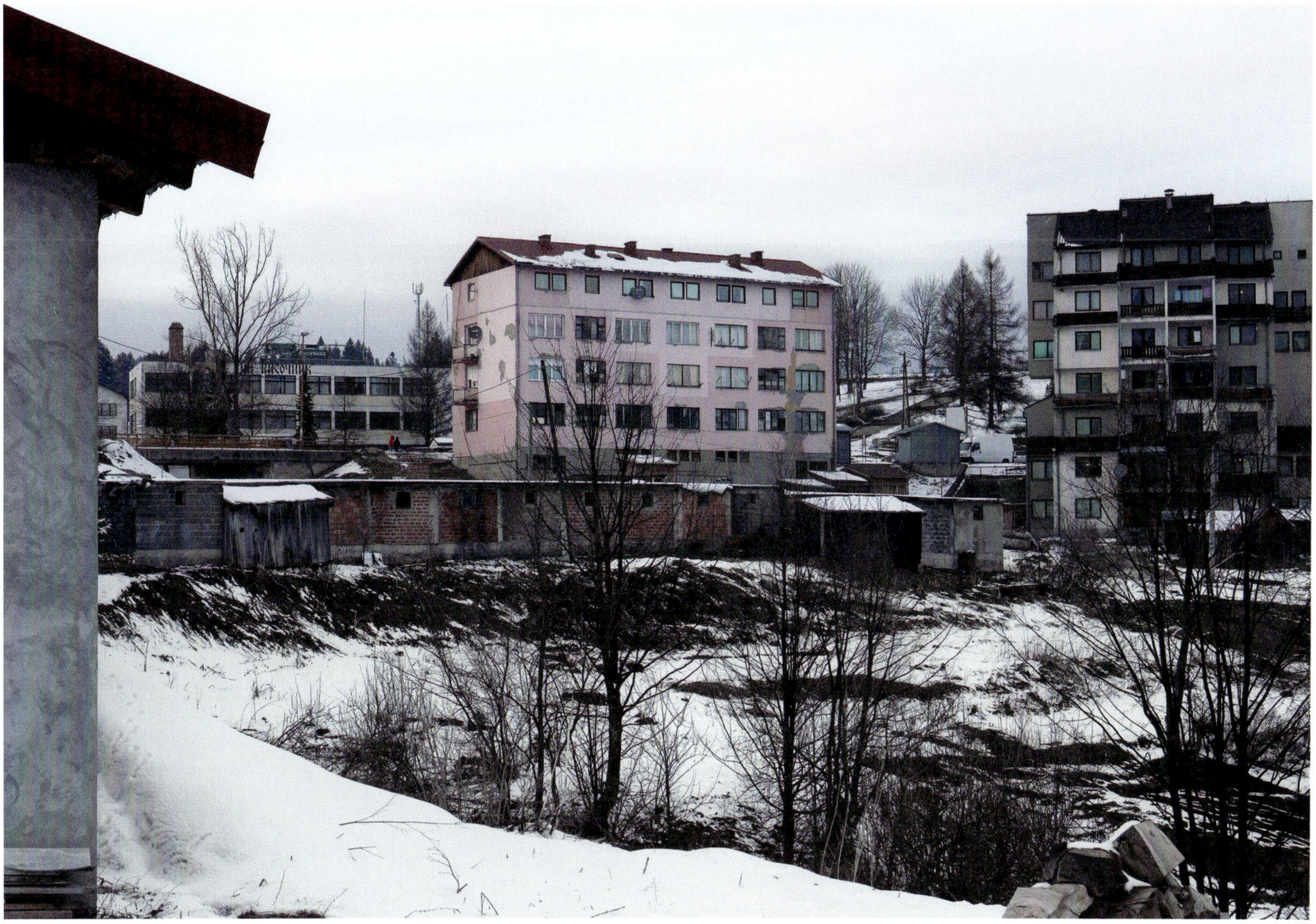

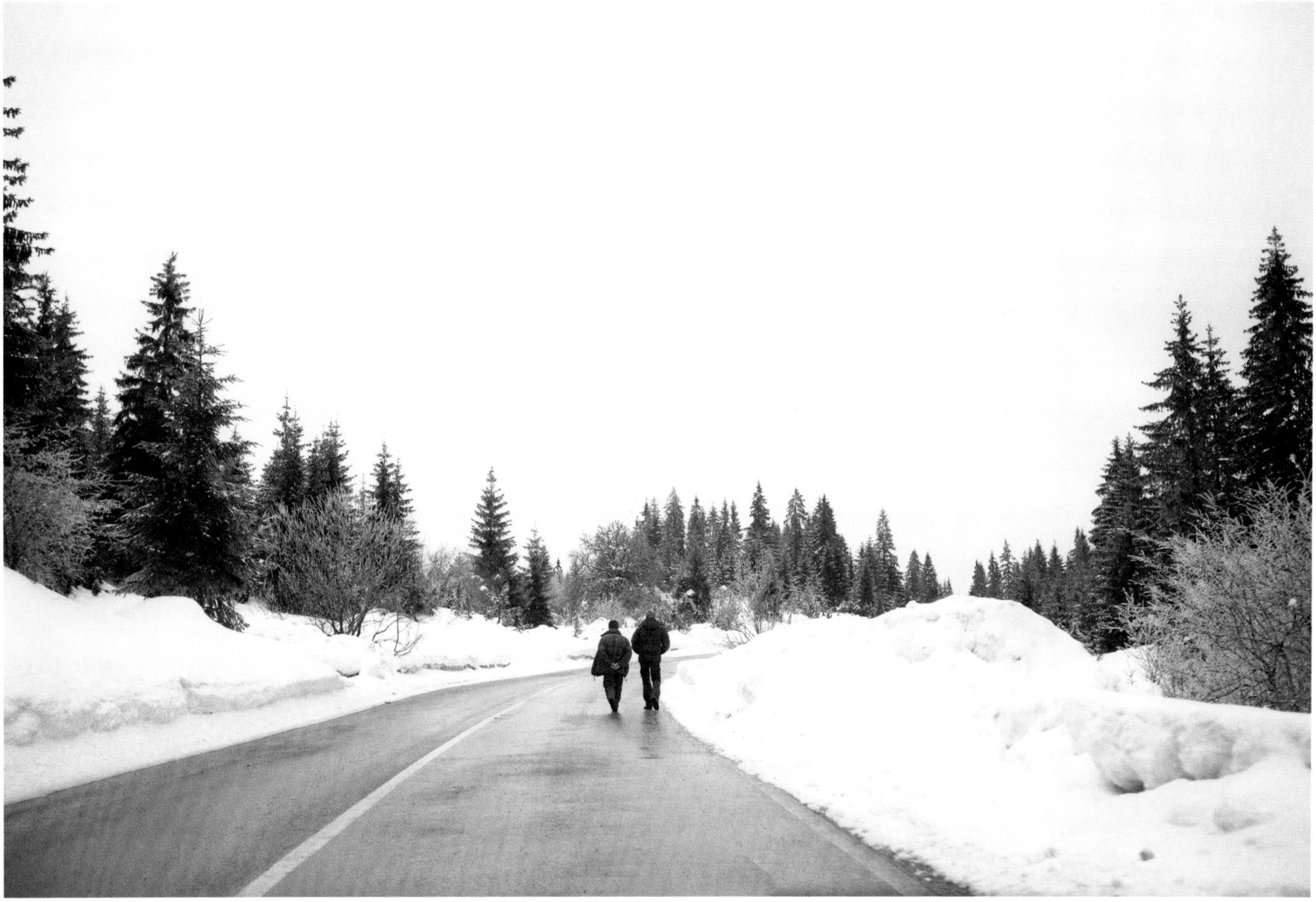

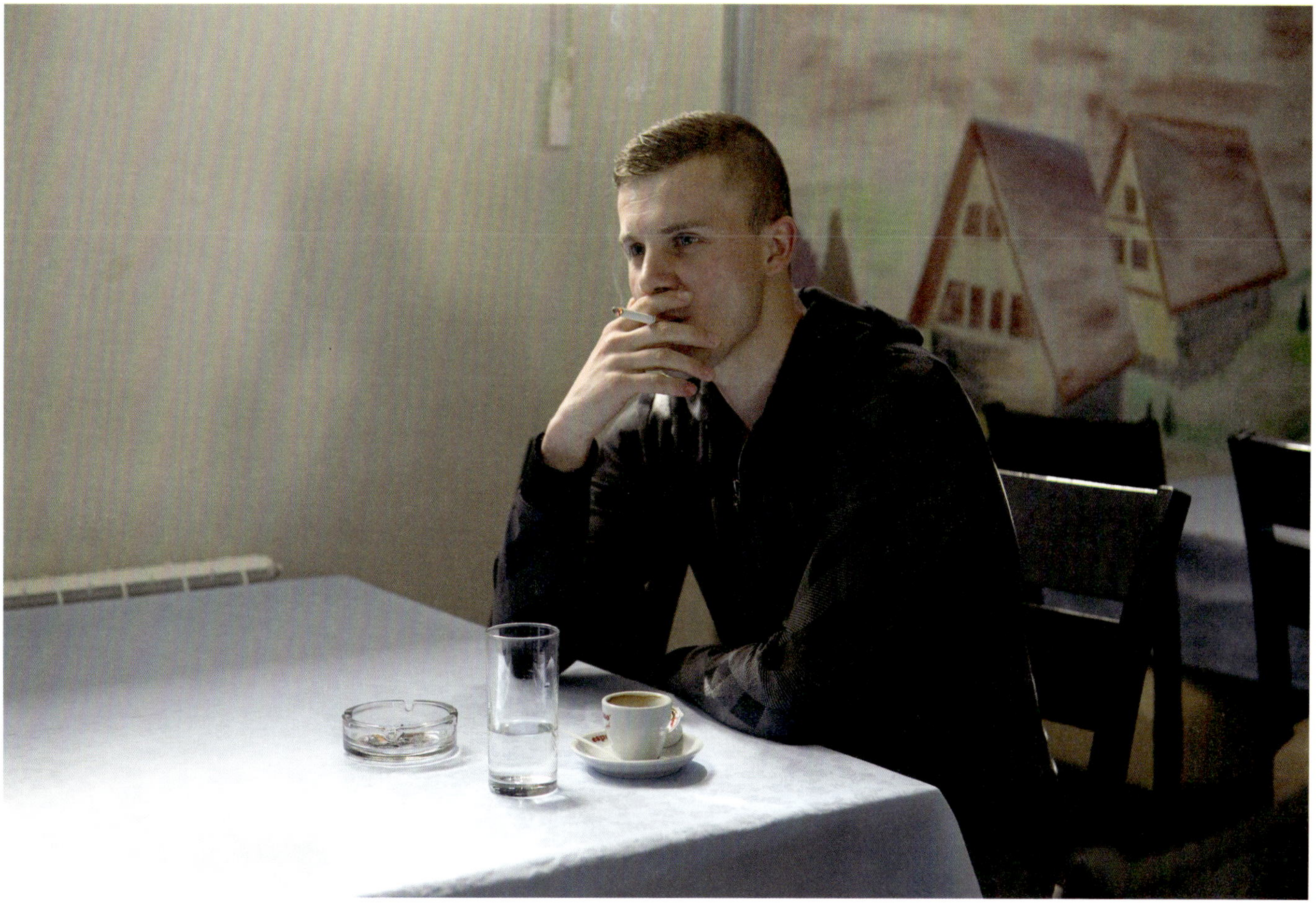

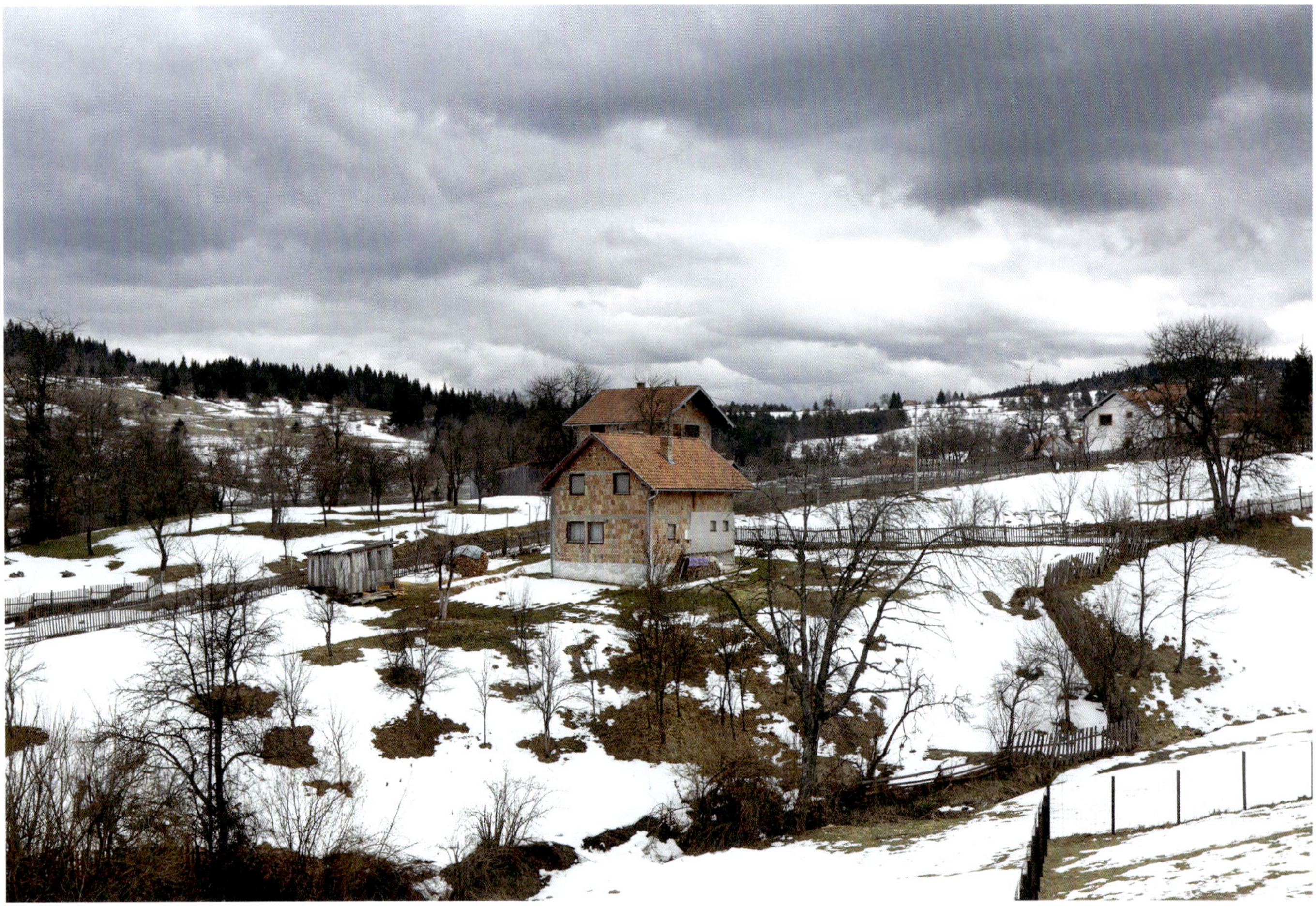

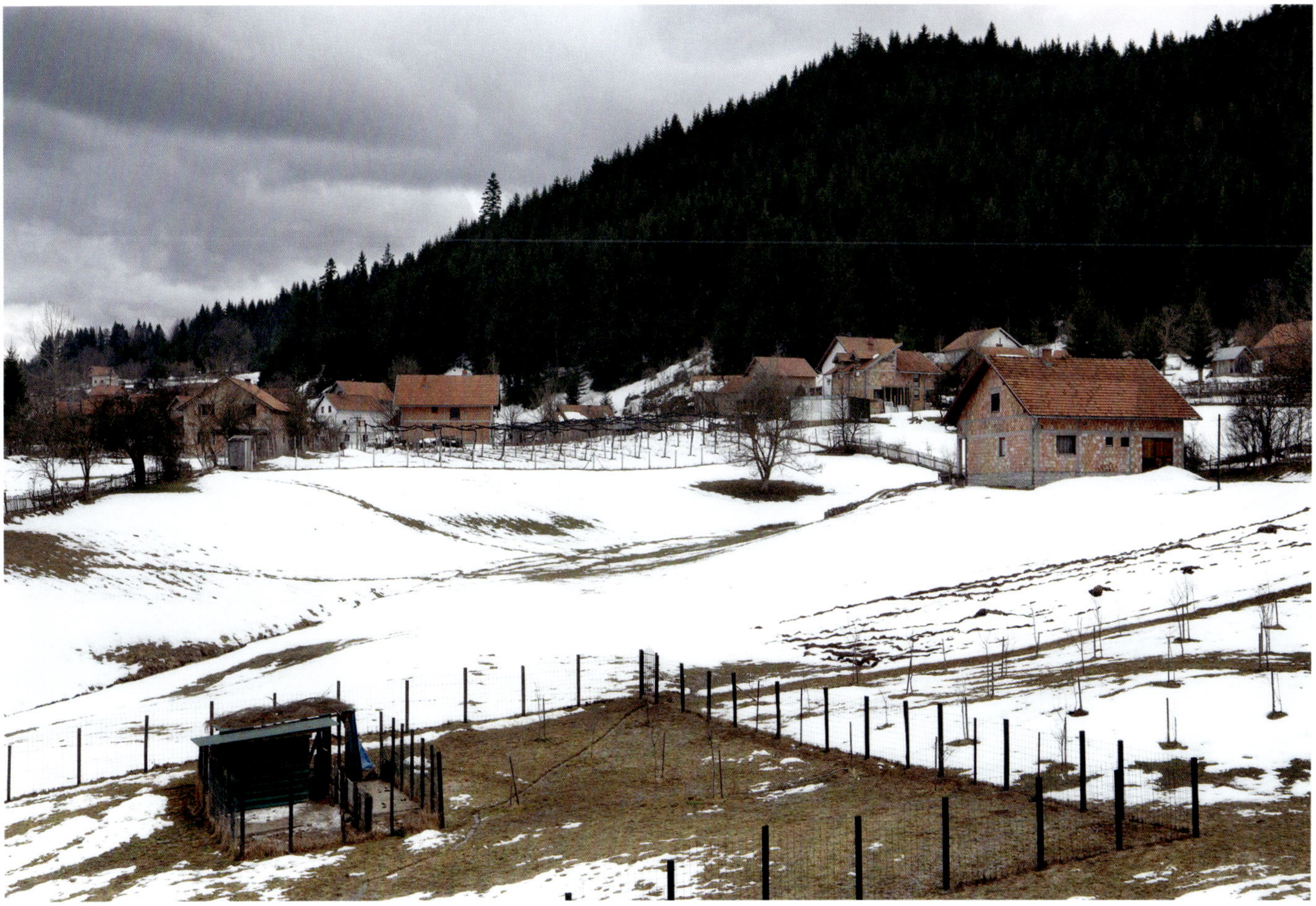

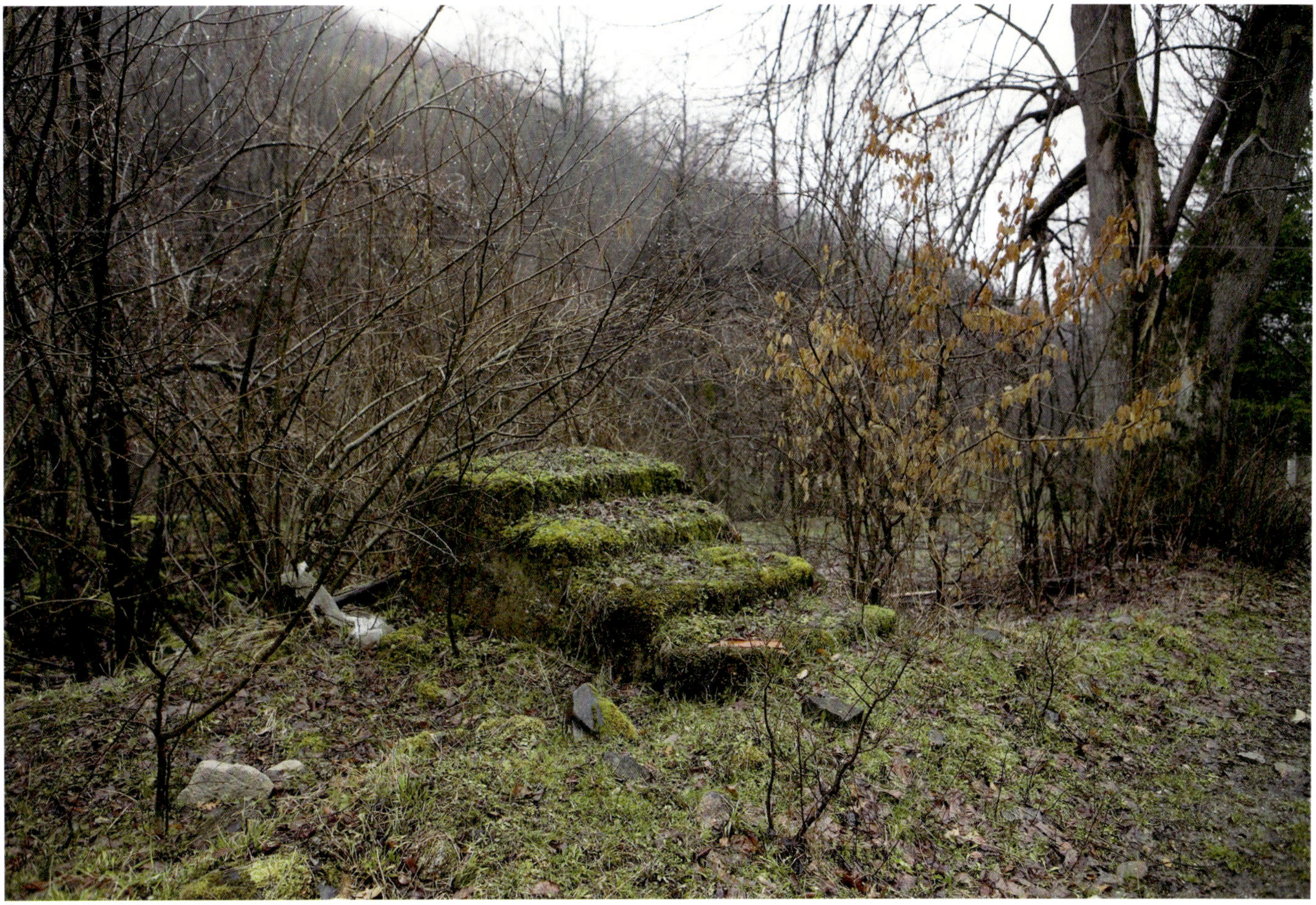

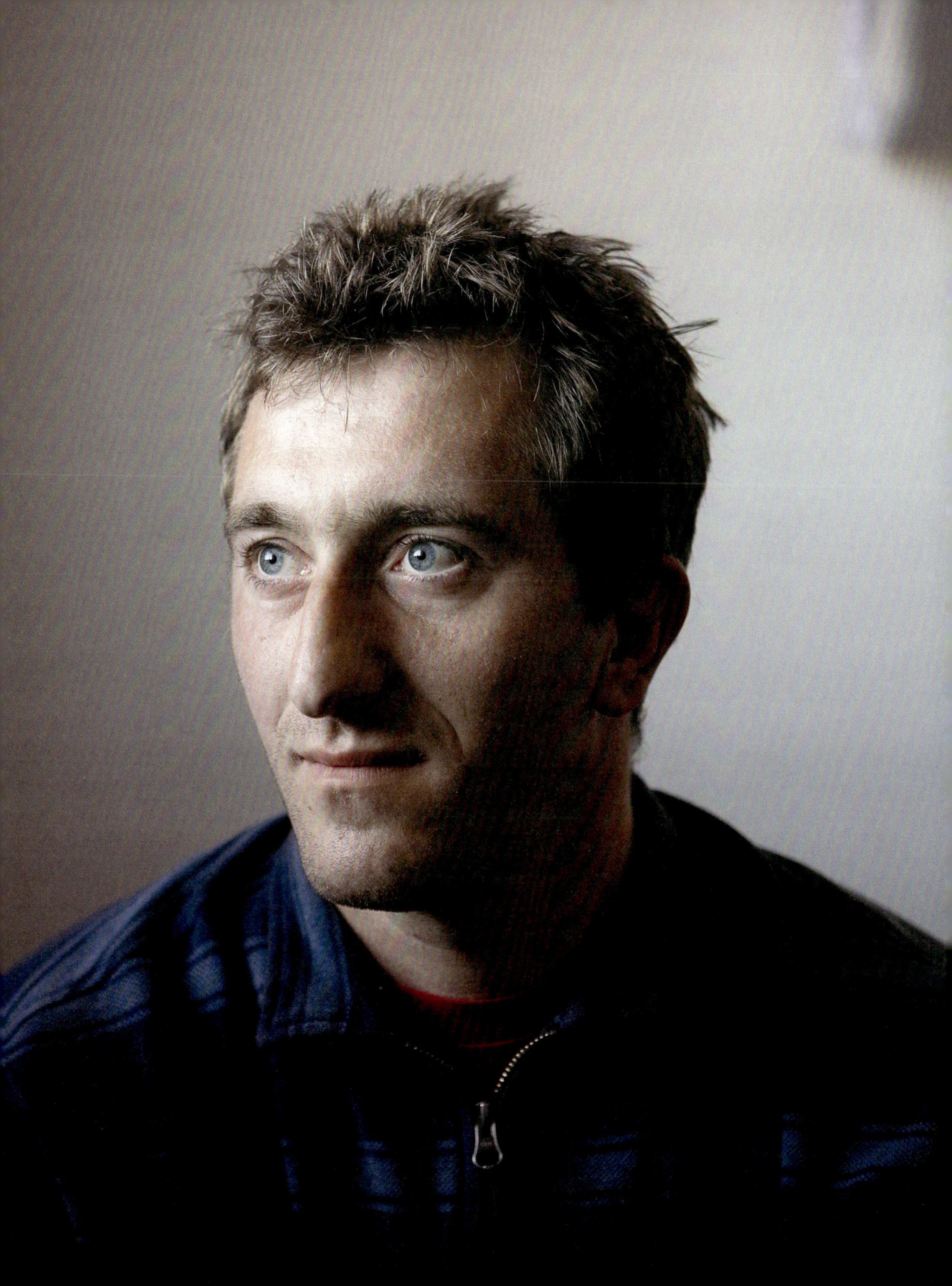

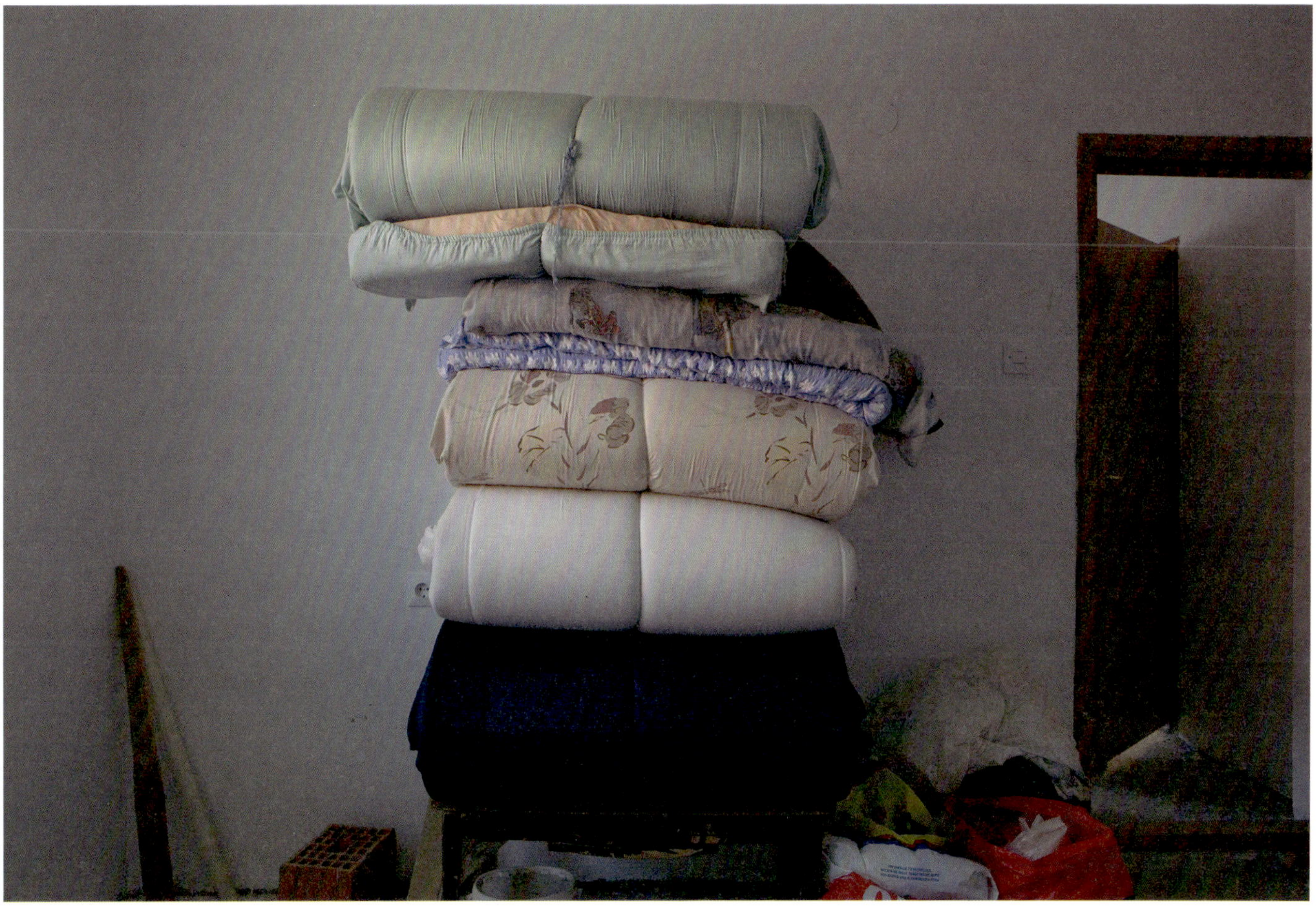

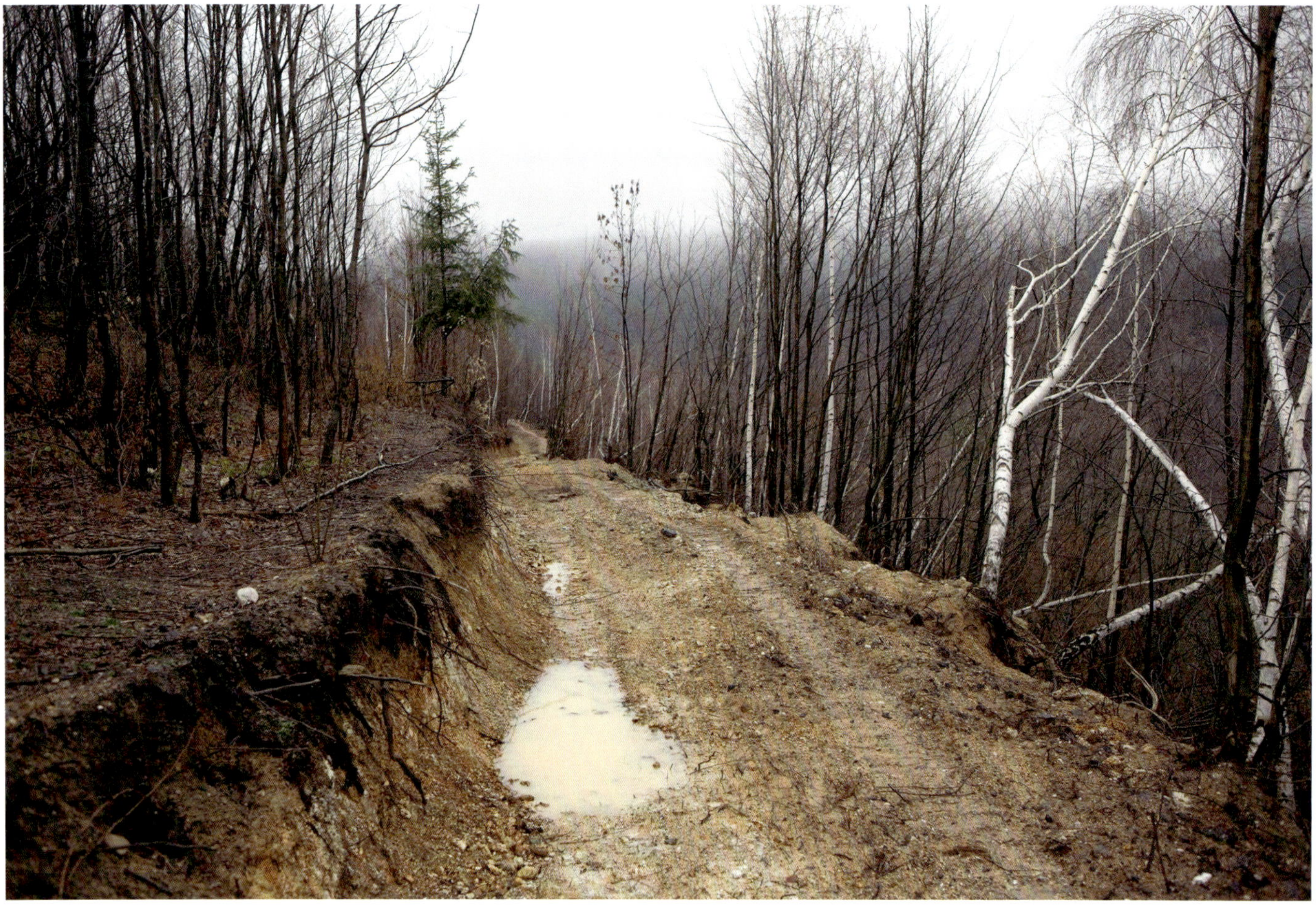

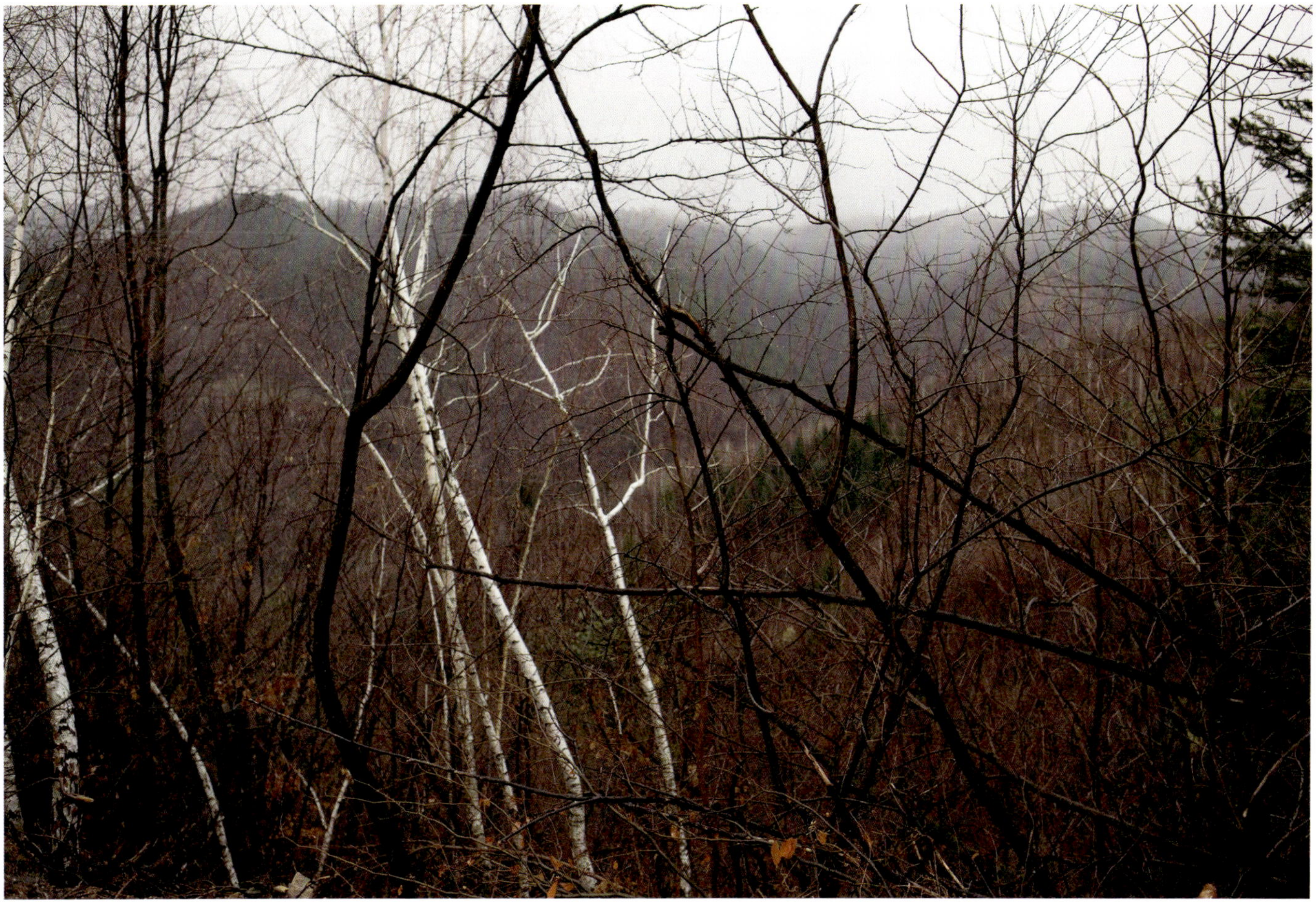

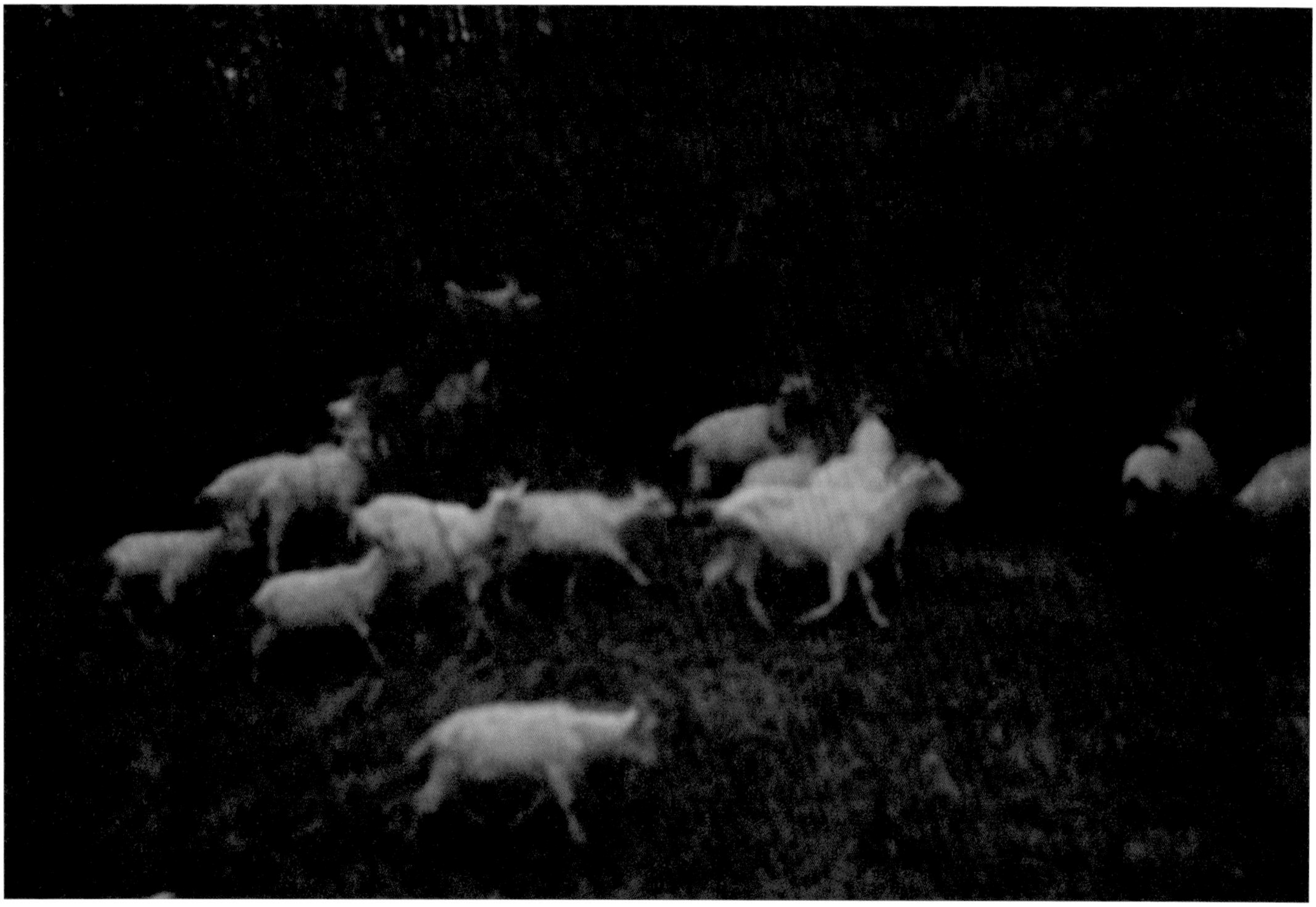

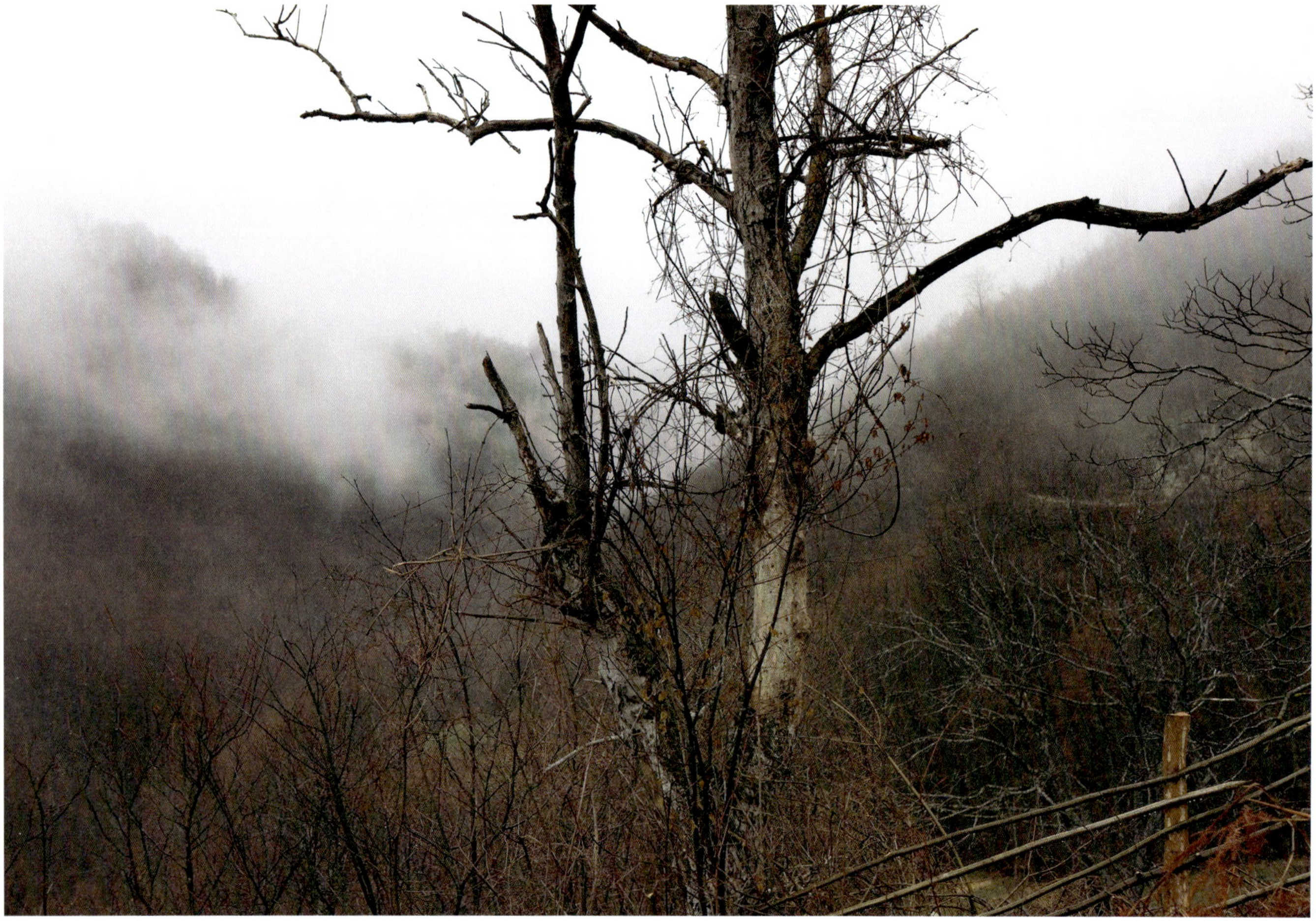

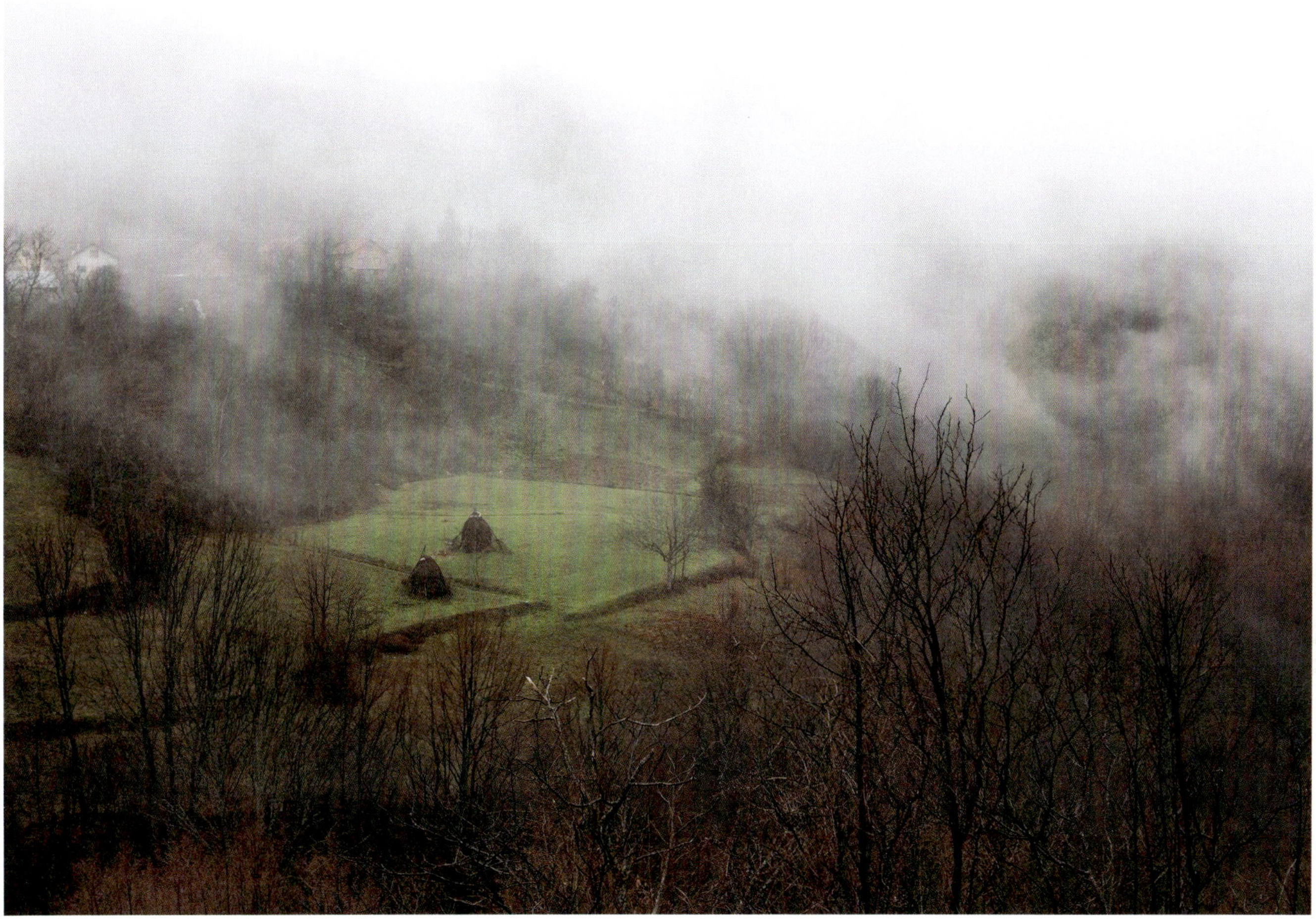

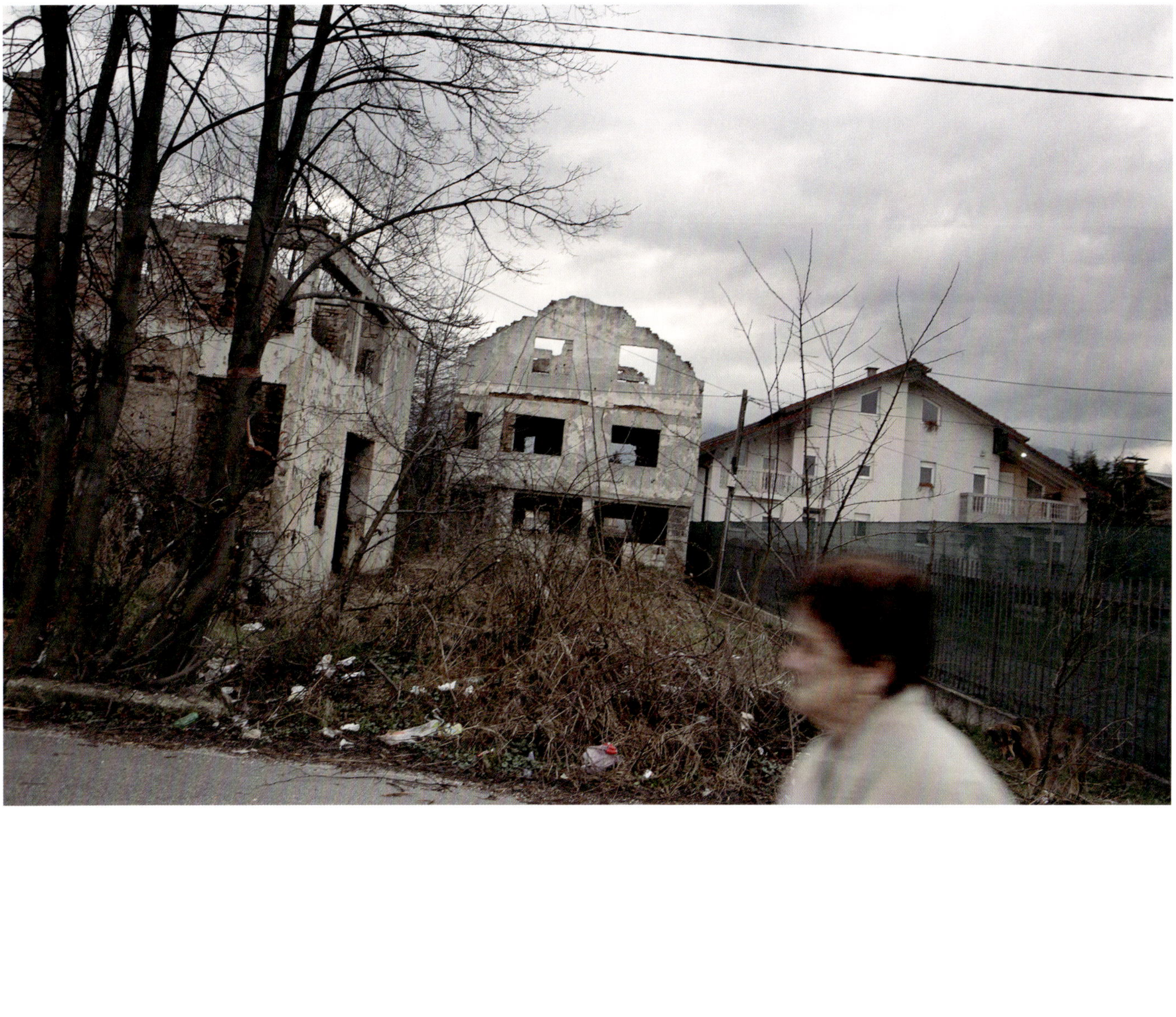

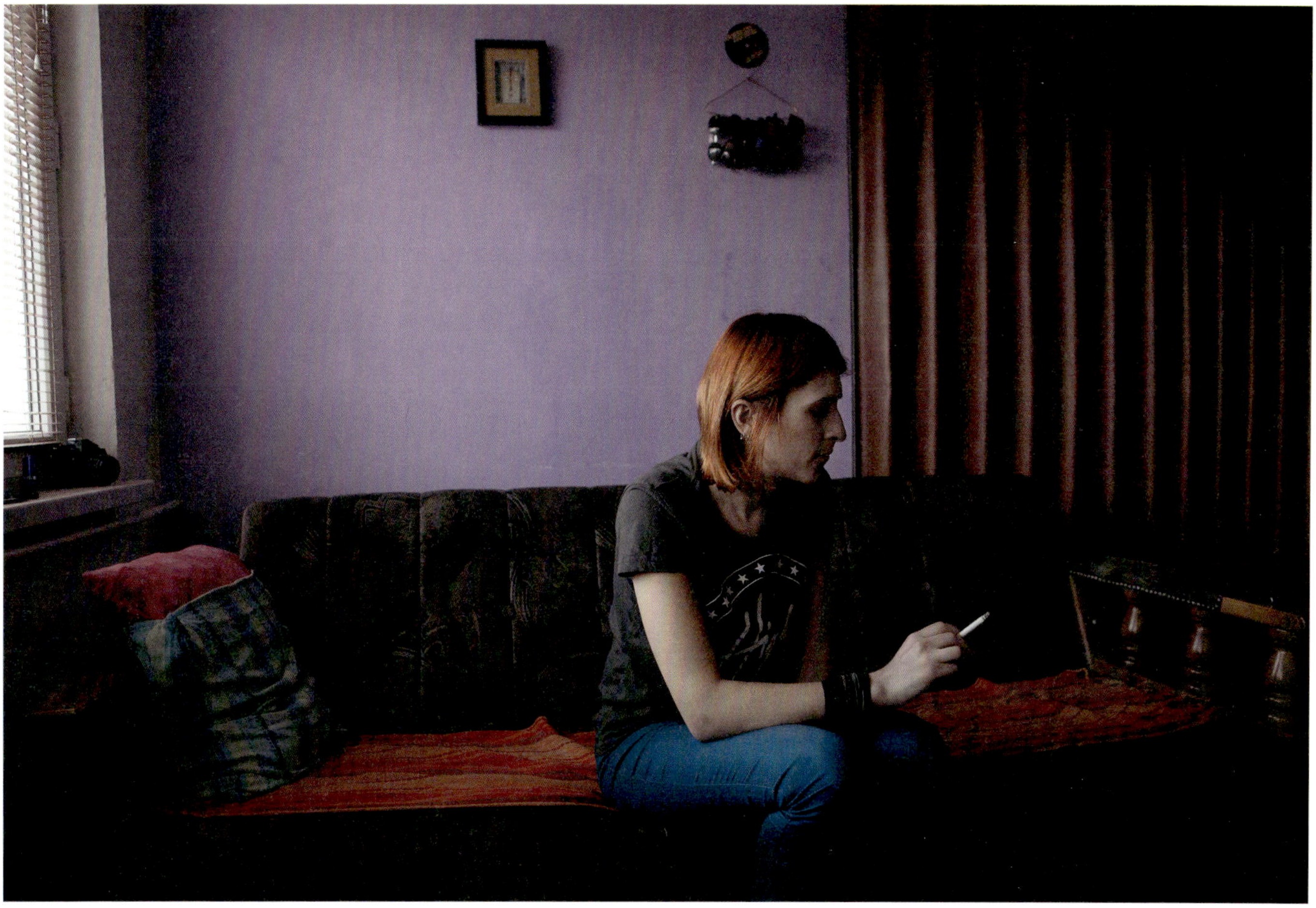

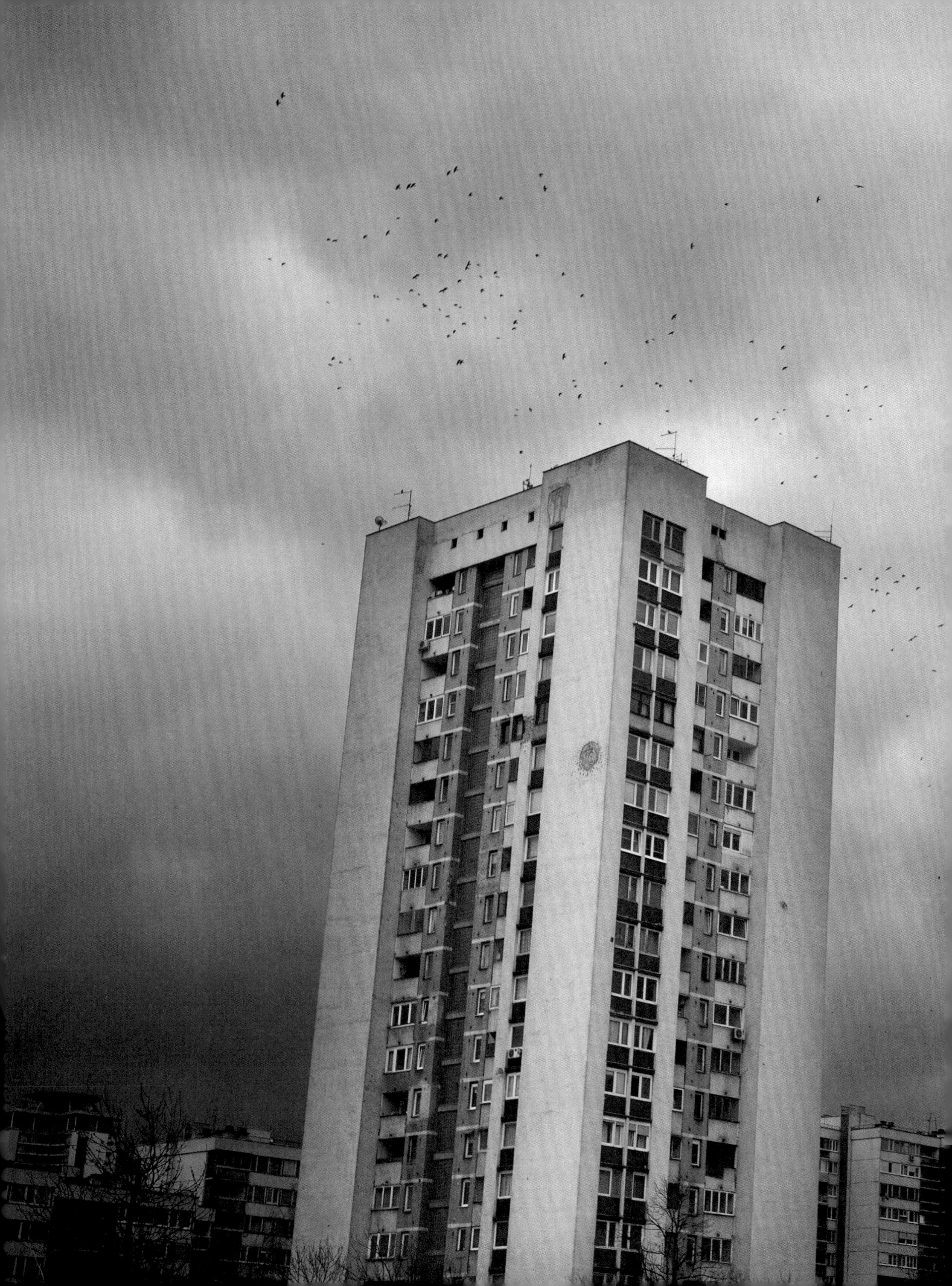

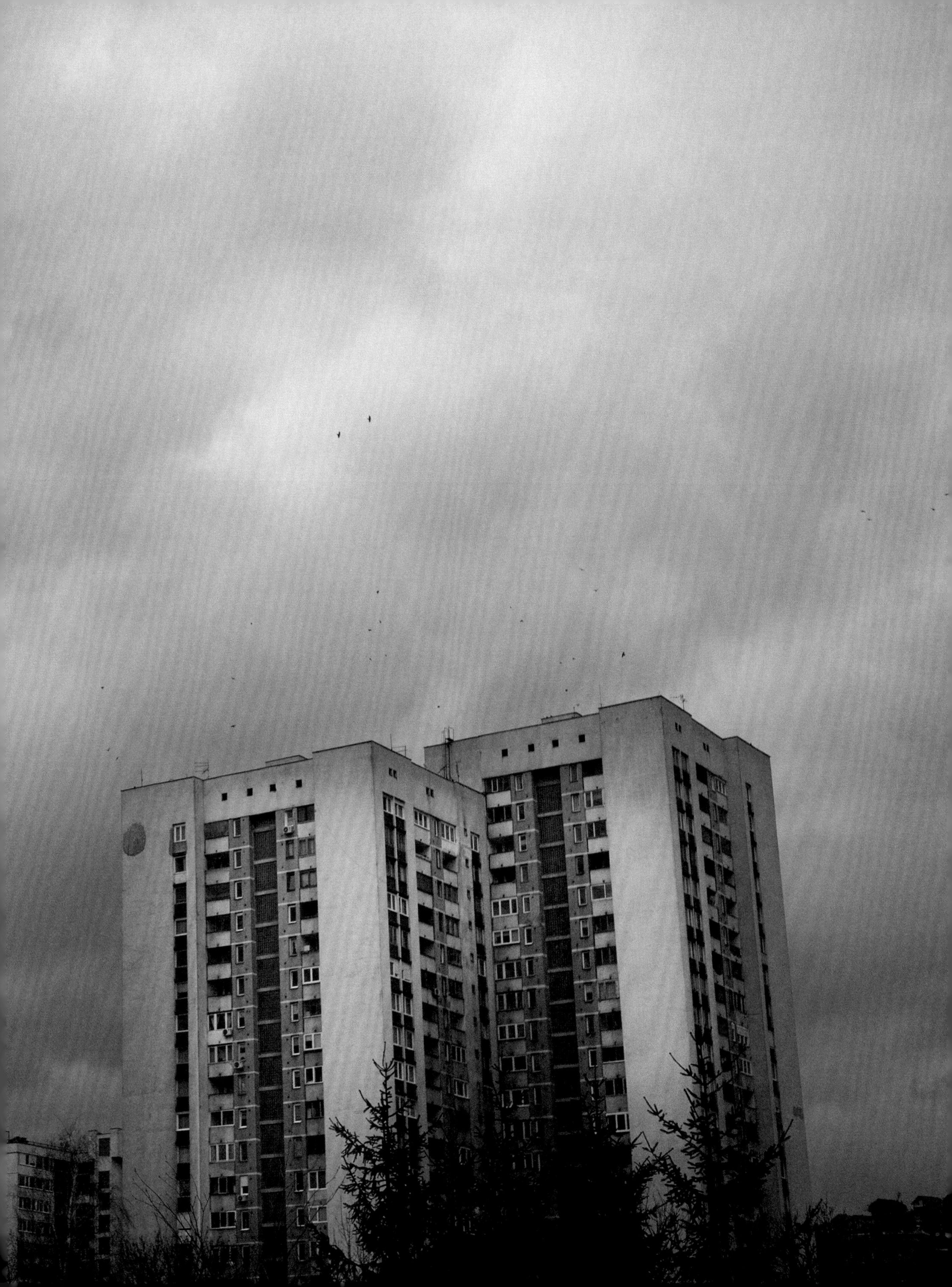

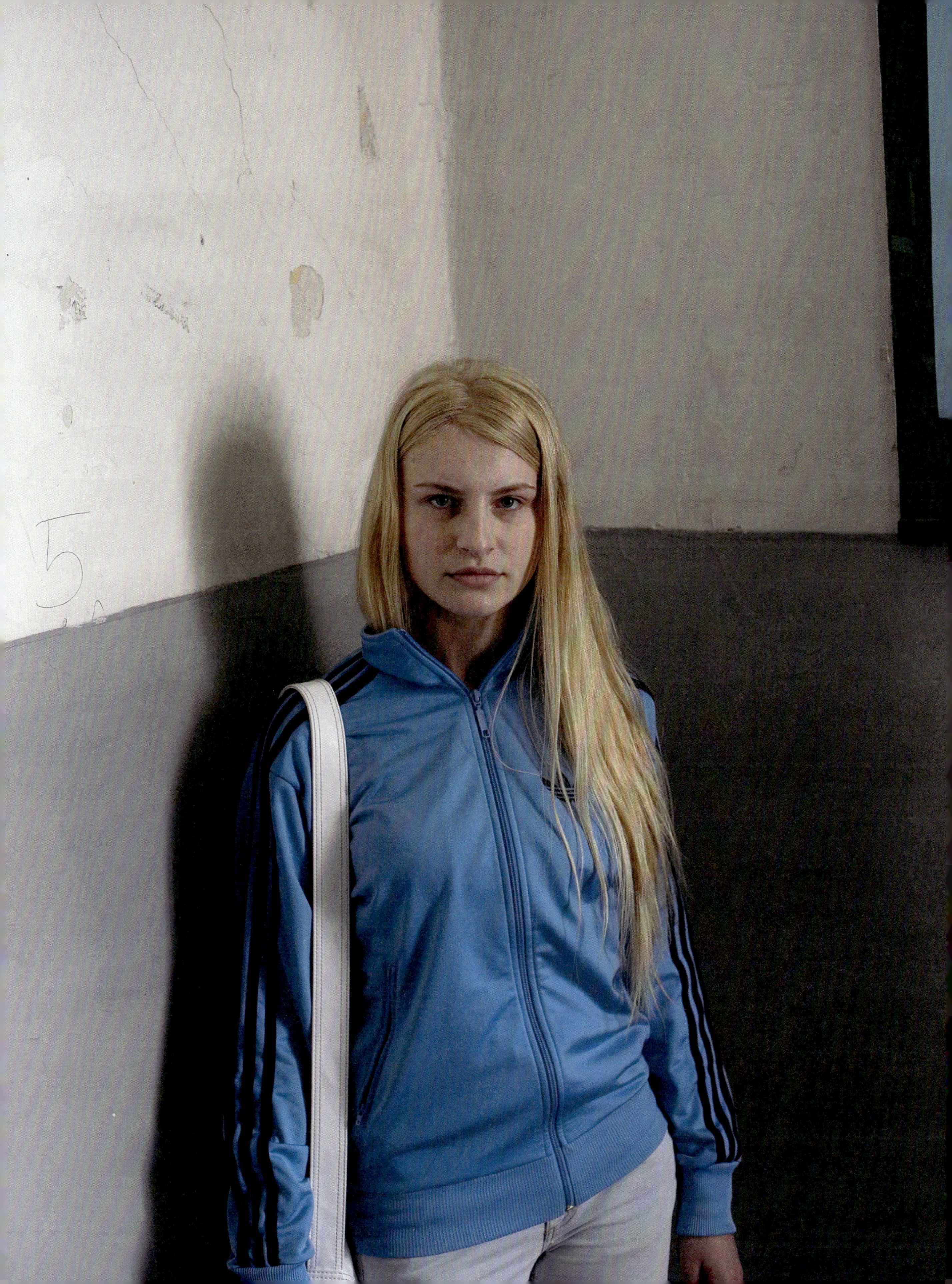

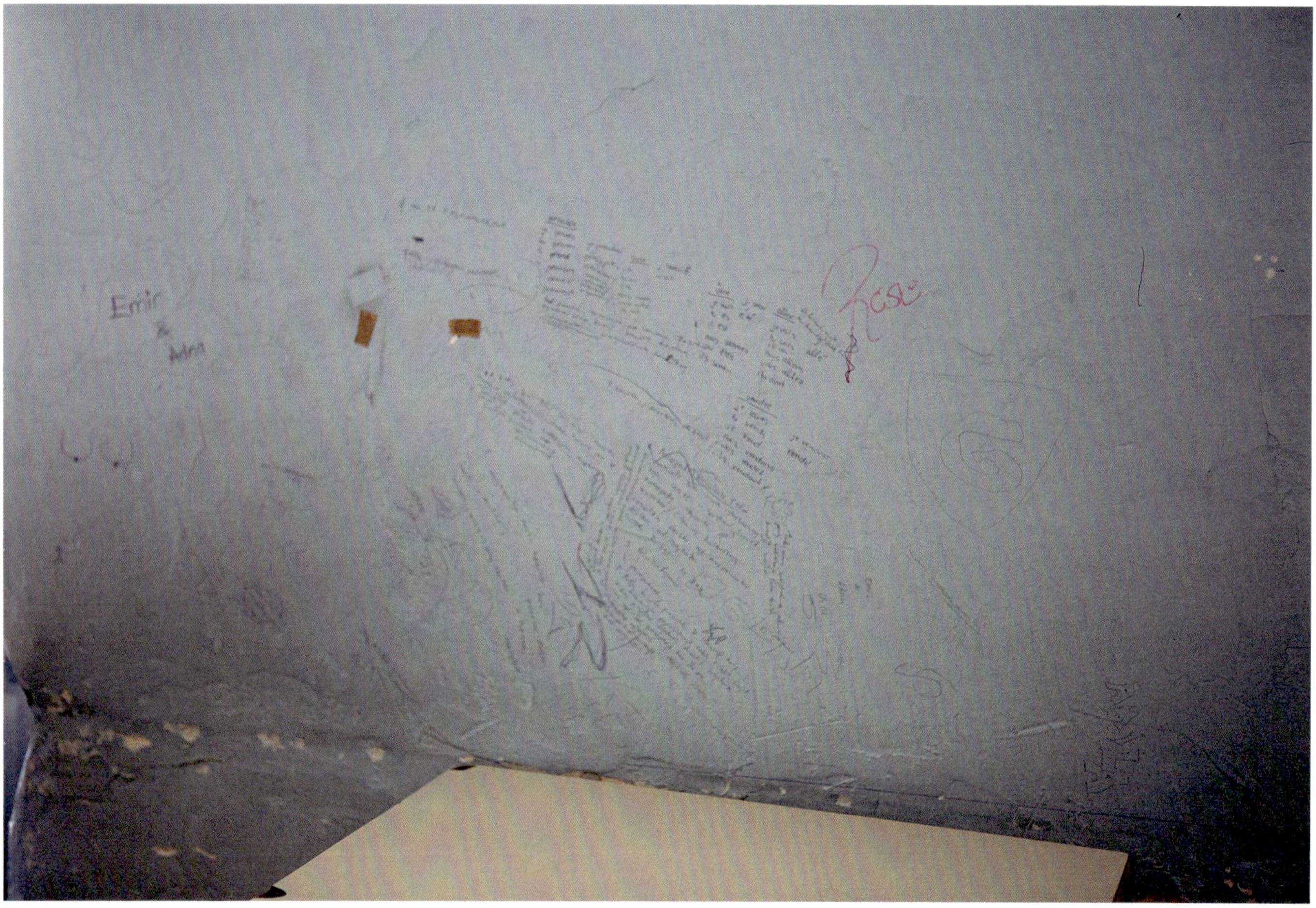
Emir
&
Adna

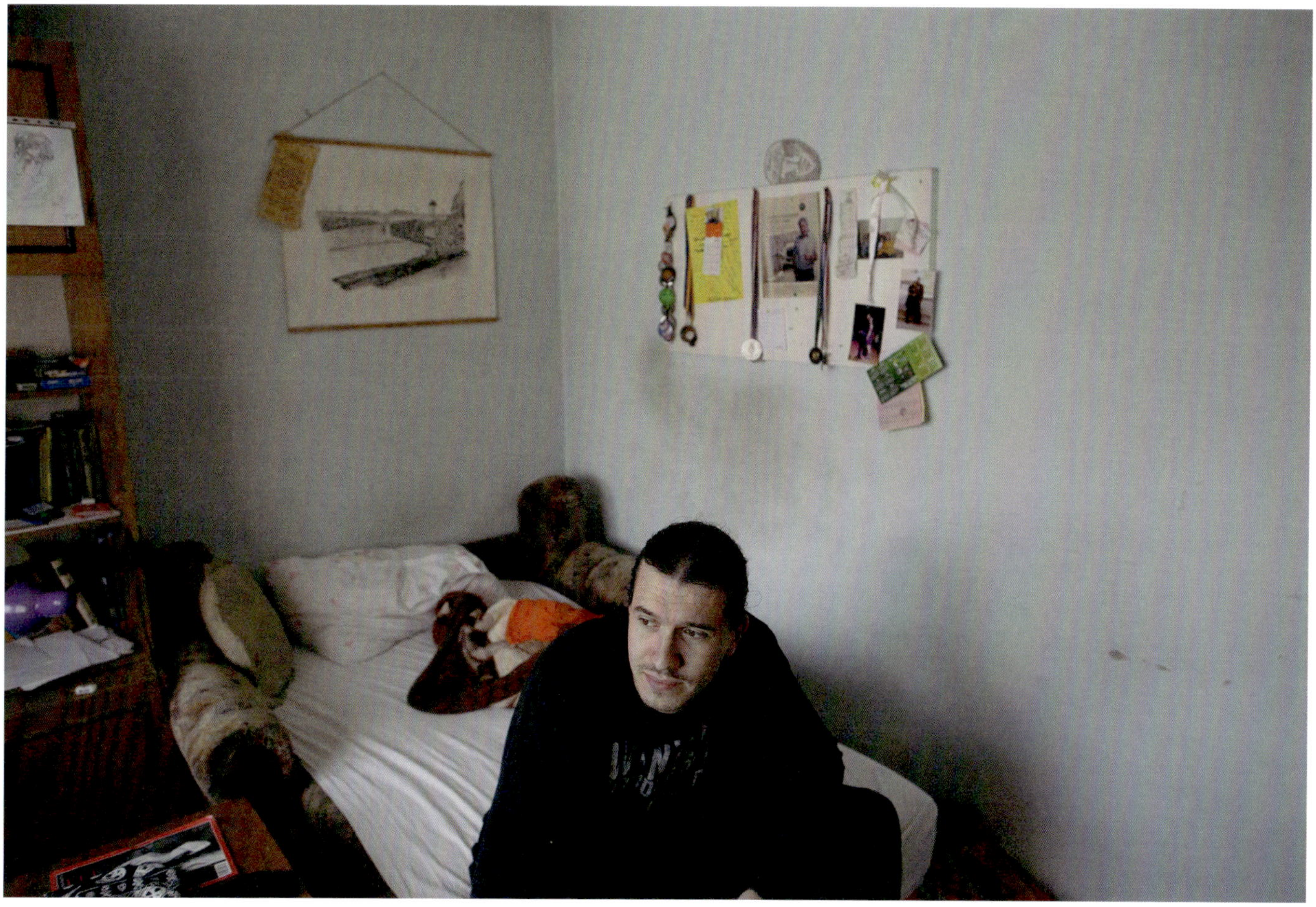

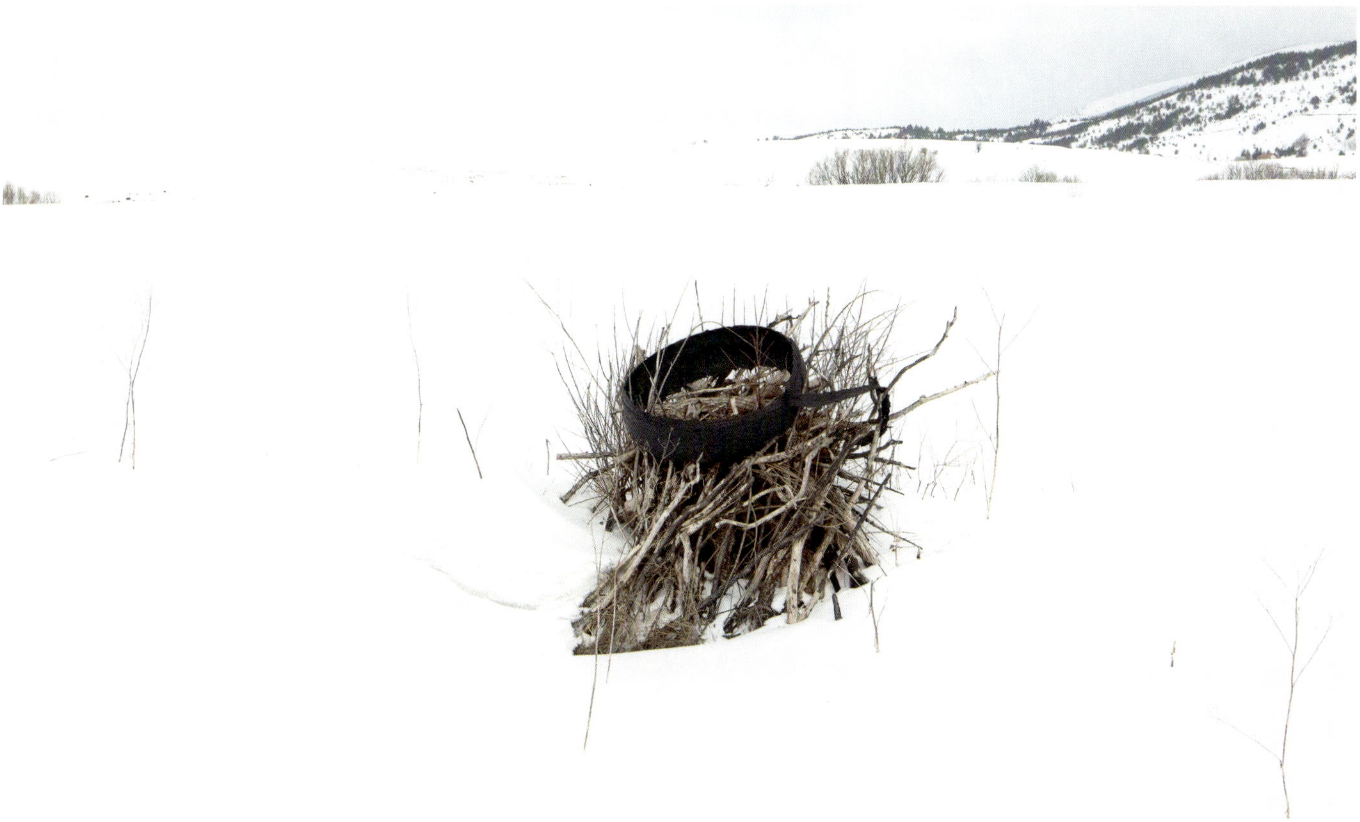

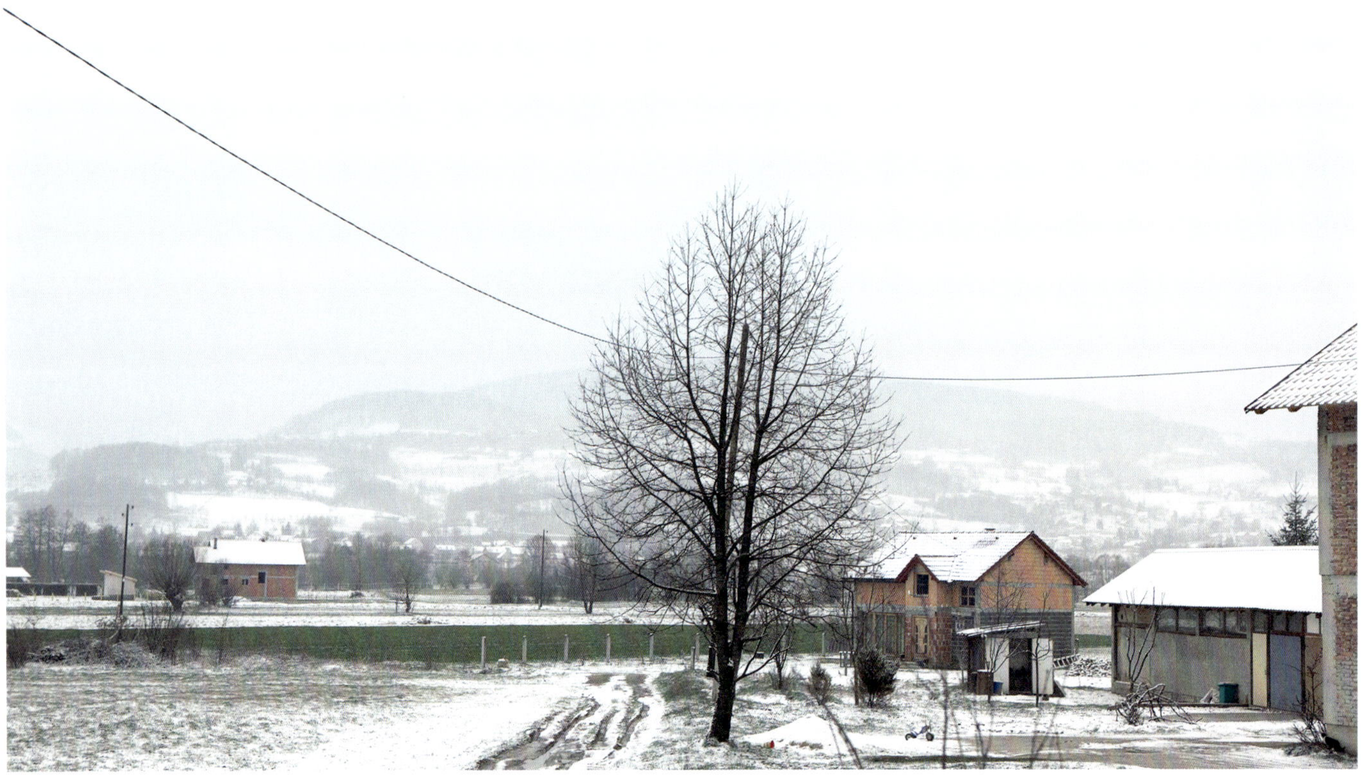

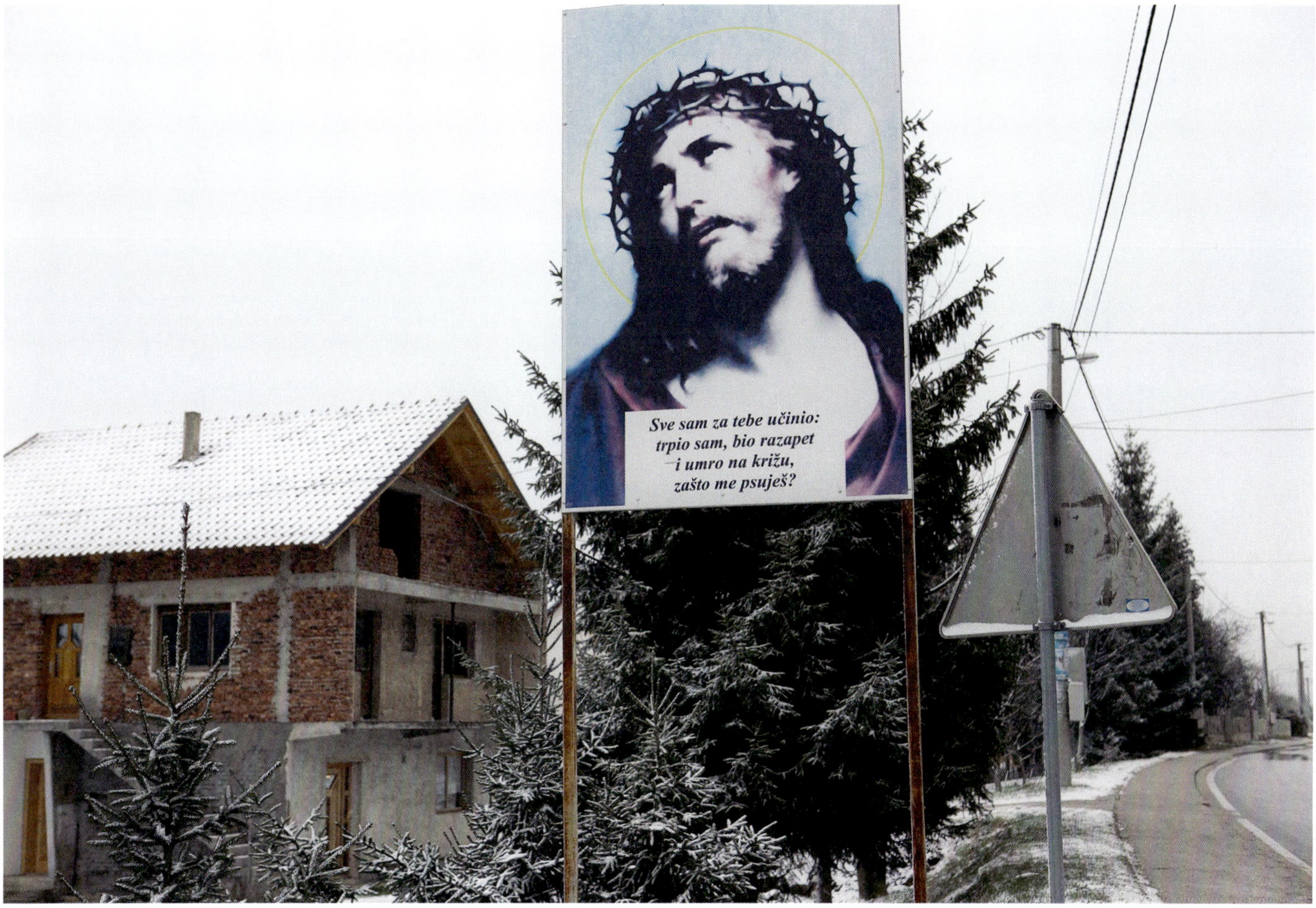
Sve sam za tebe učinio:
trpio sam, bio razapet
i umro na križu,
zašto me psuješ?

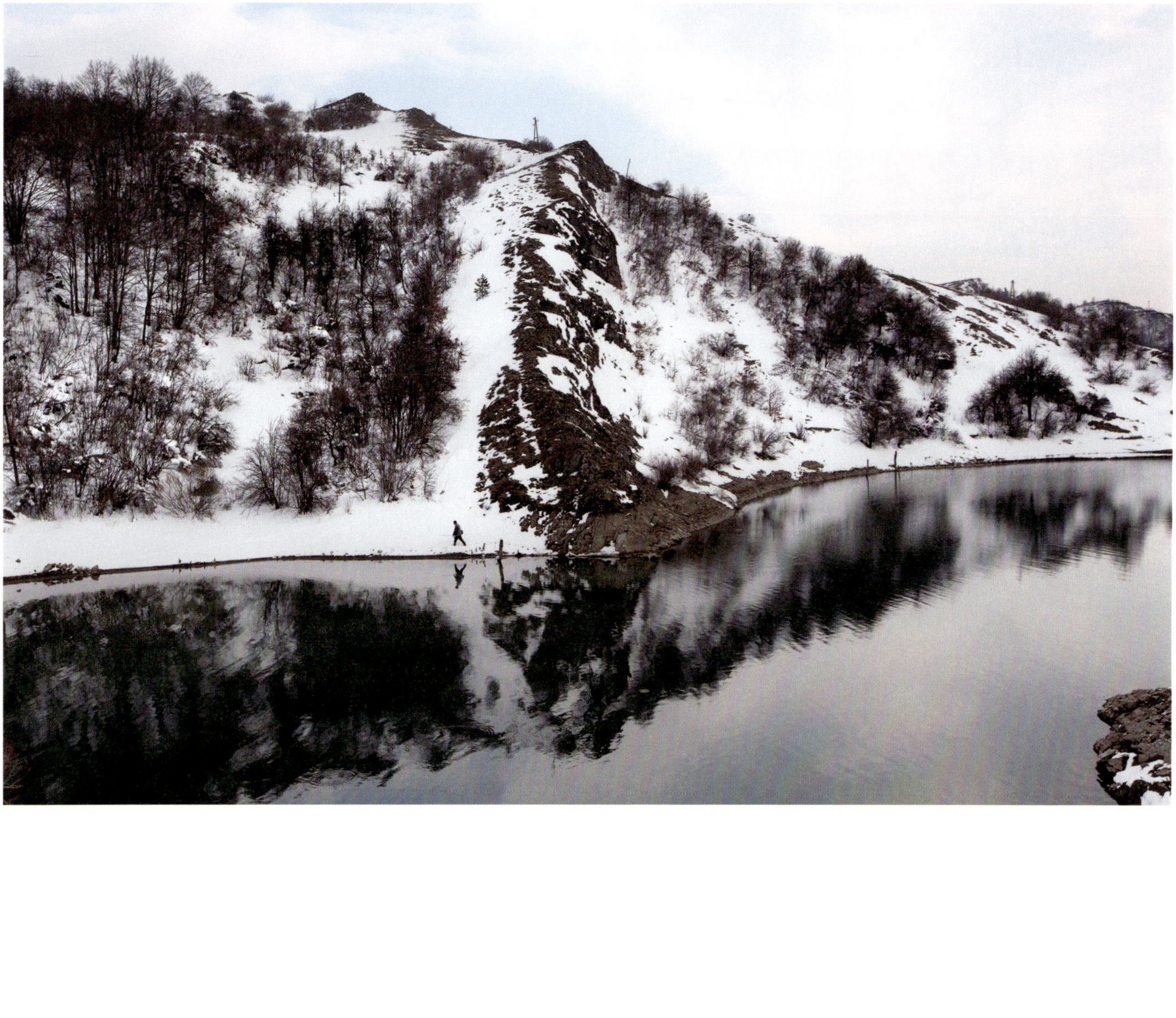

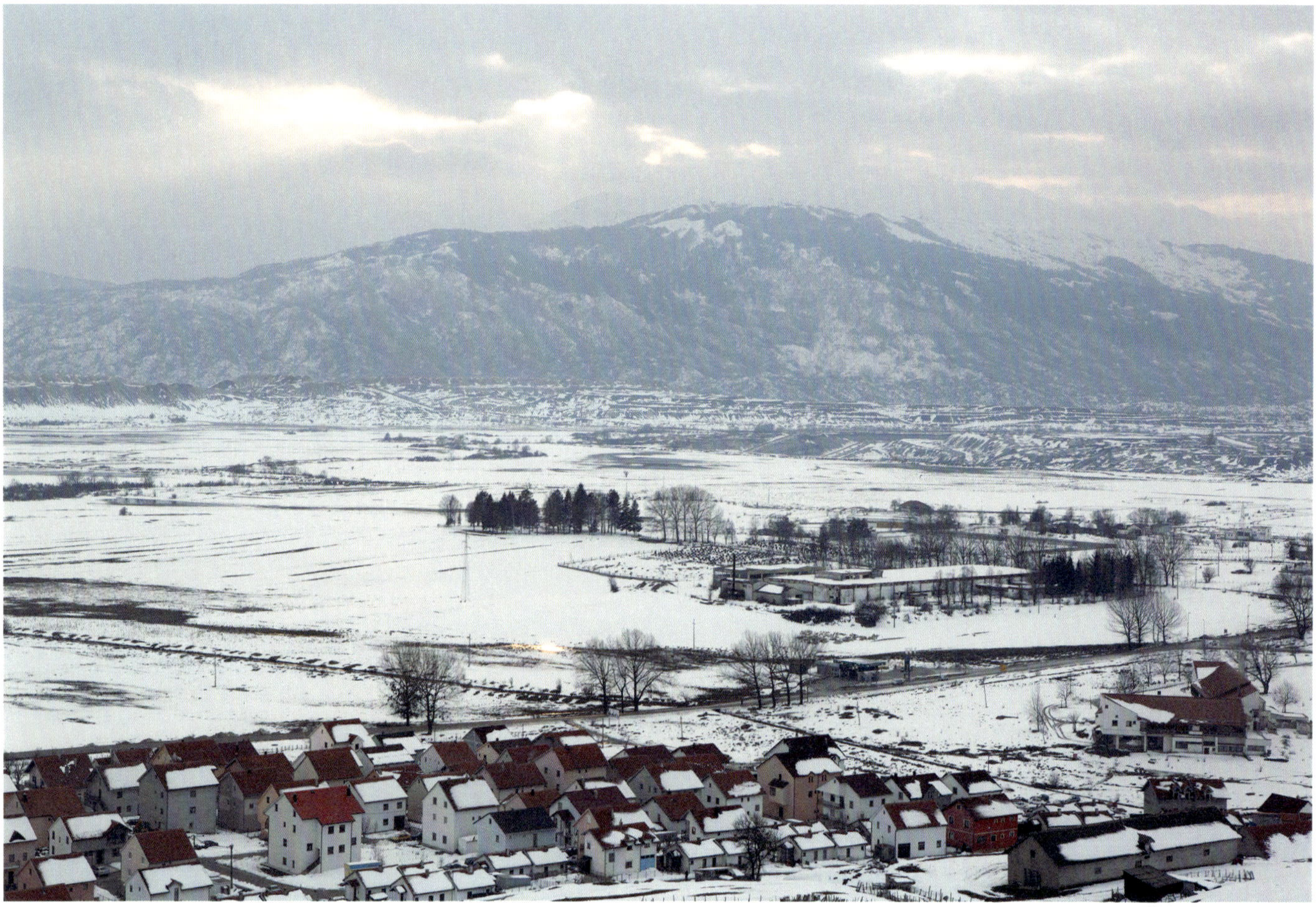

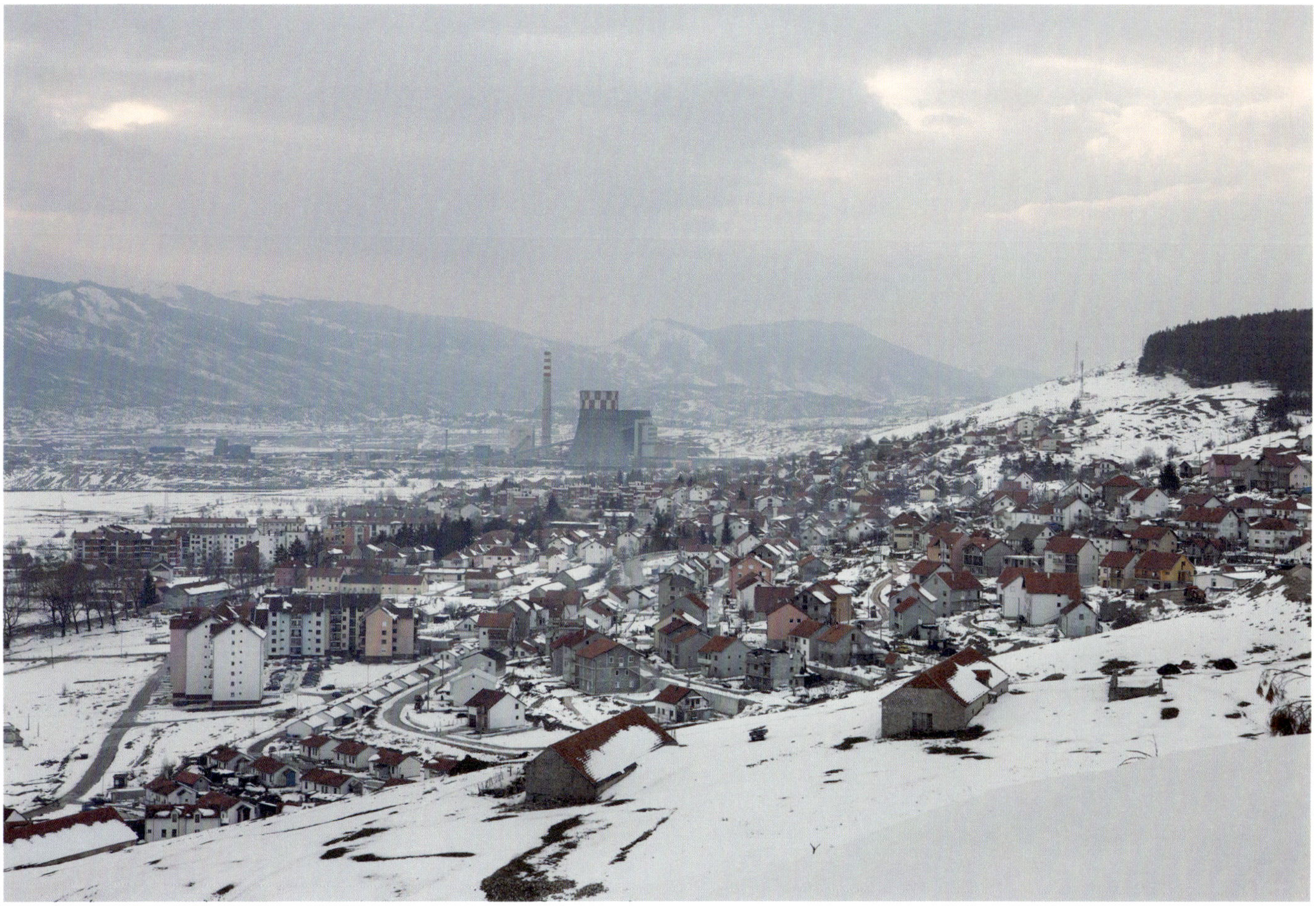

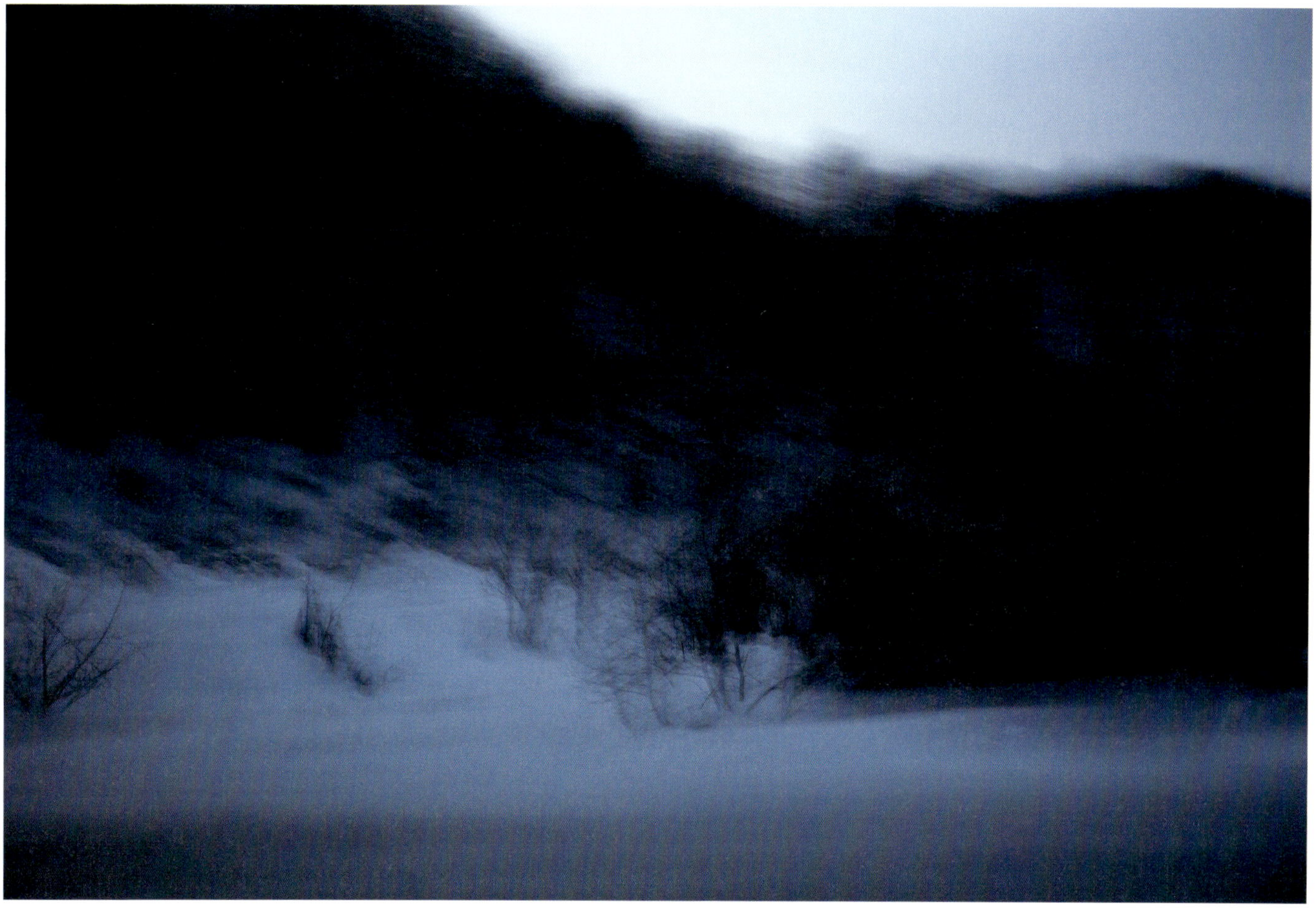

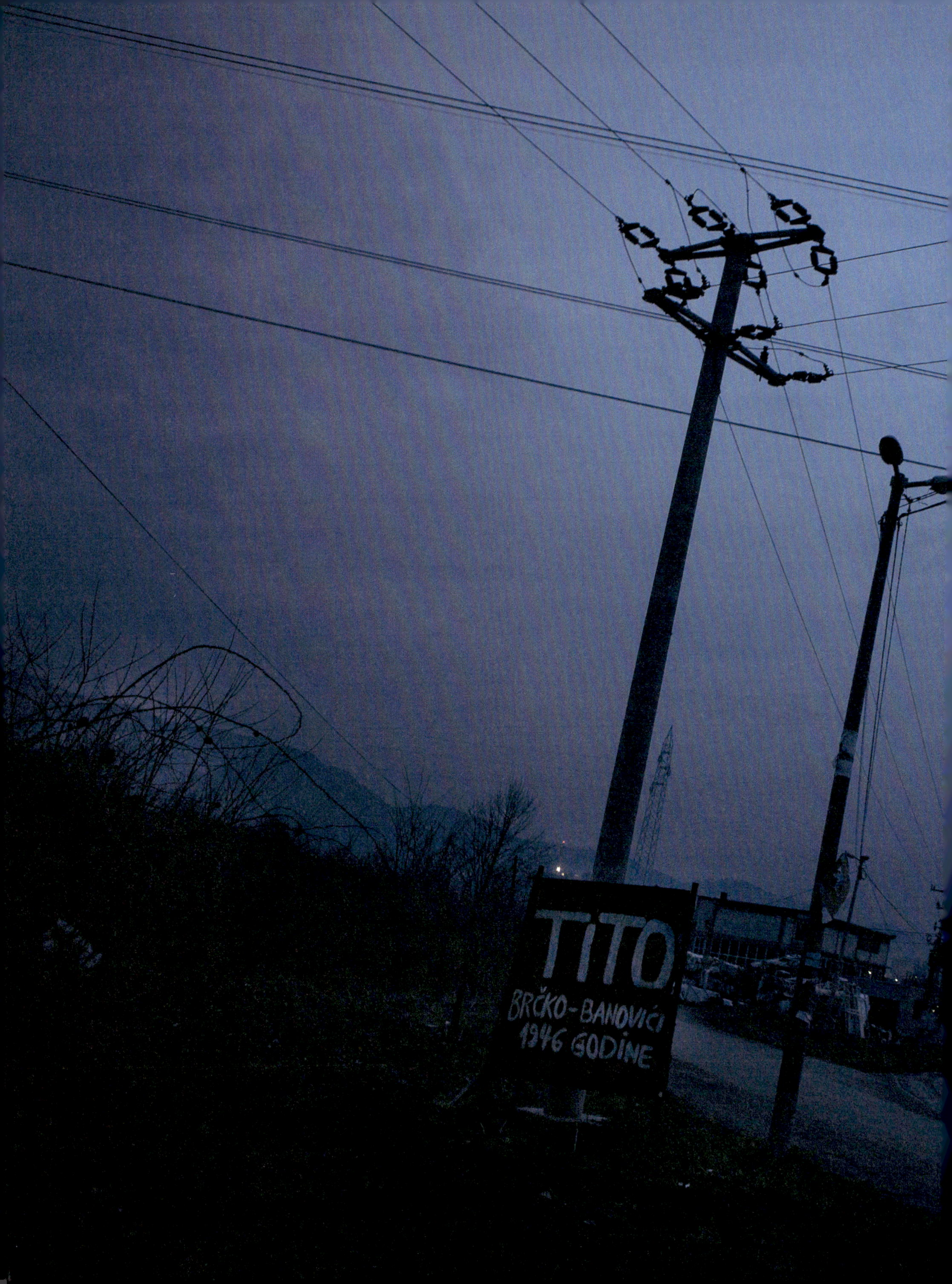
TITO
BRČKO-BANOVIĆI
1946 GODINE

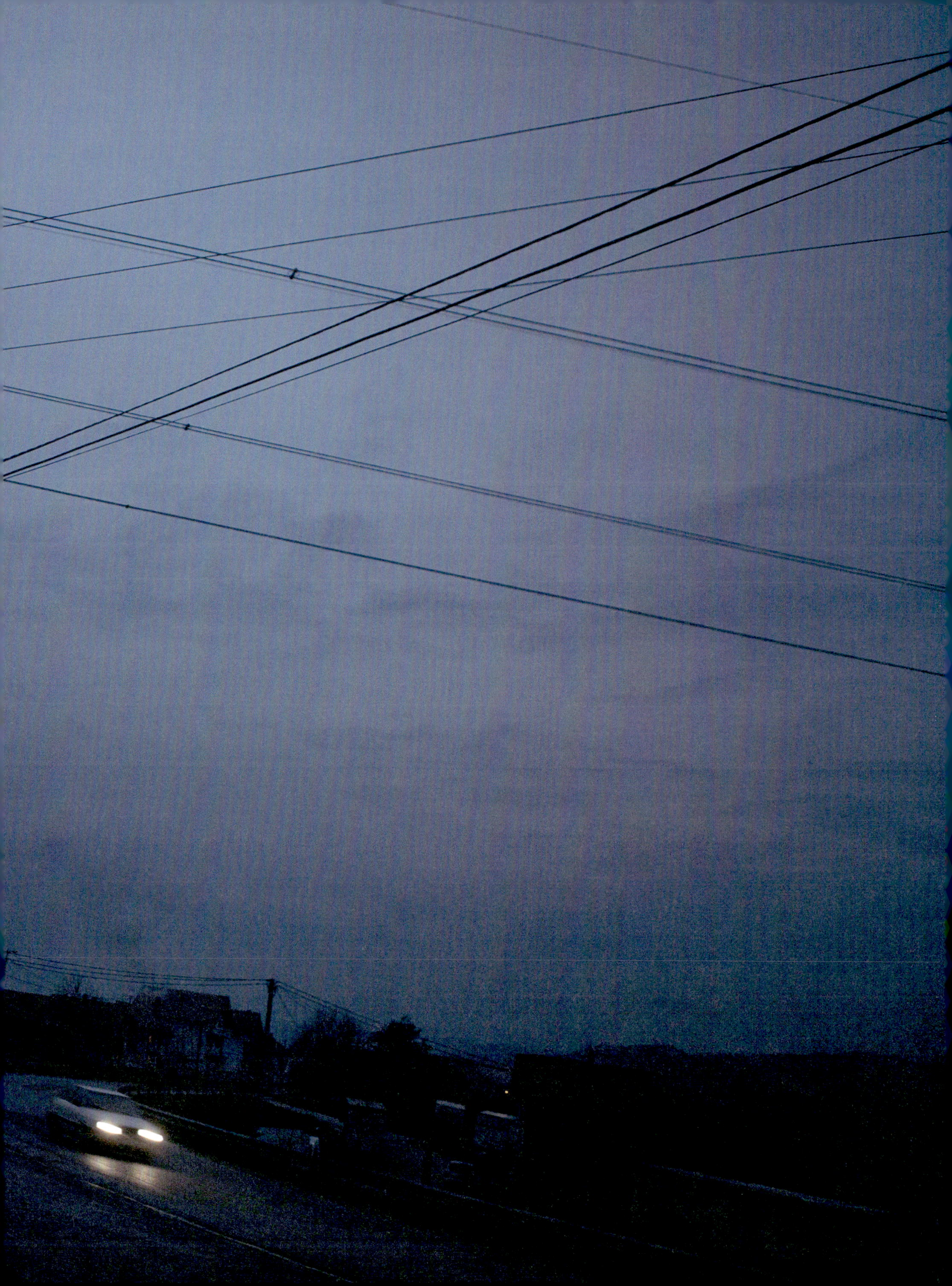

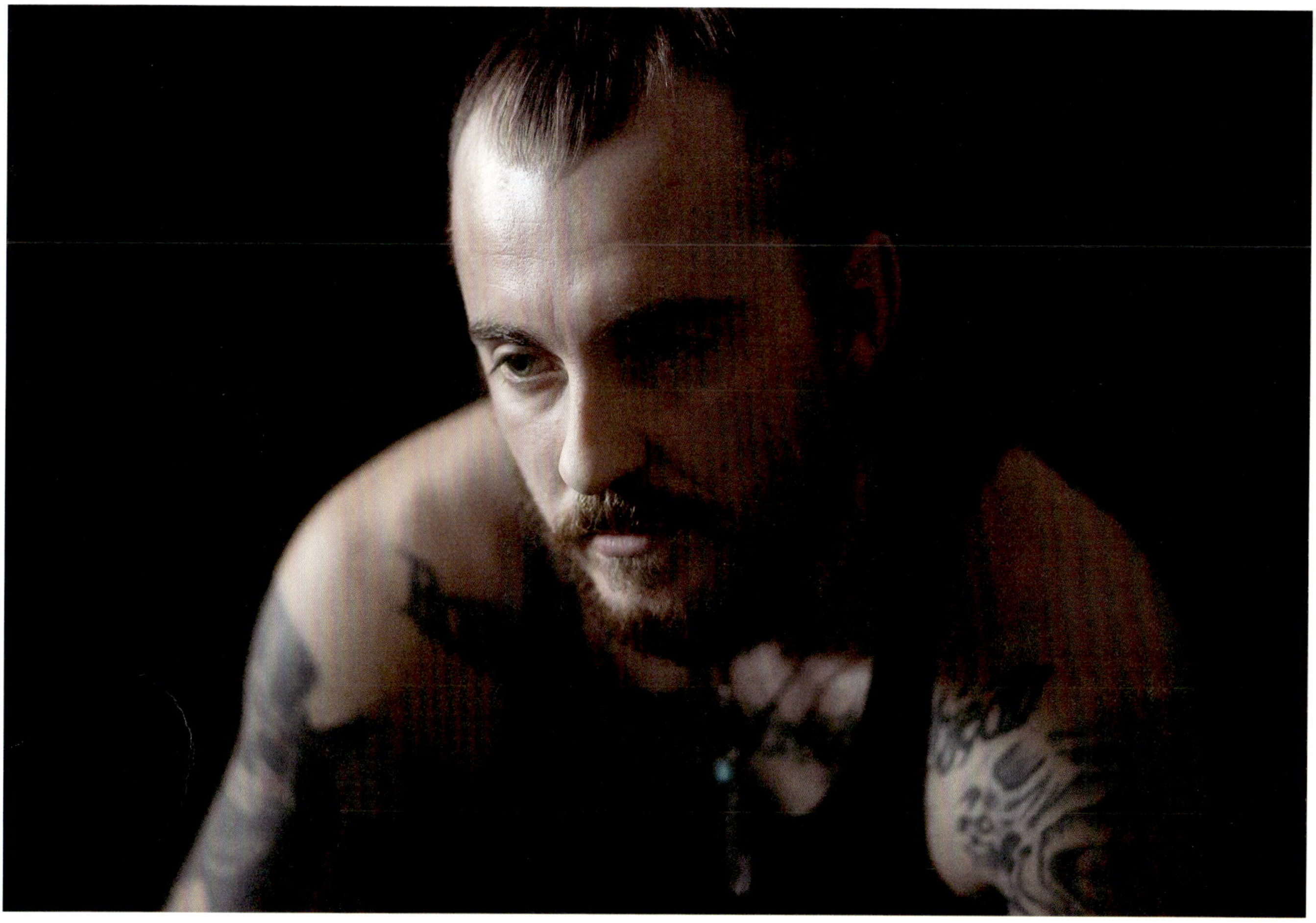

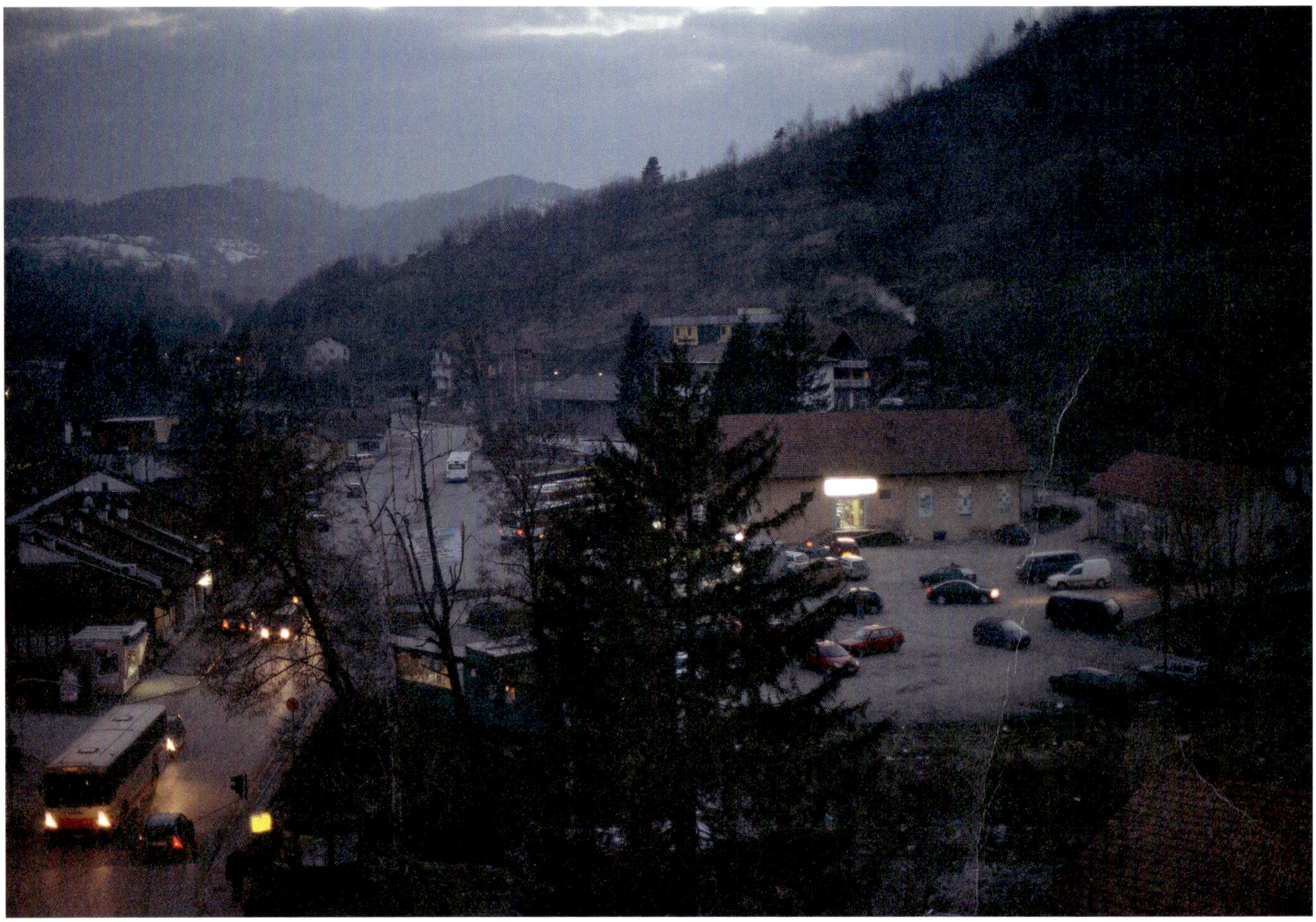

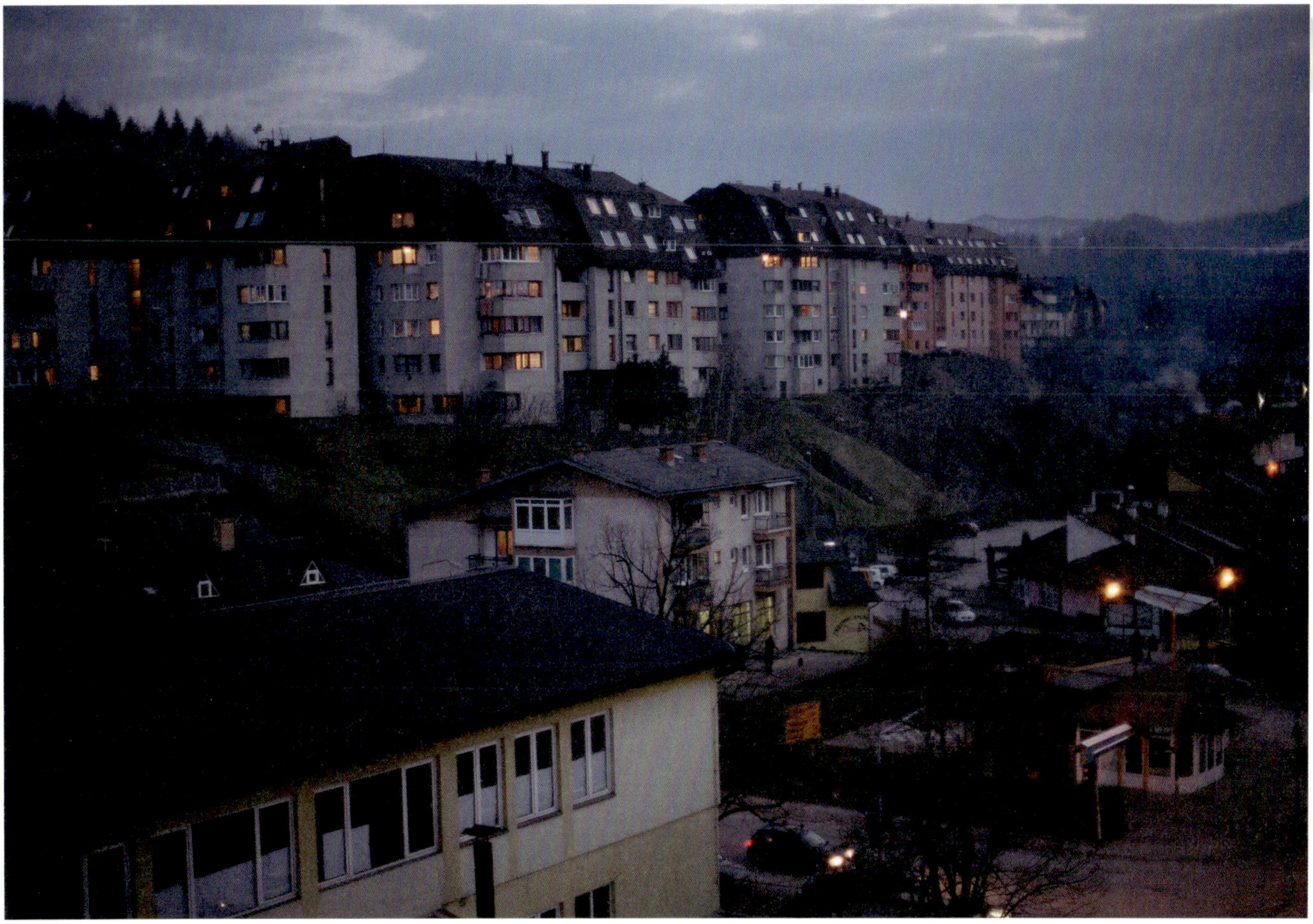

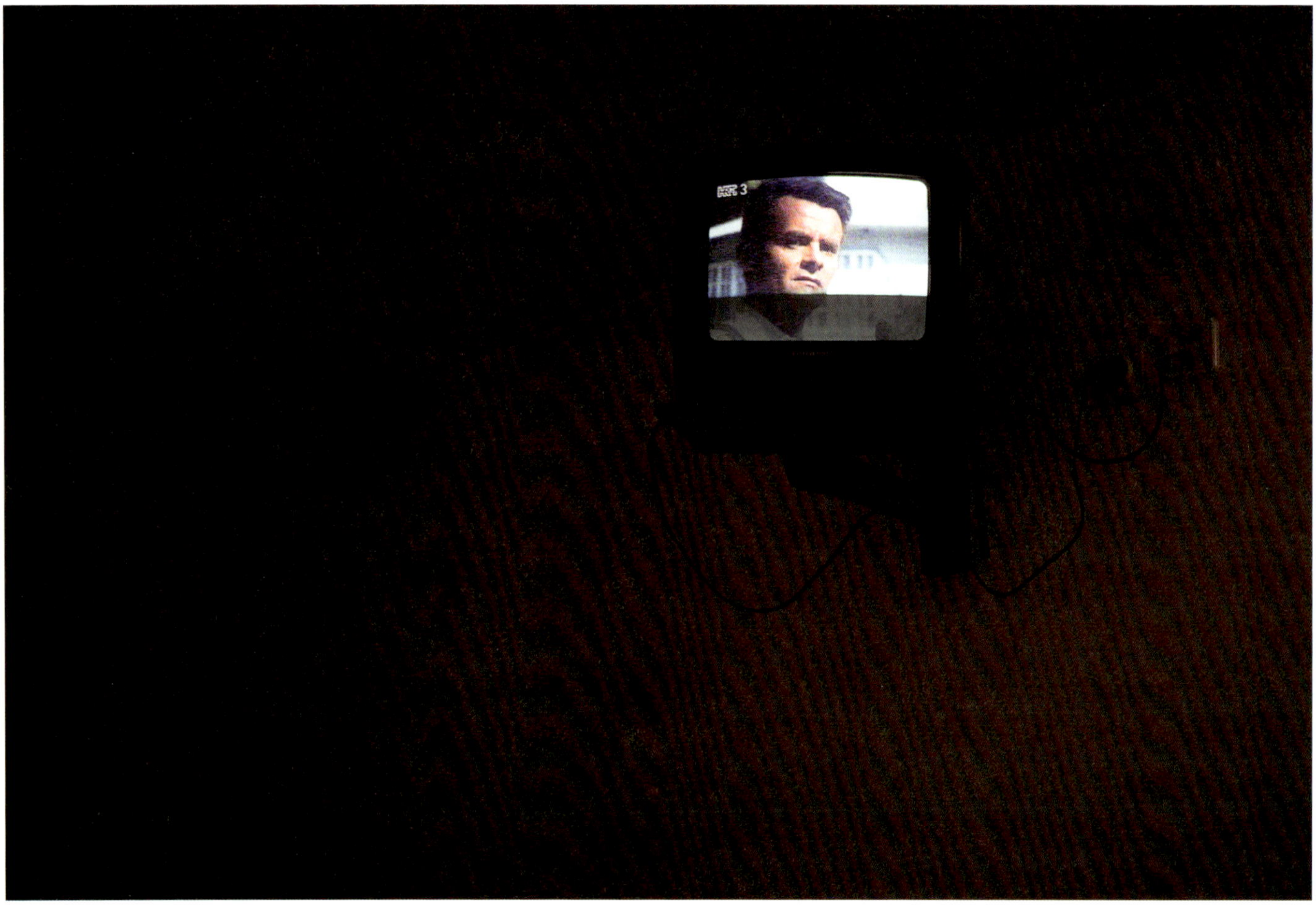

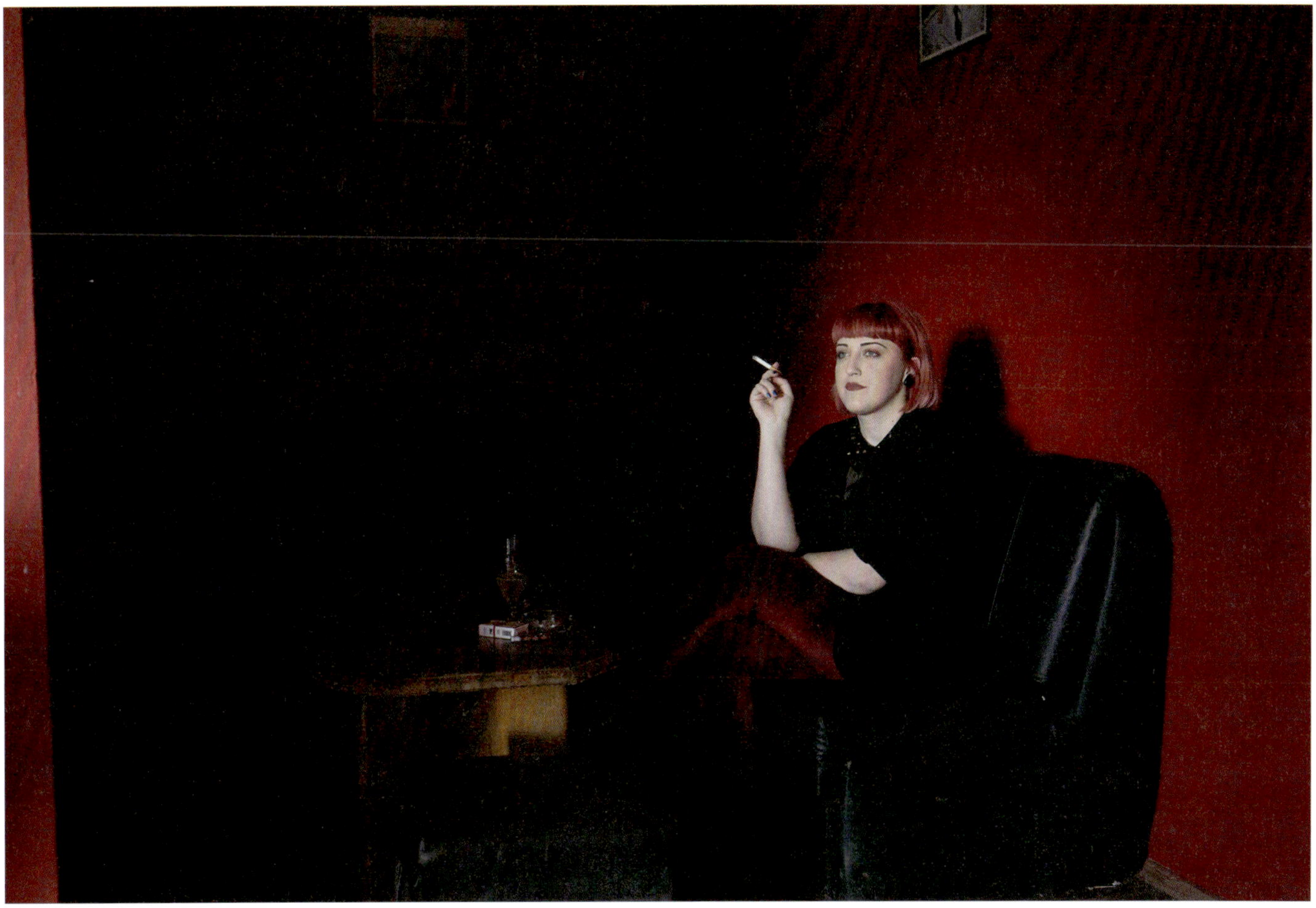

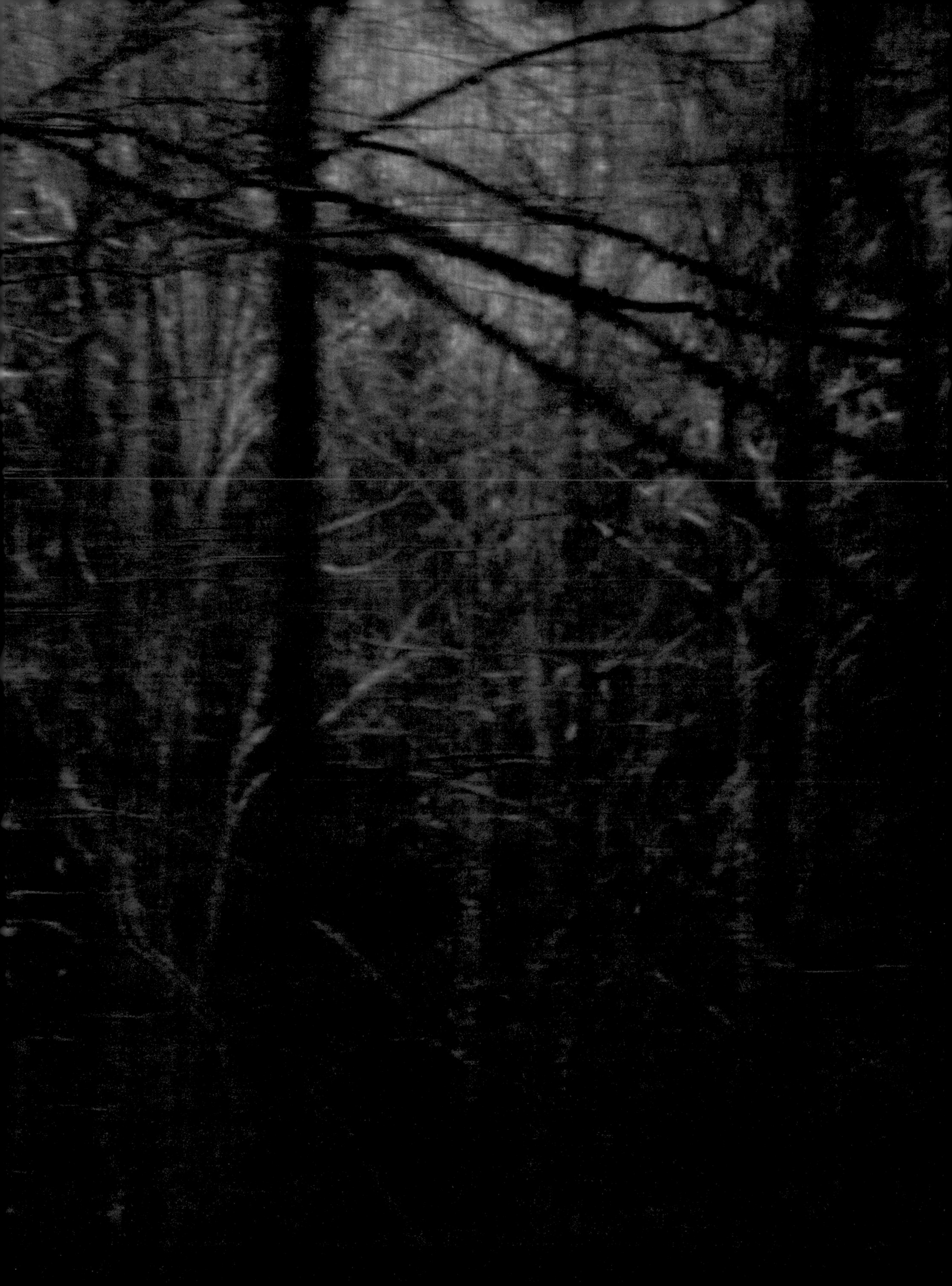

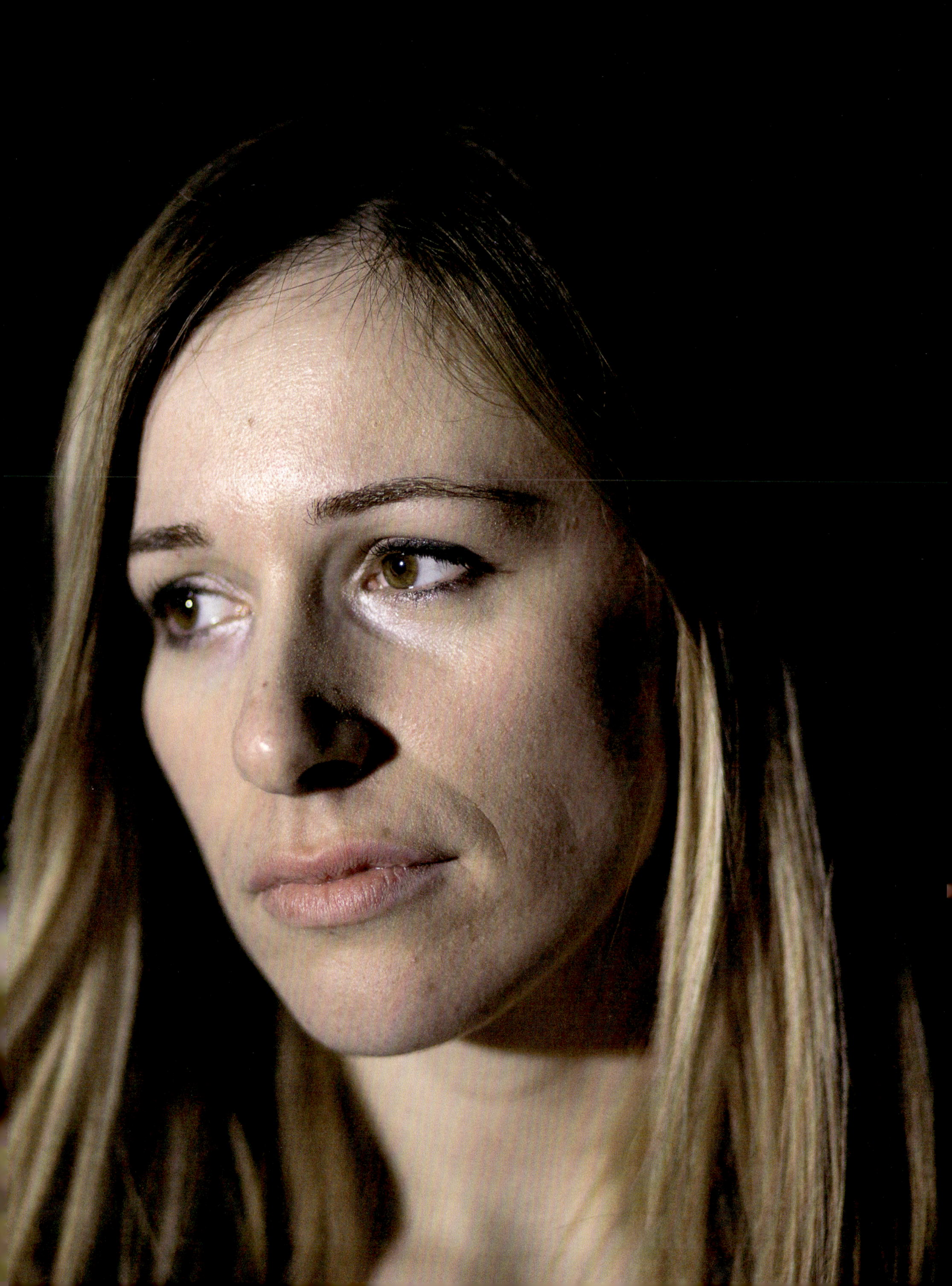

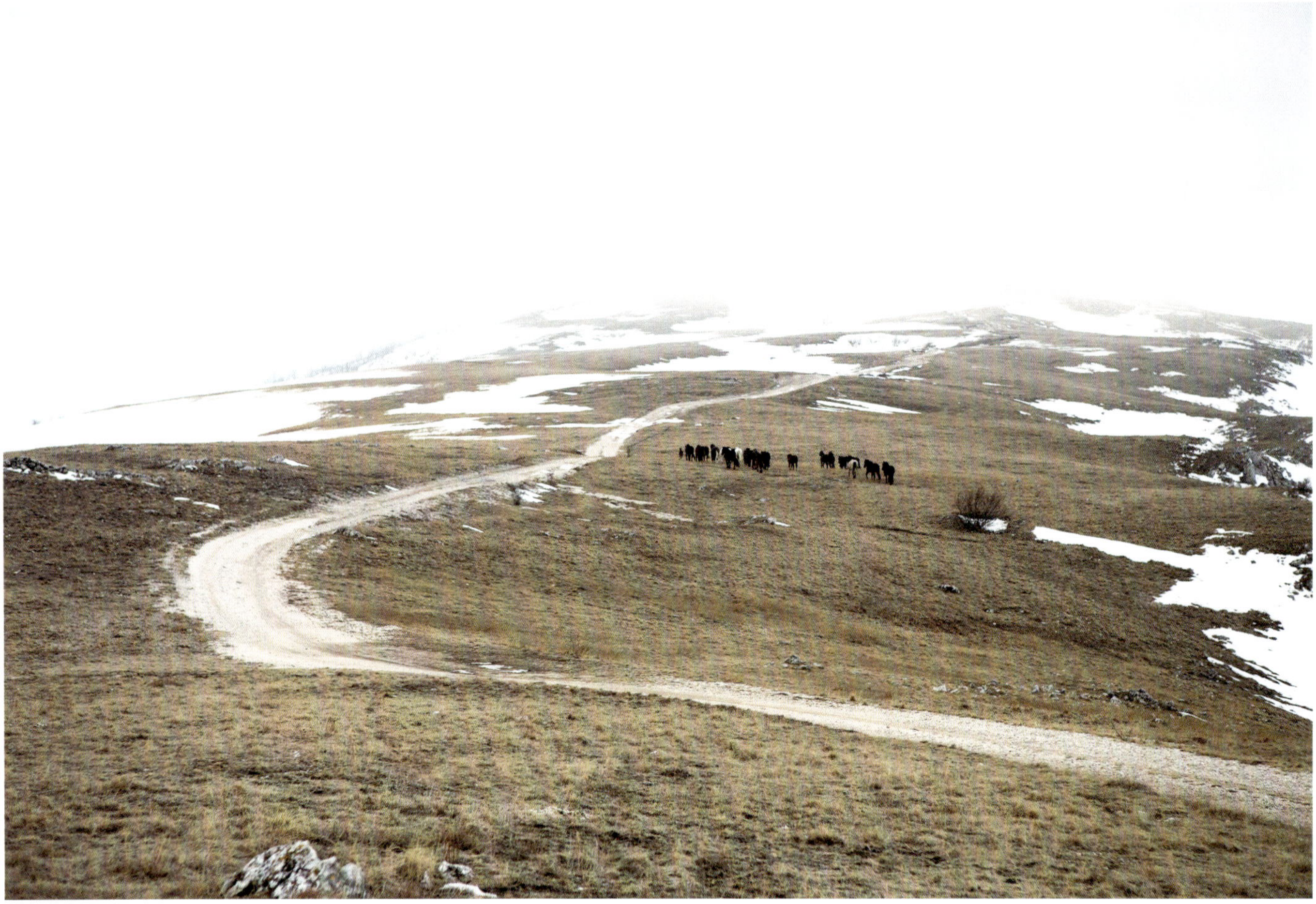

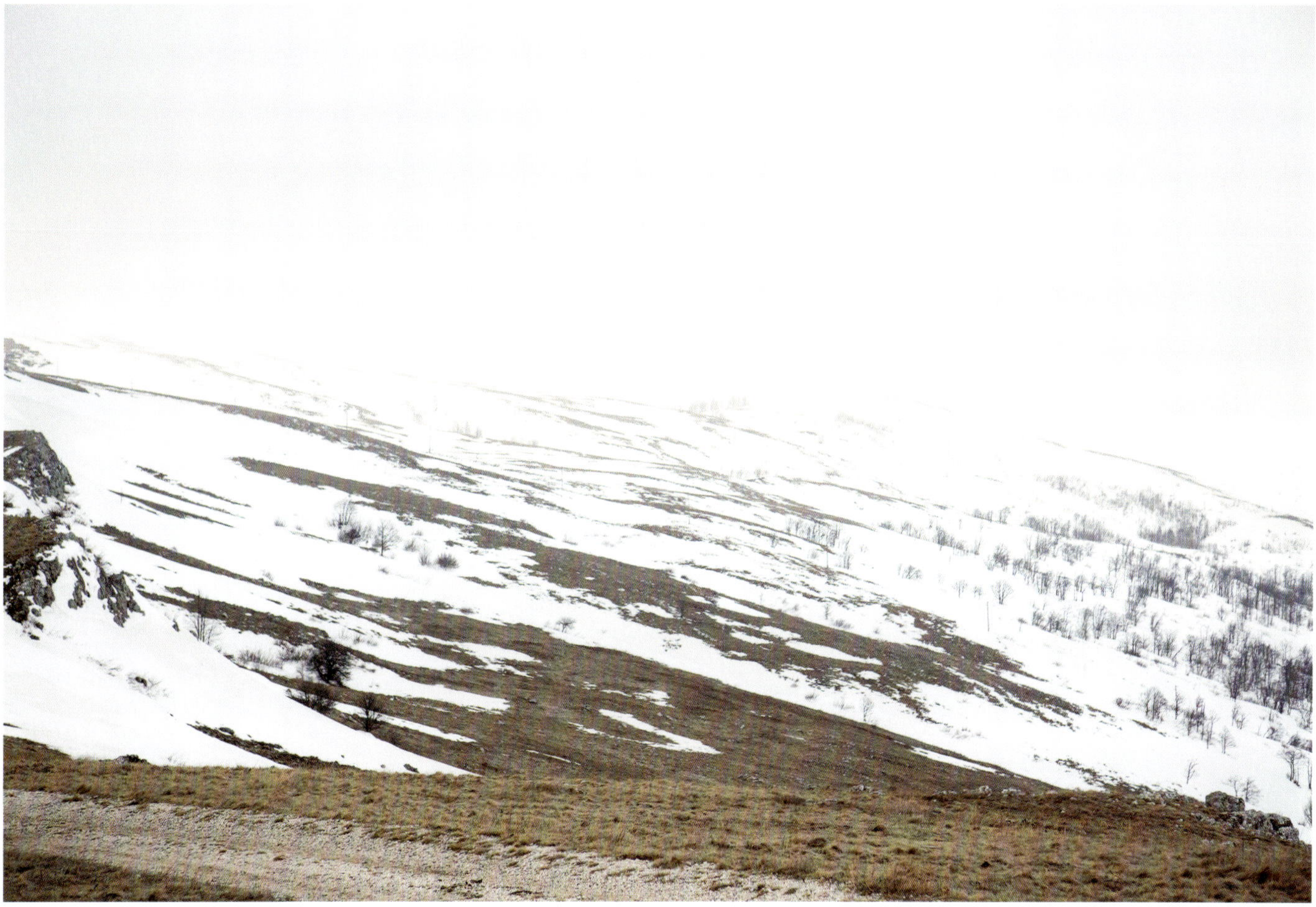

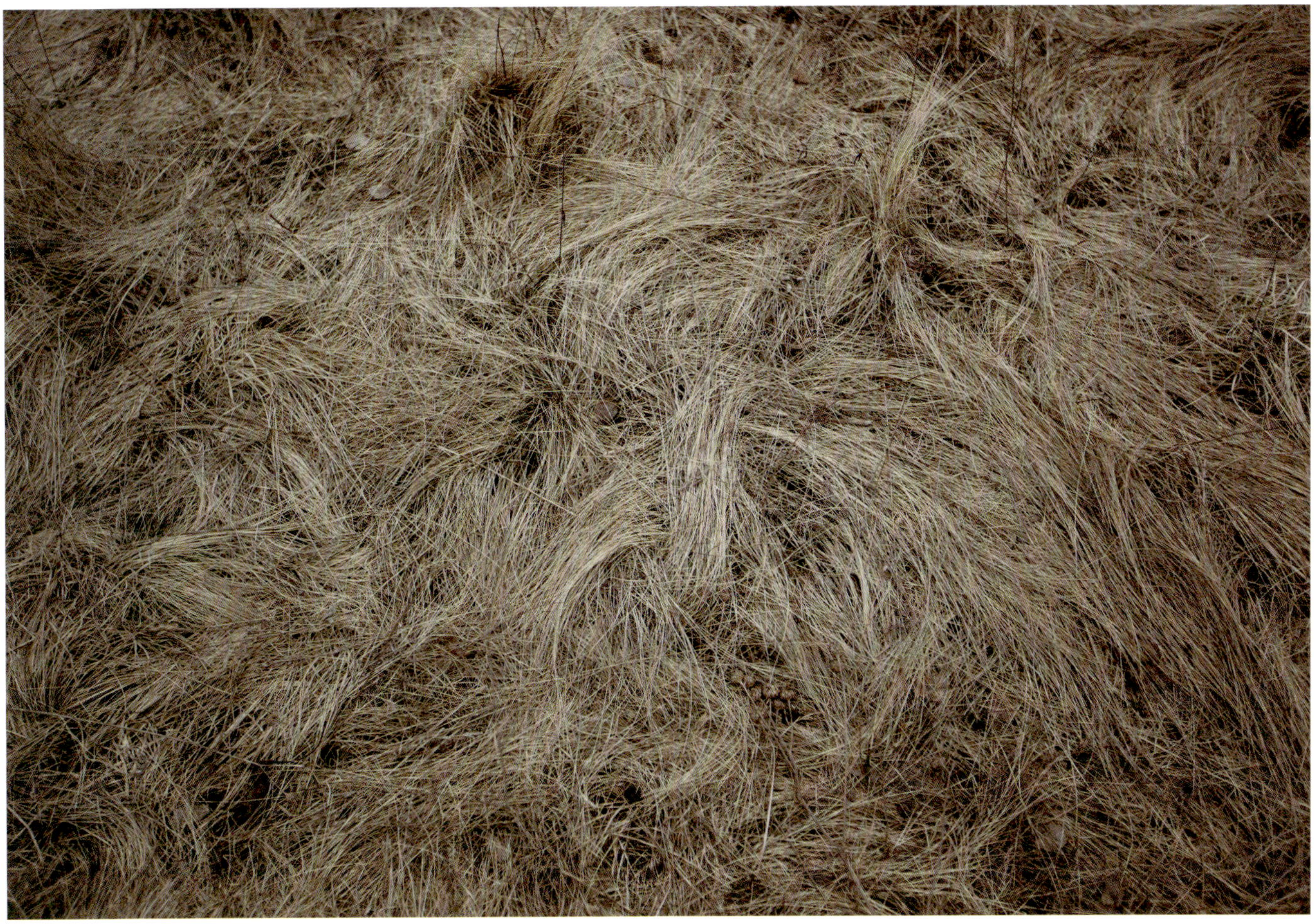

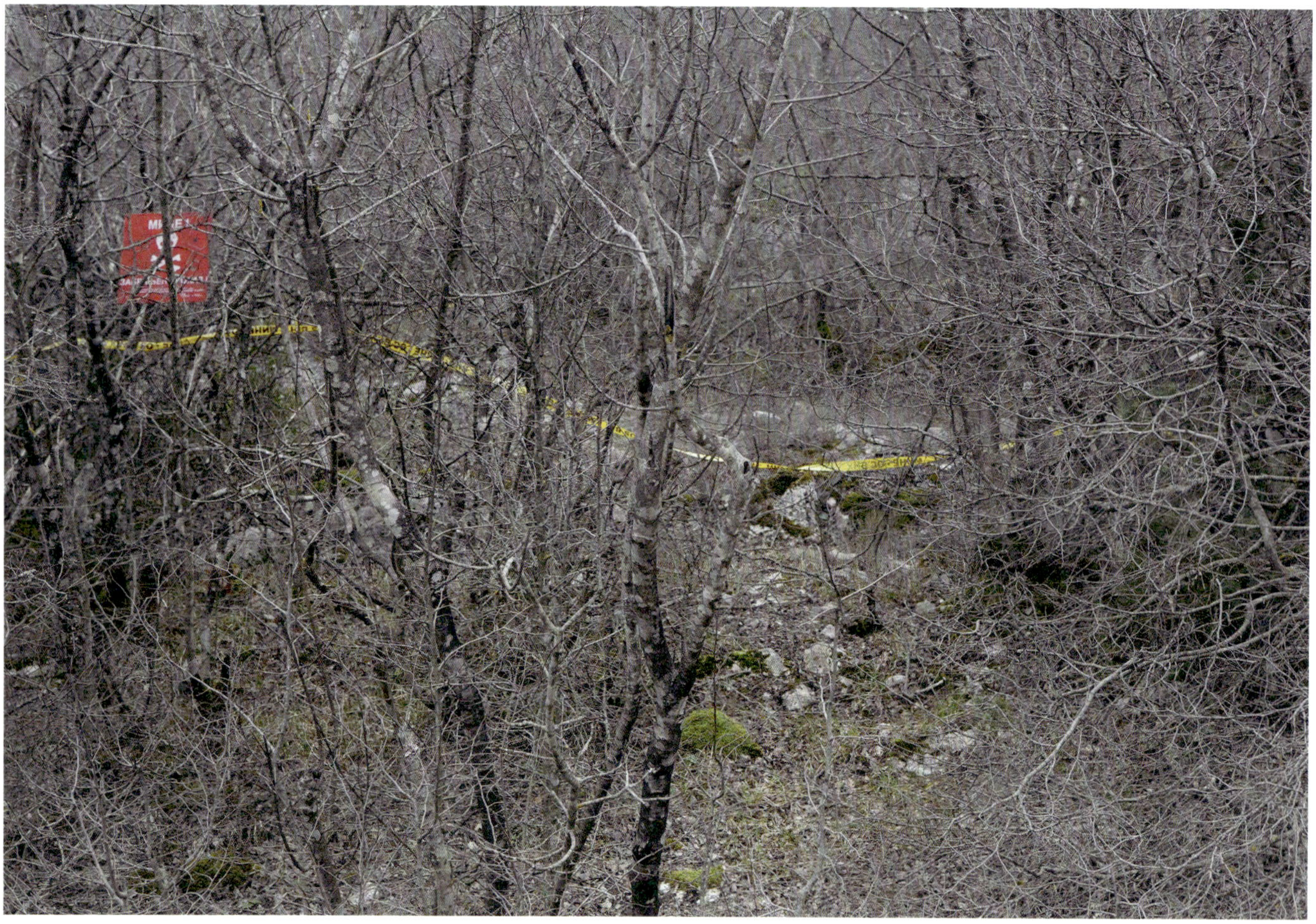

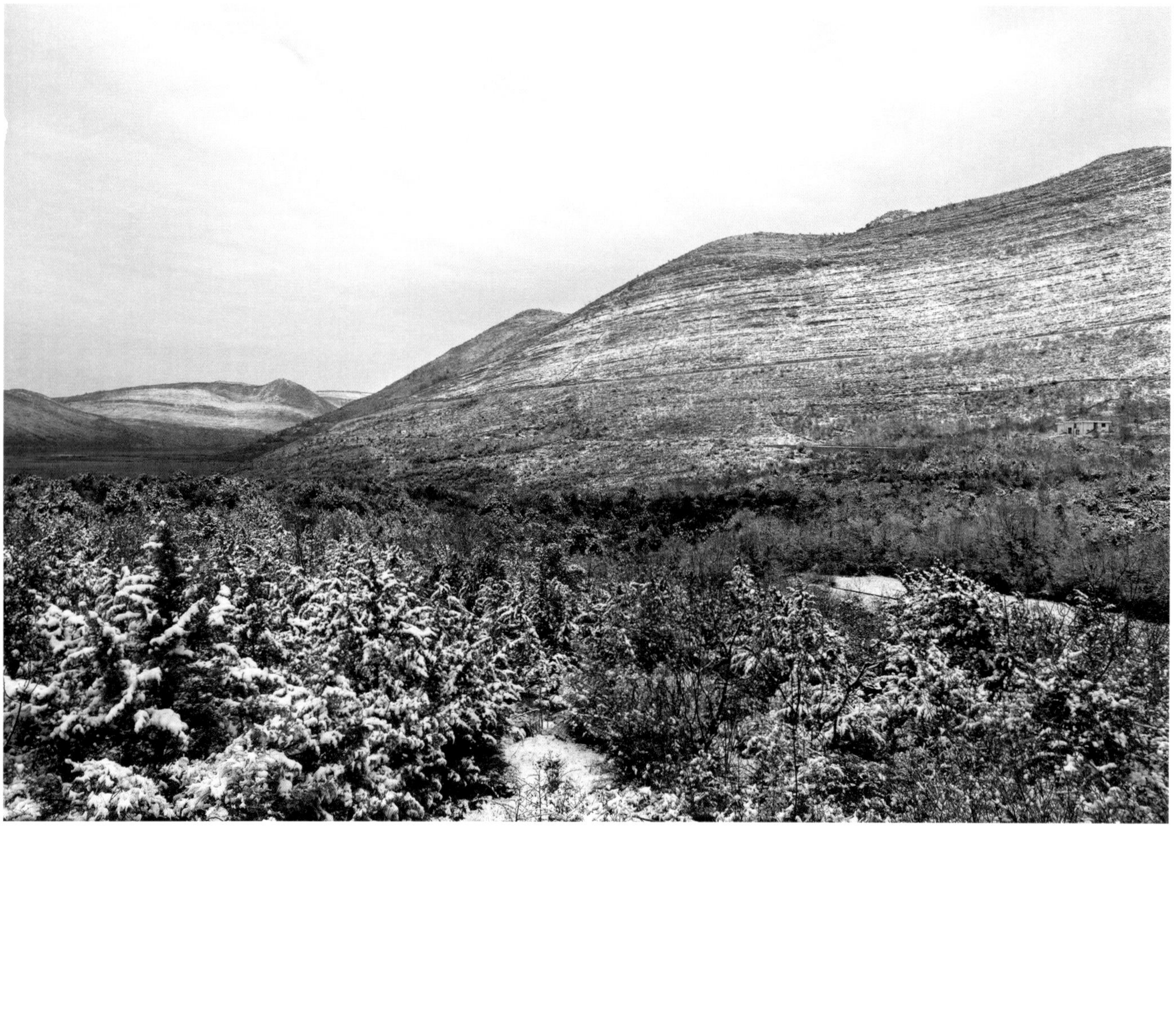

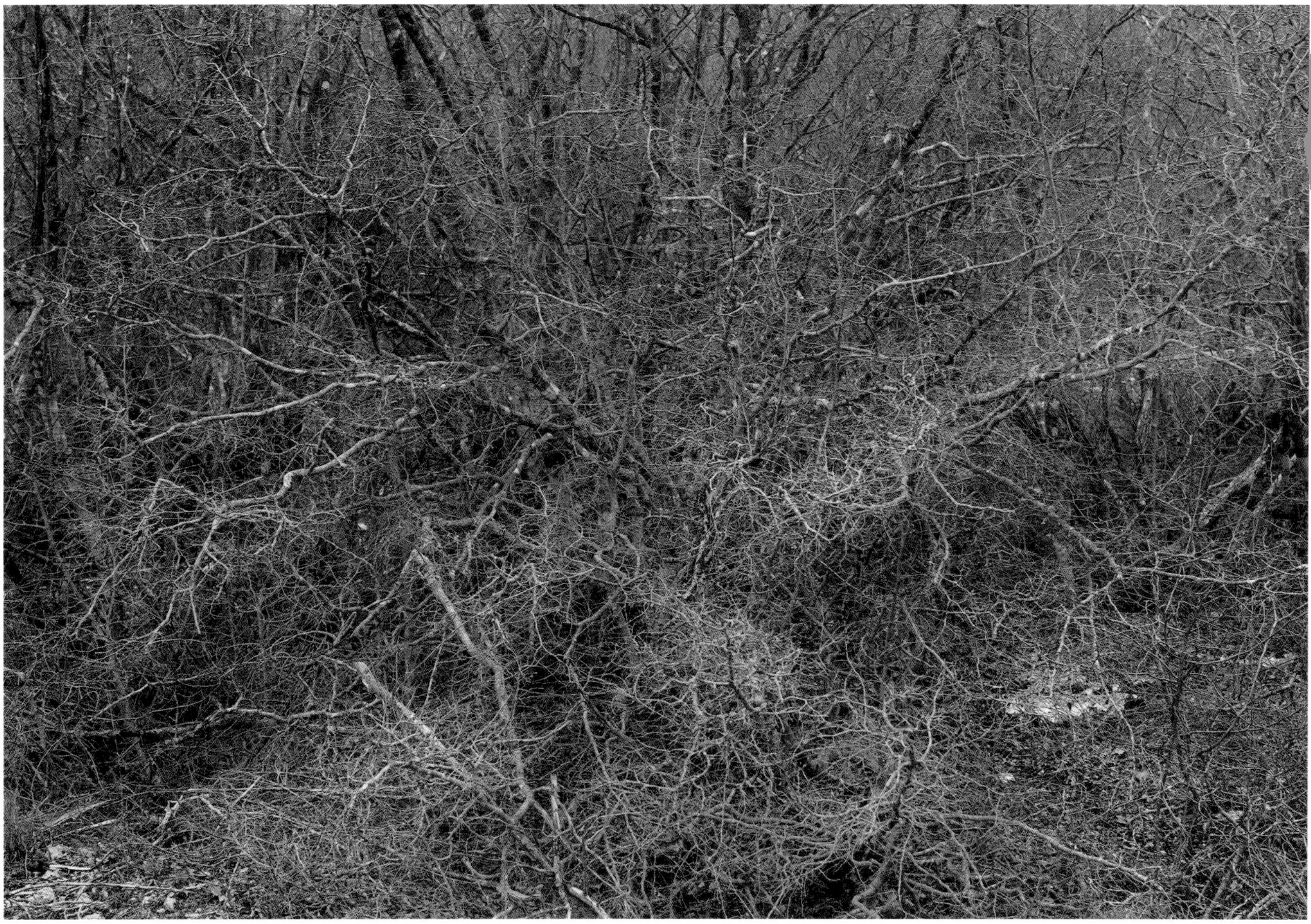

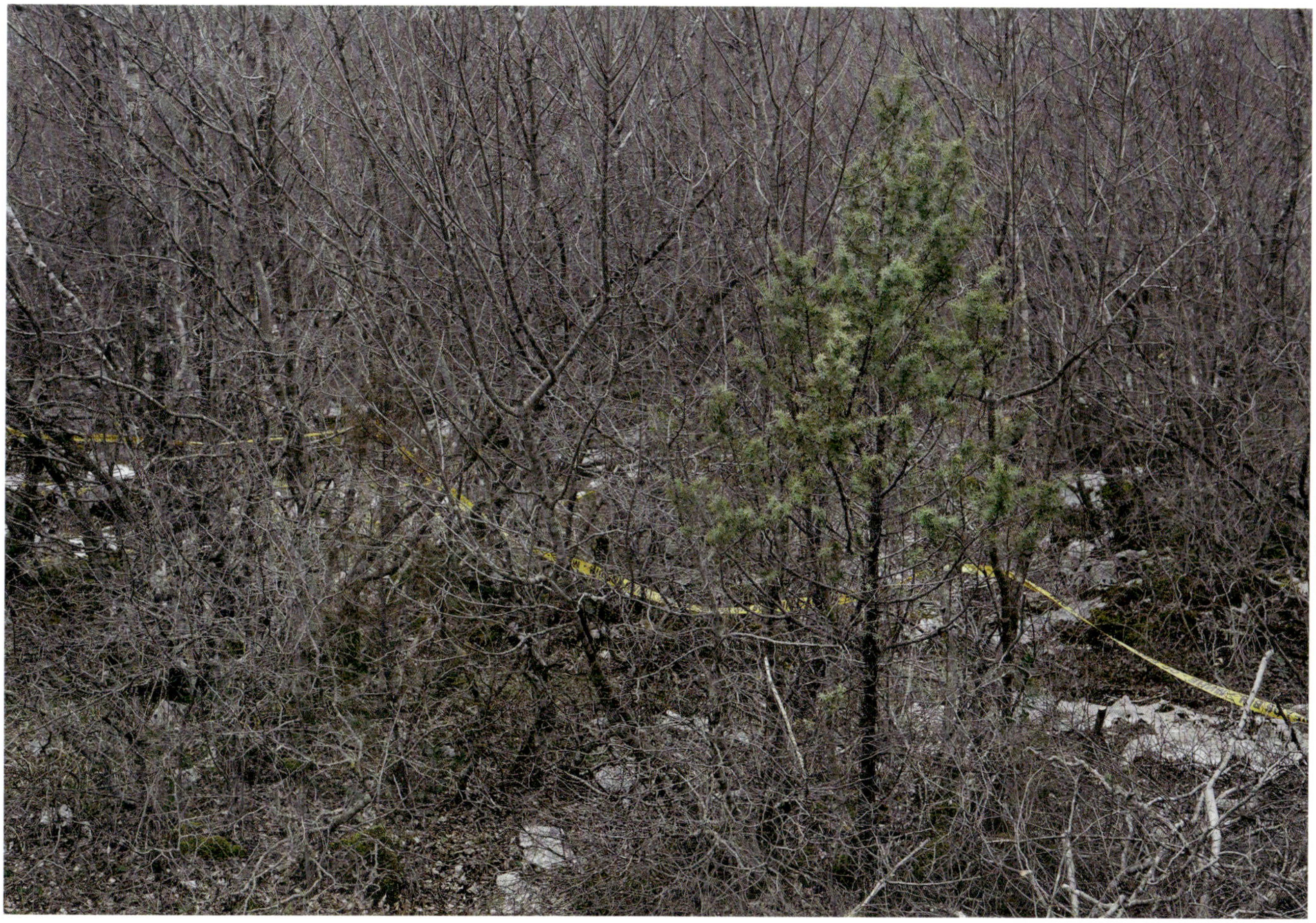

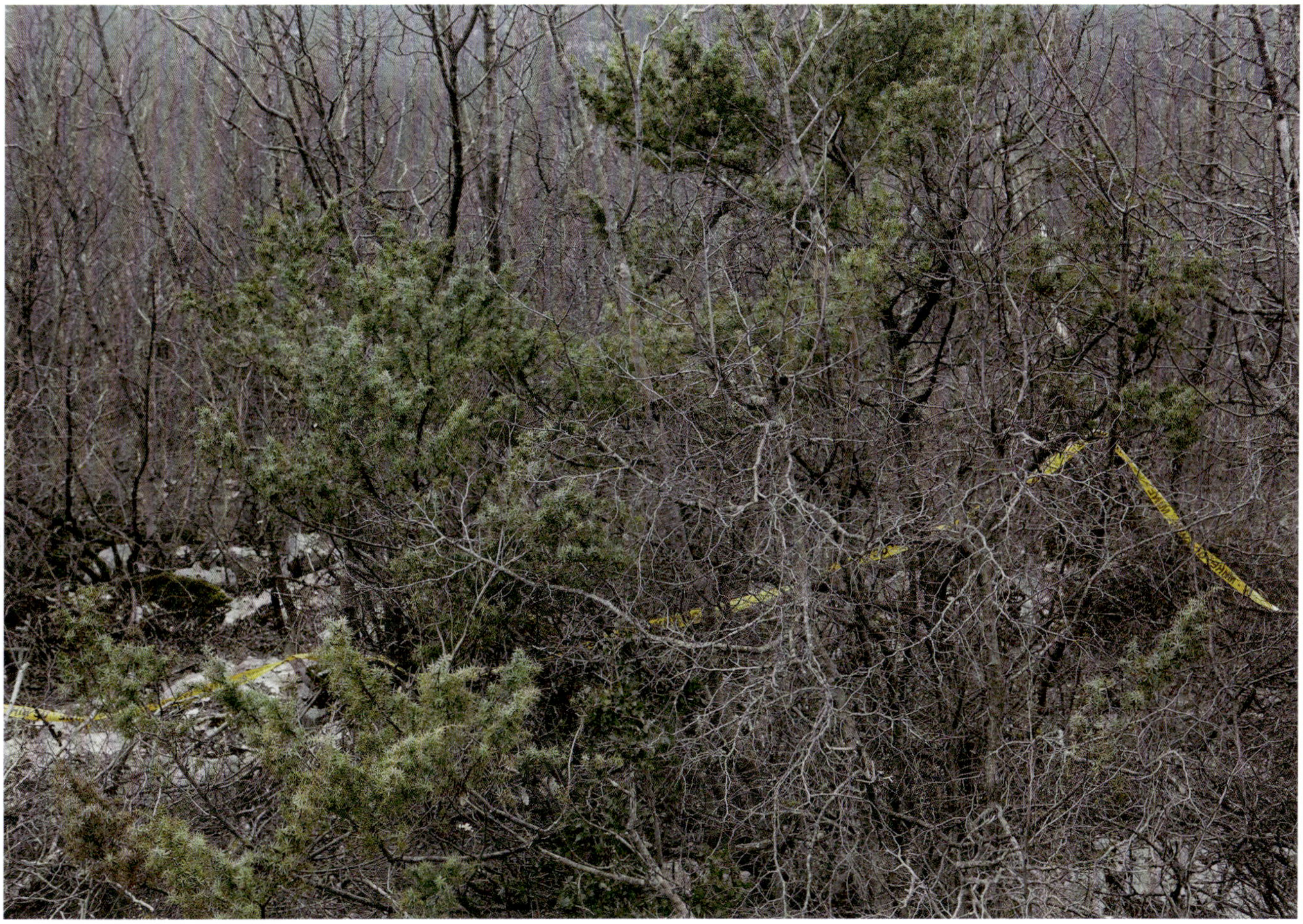

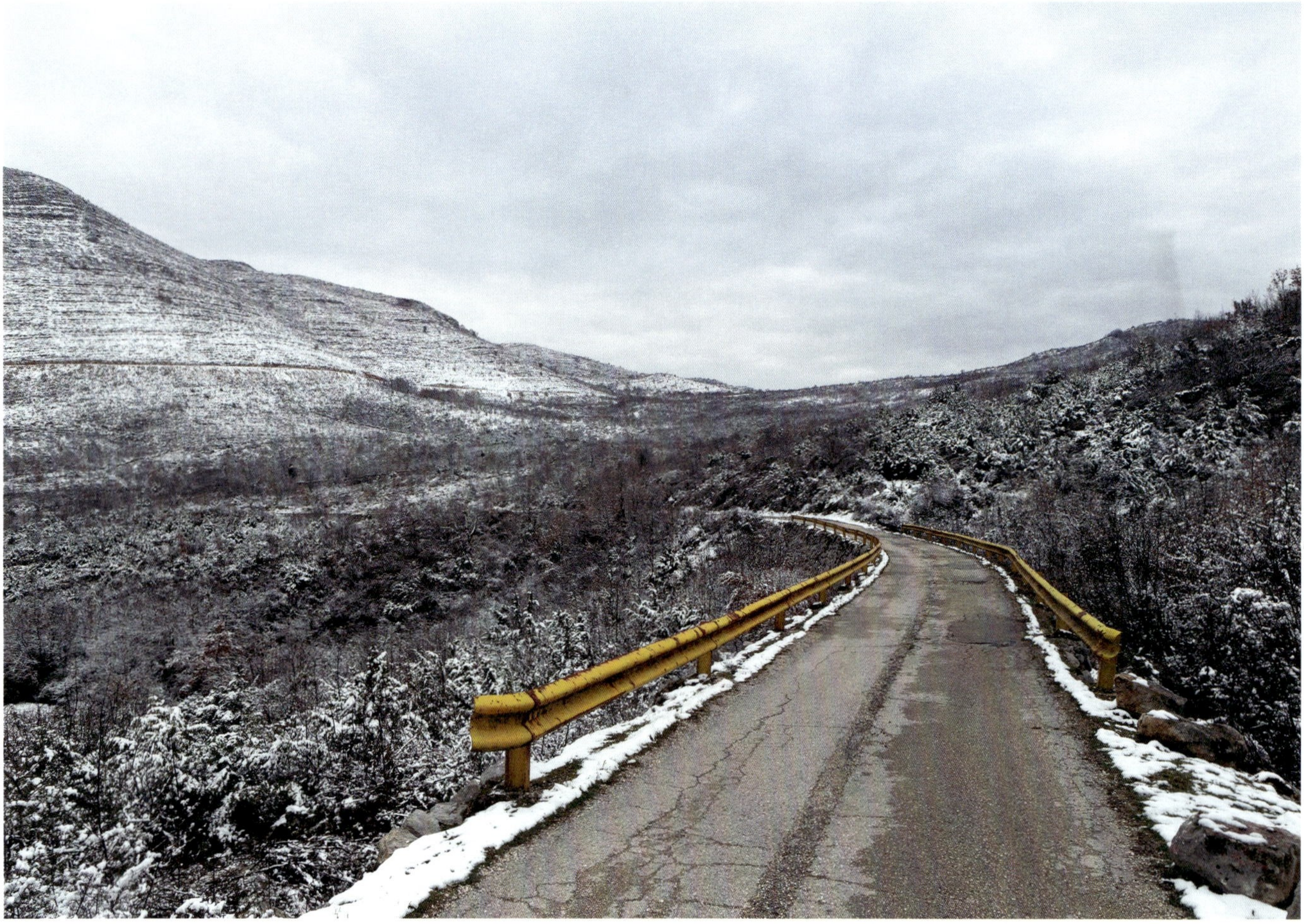

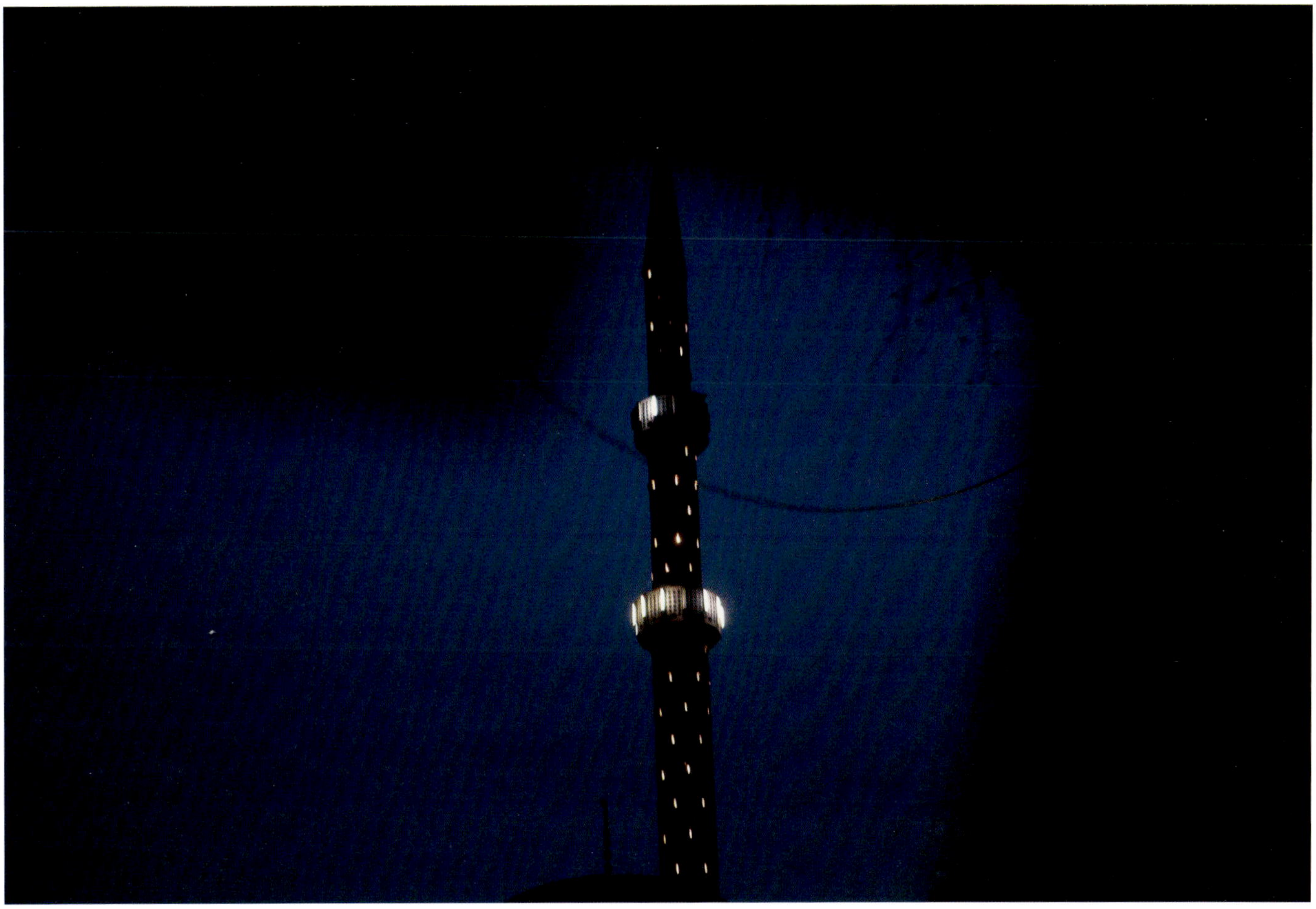

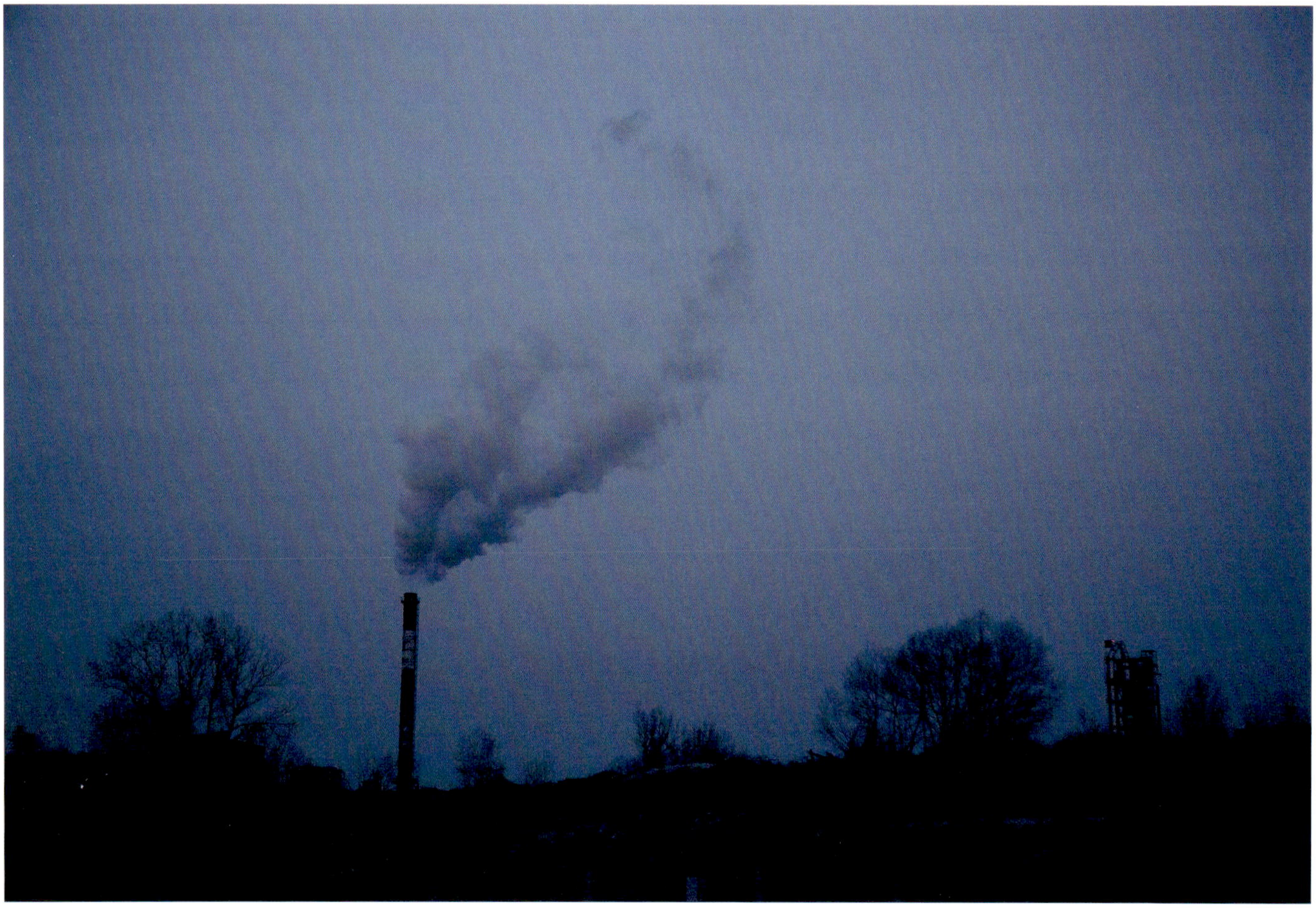

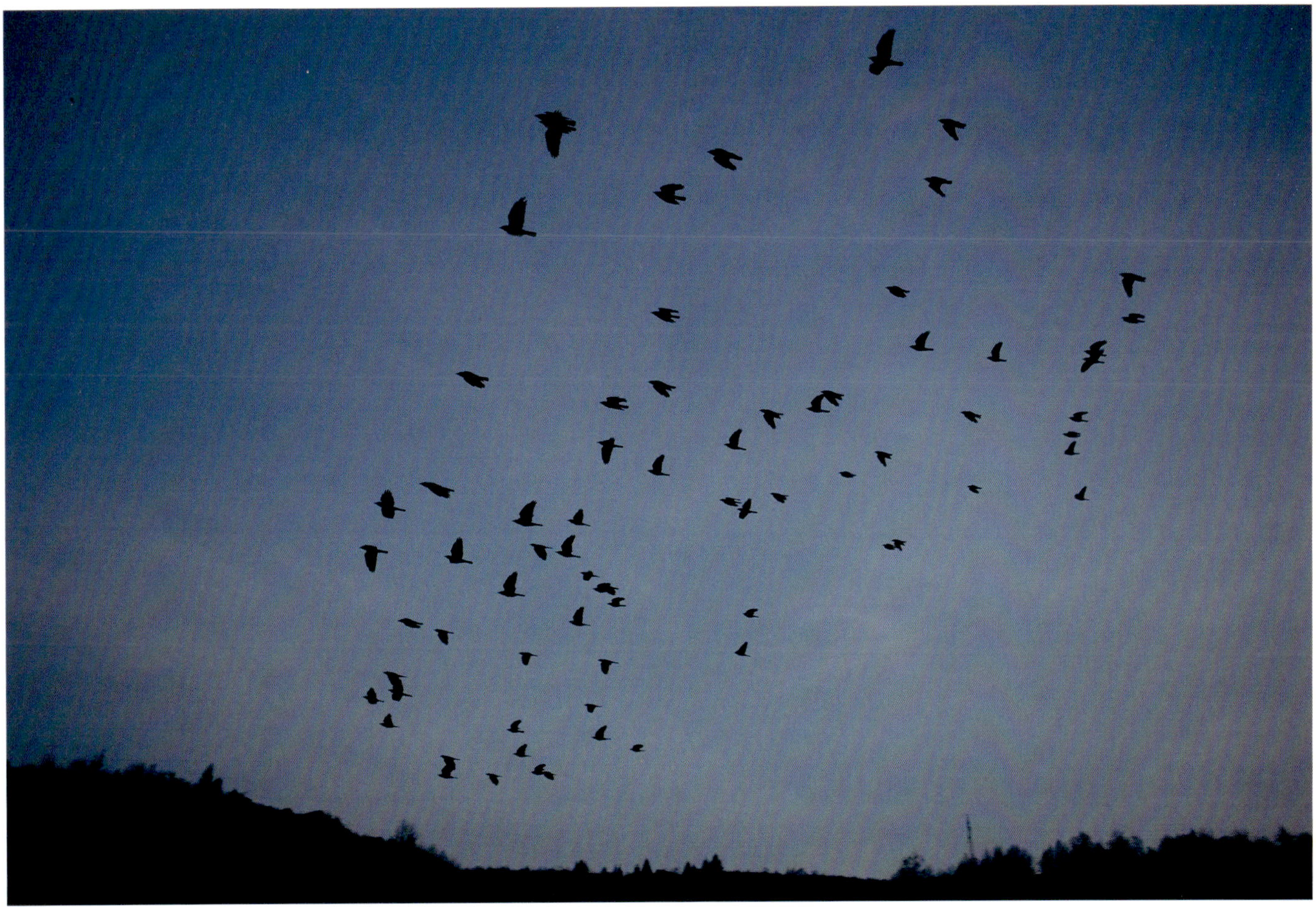

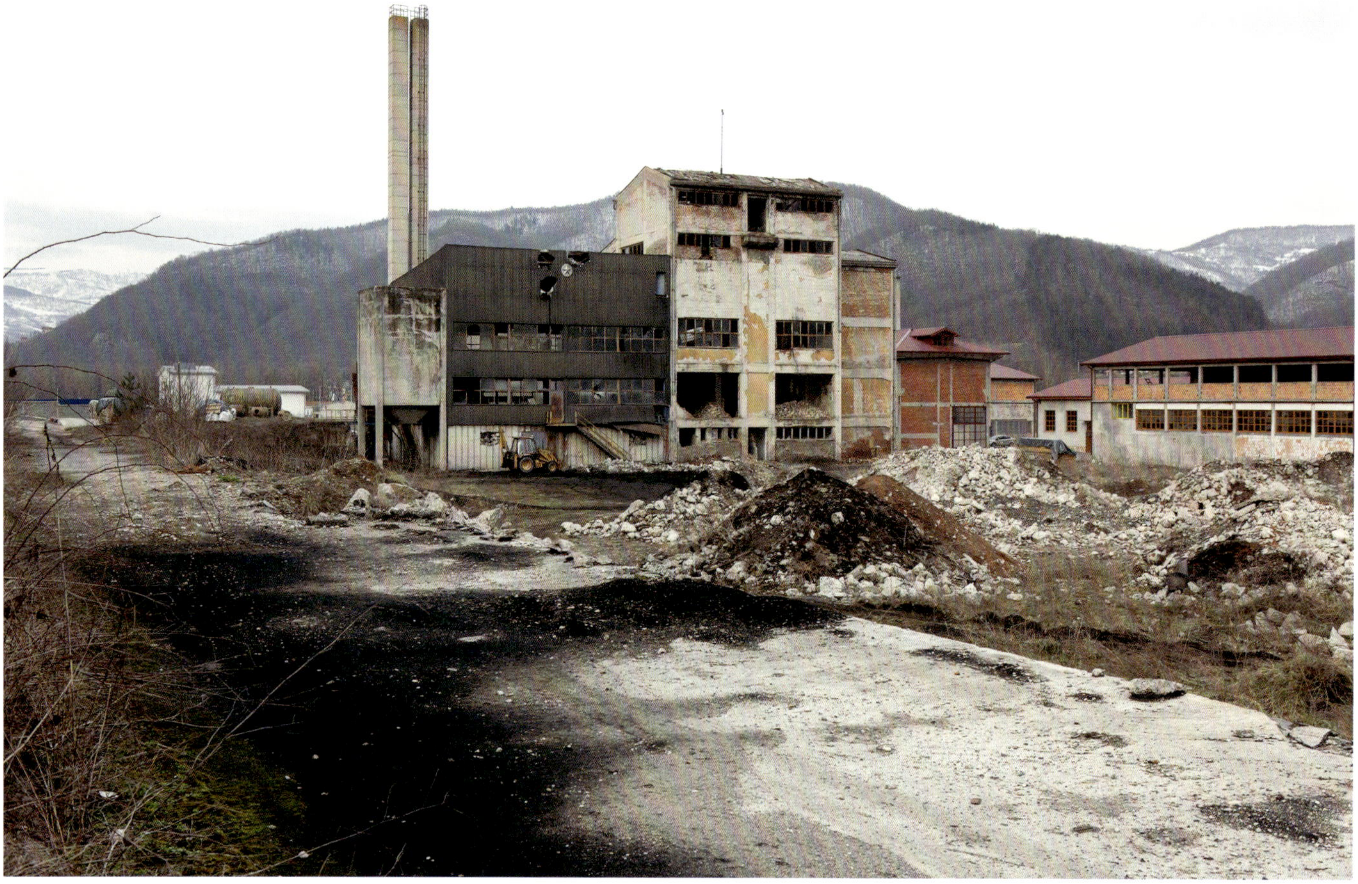

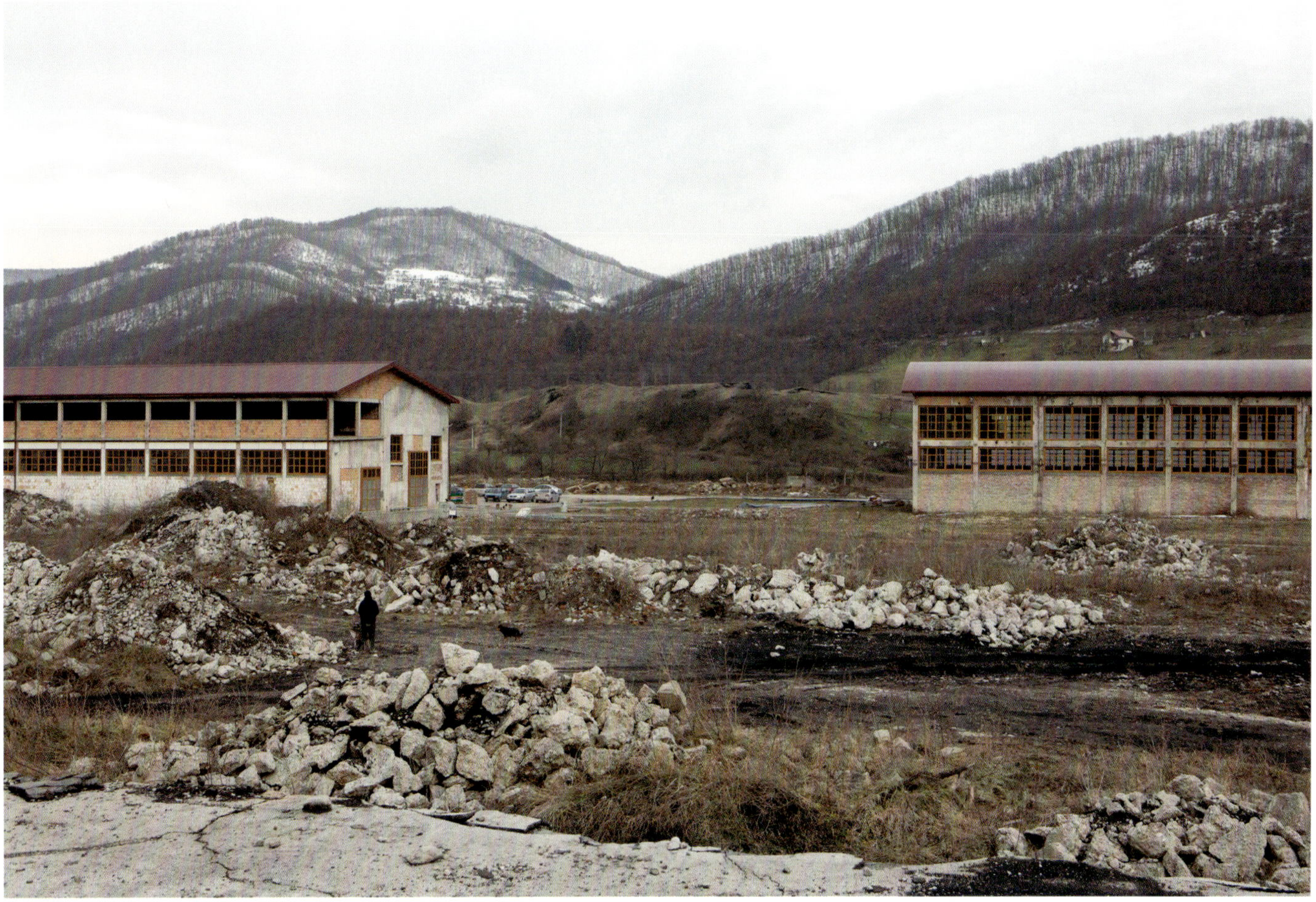

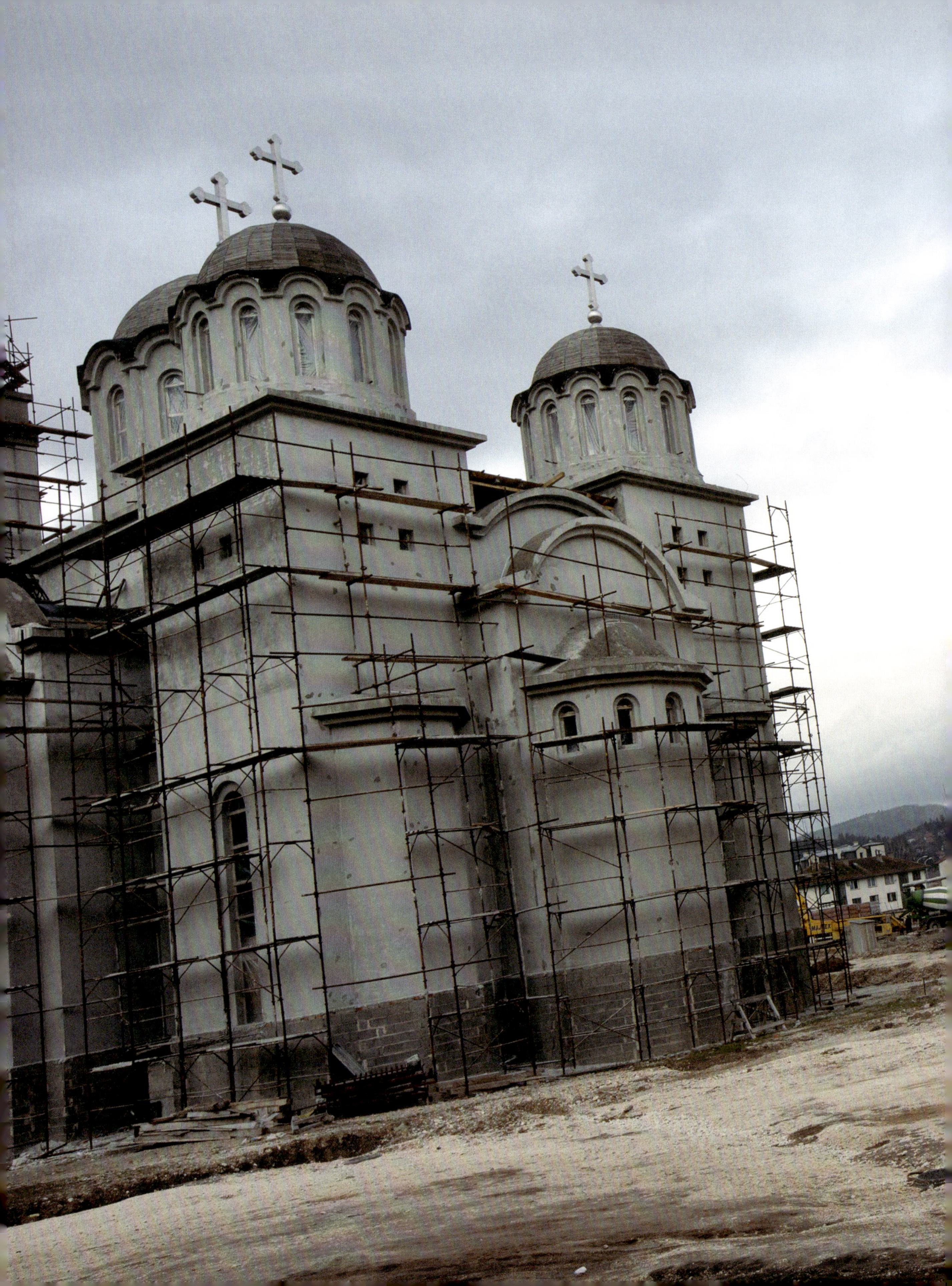

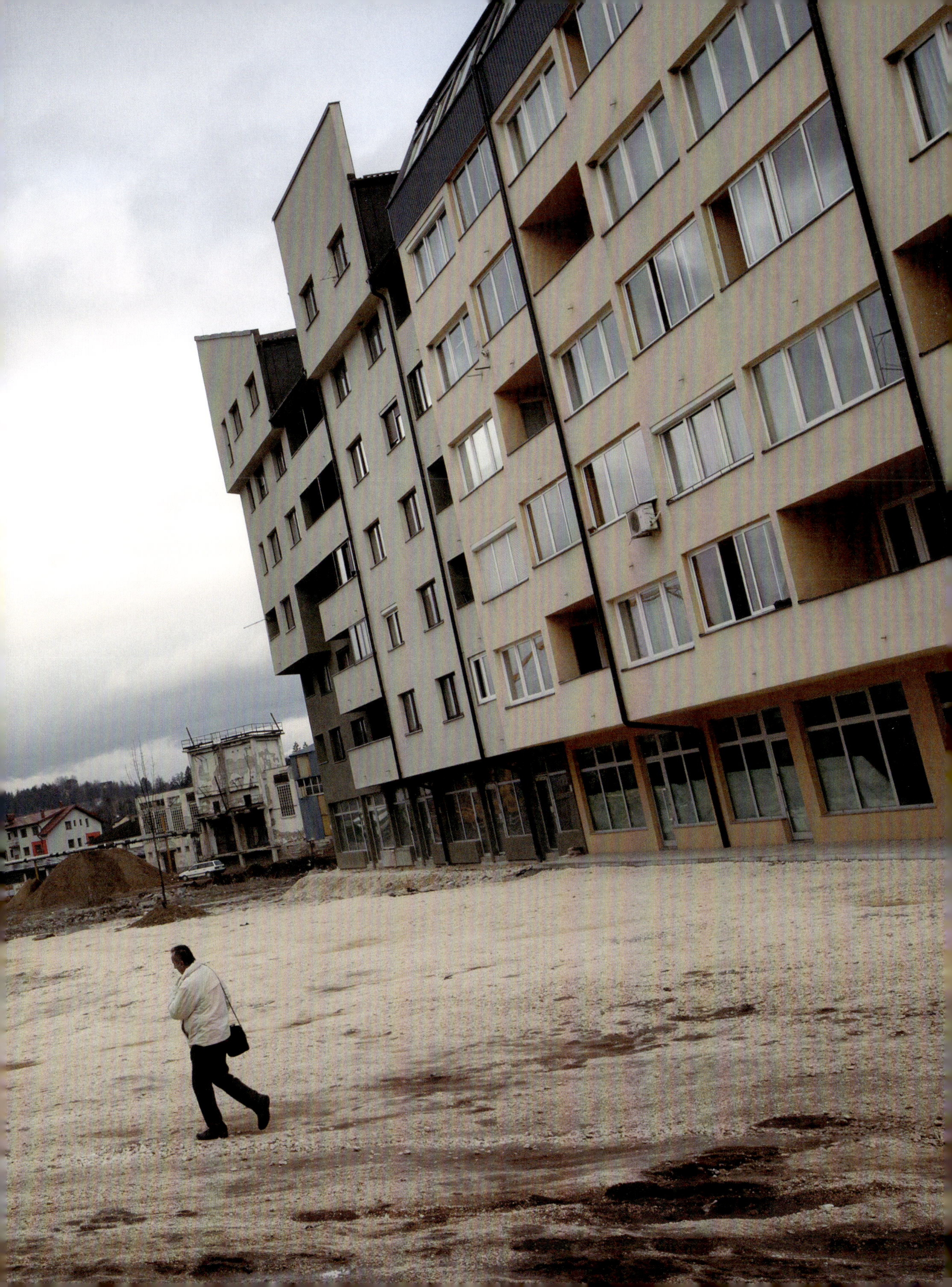

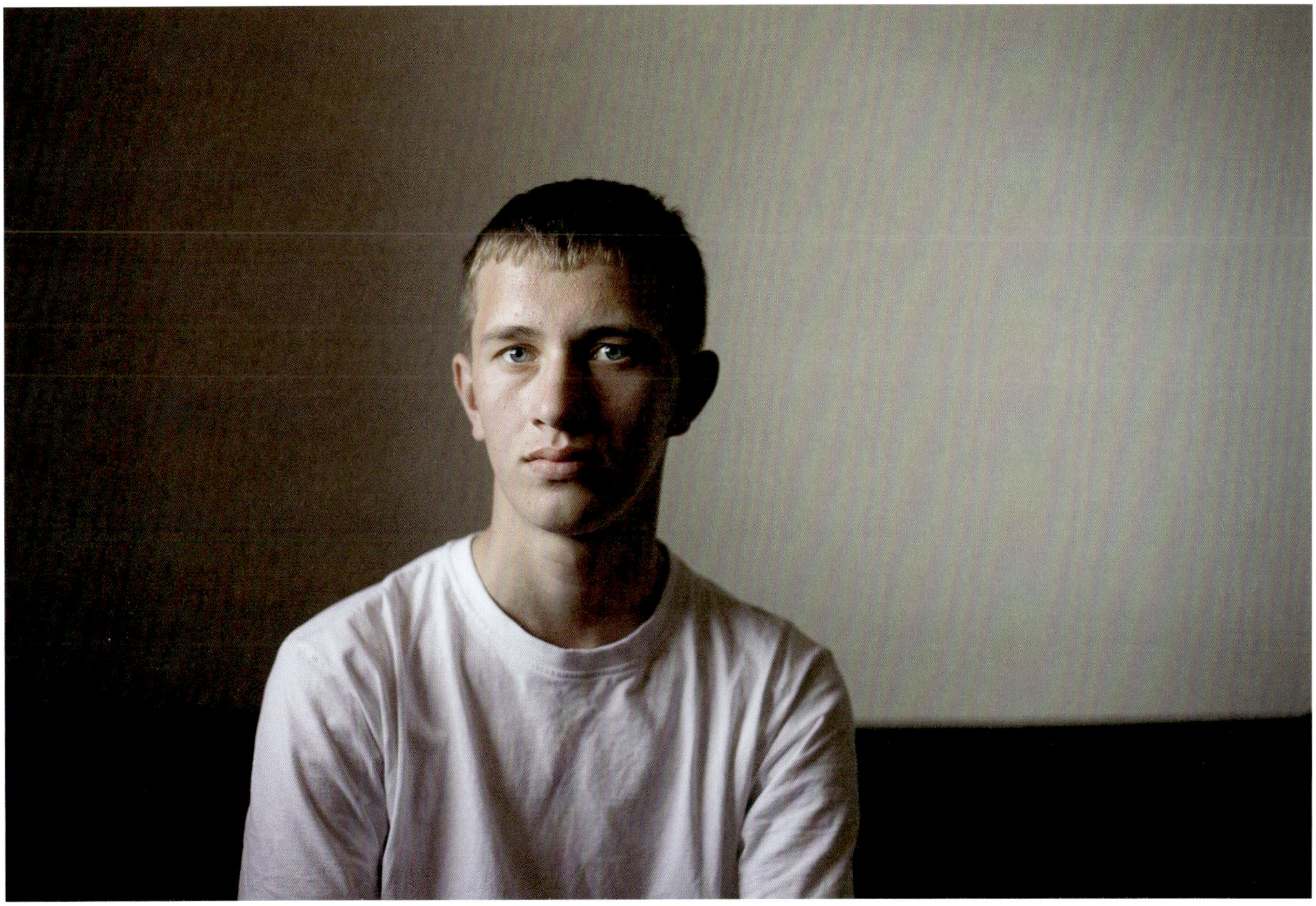

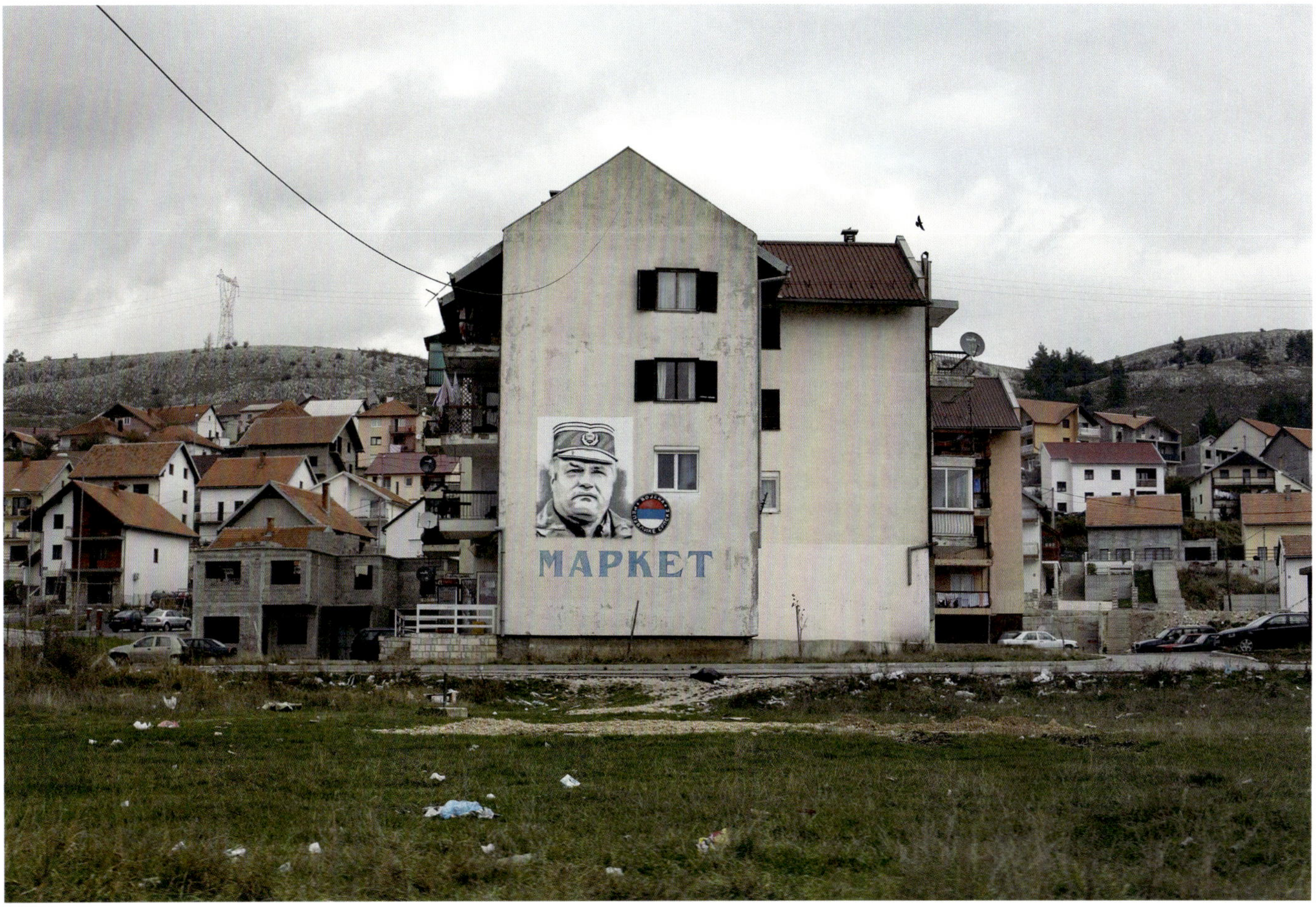
МАРКЕТ

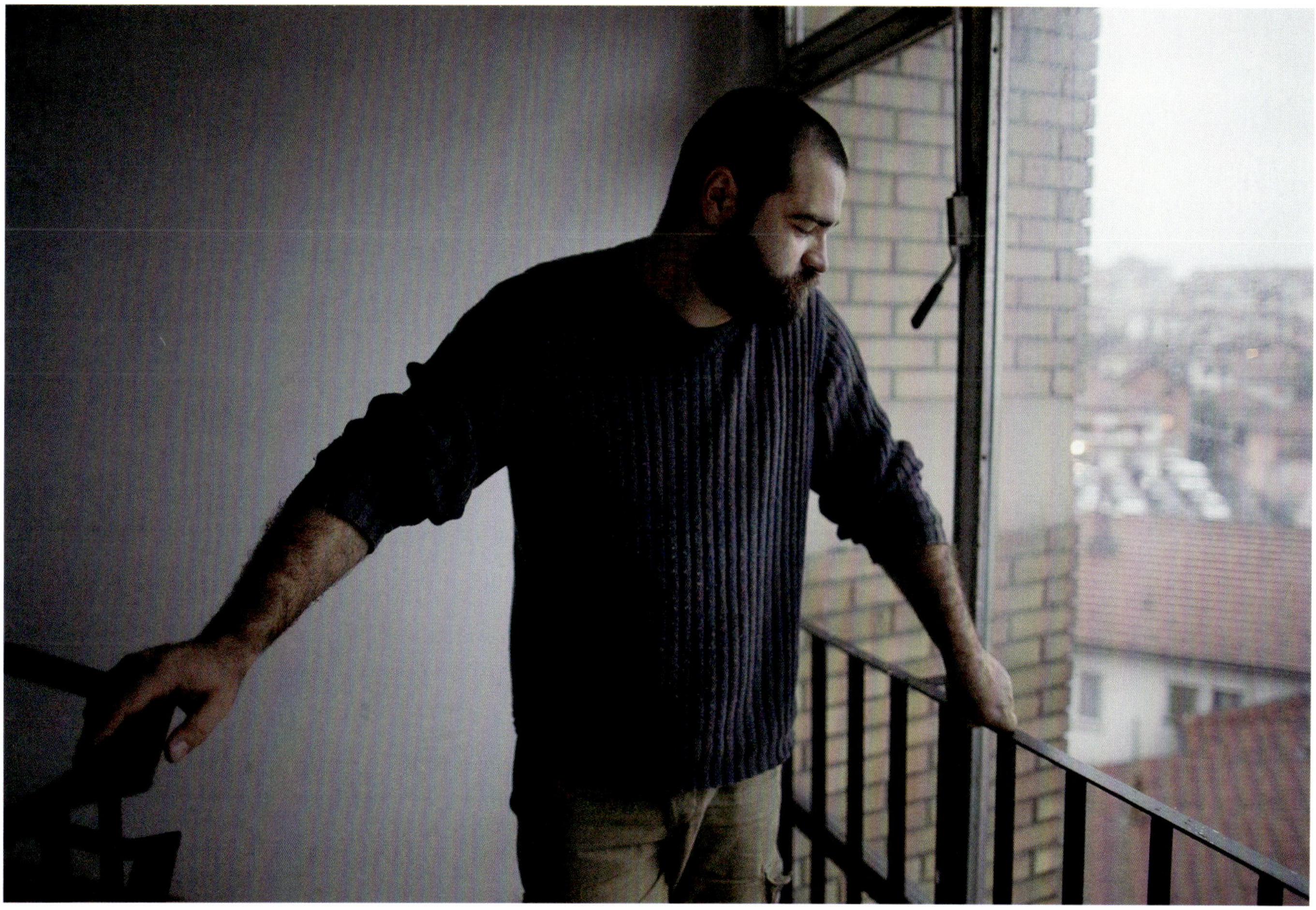

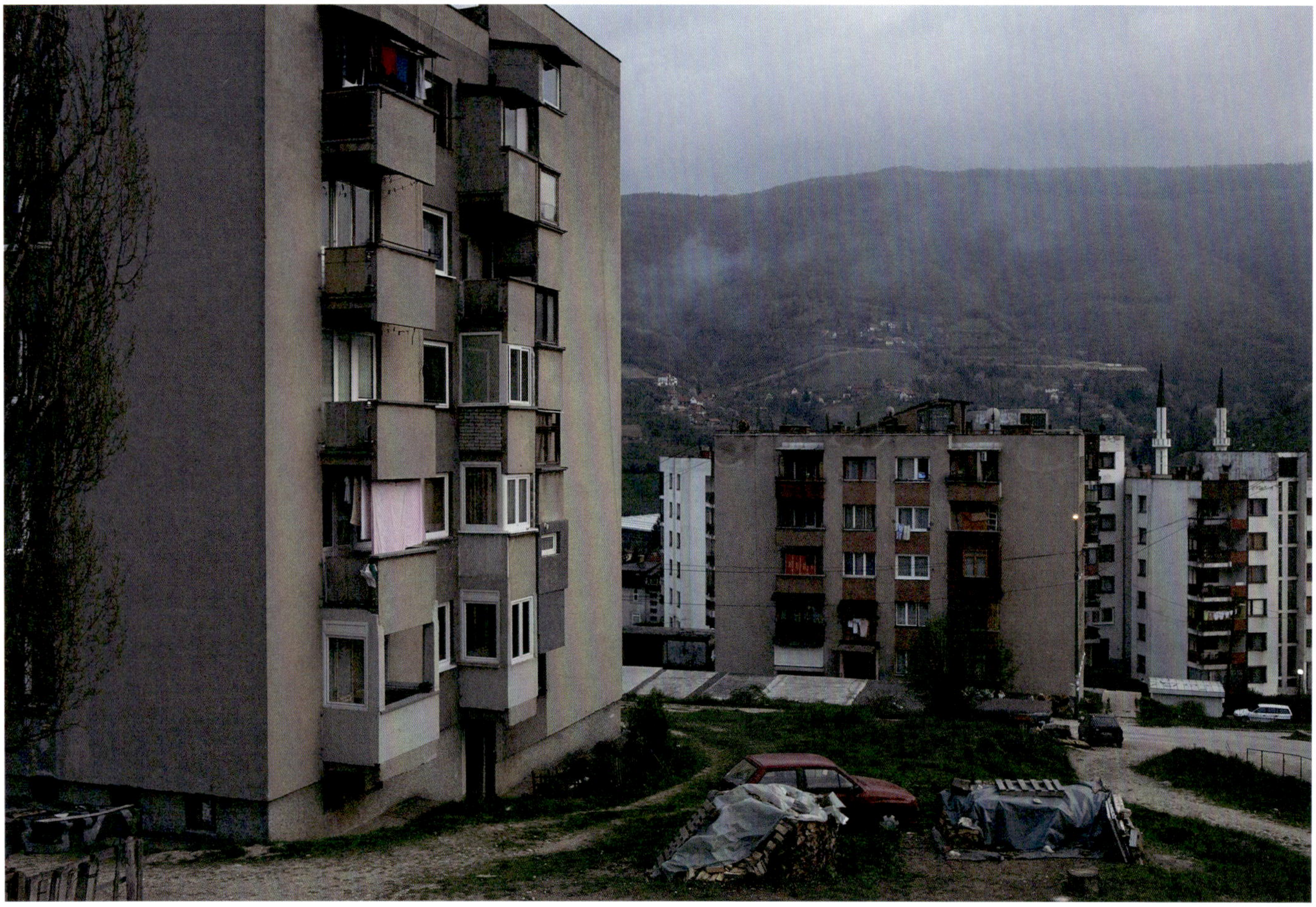

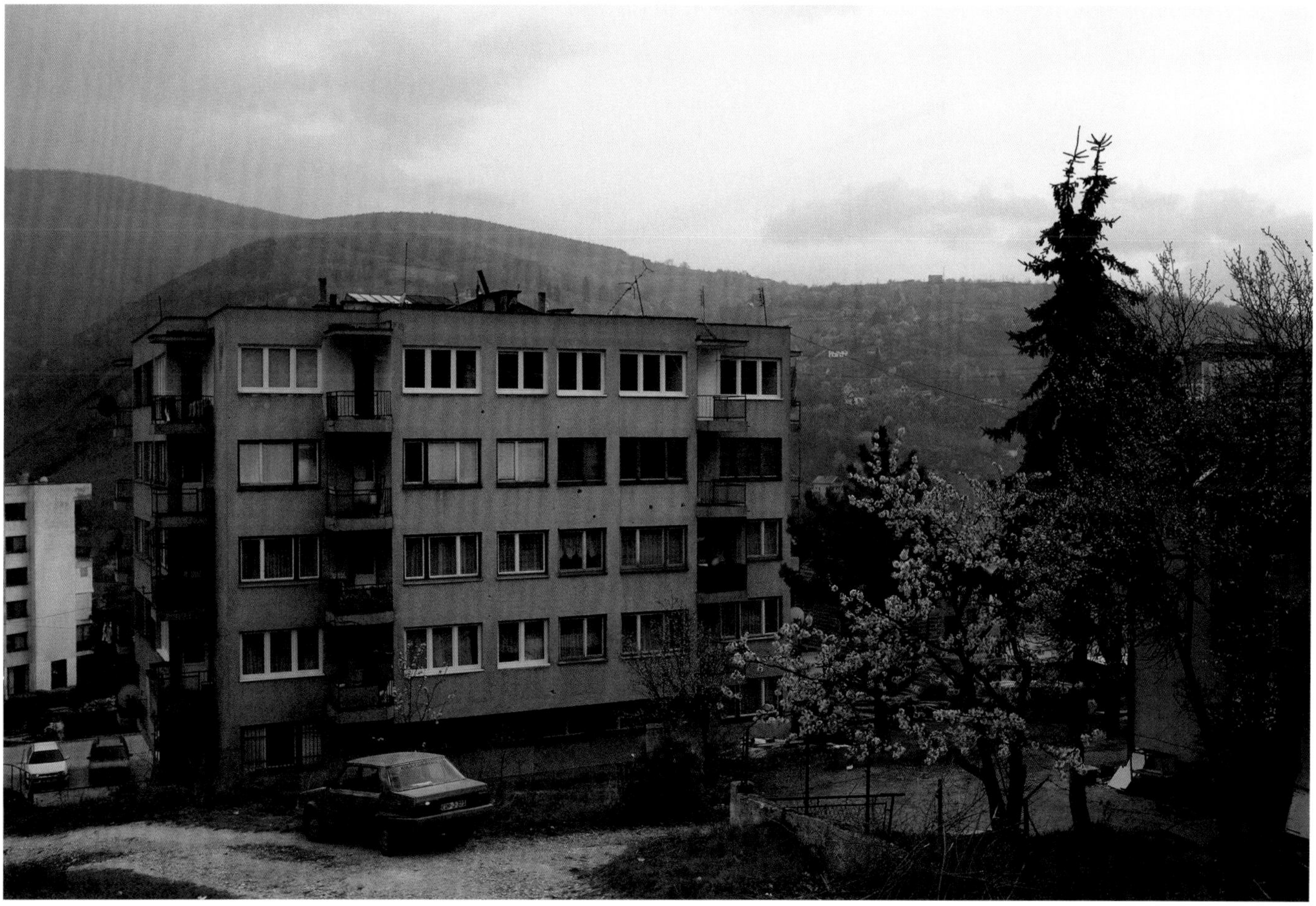

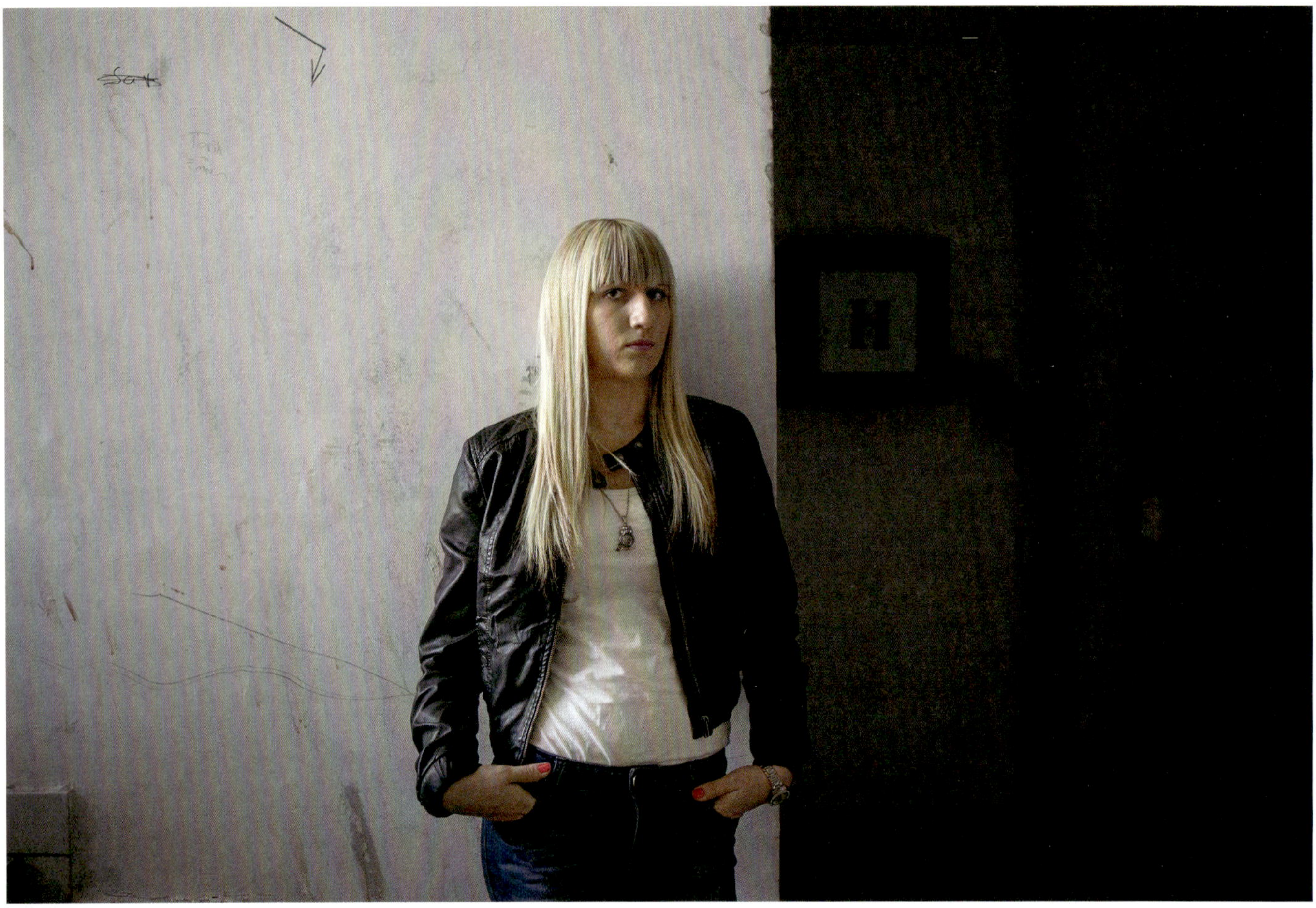

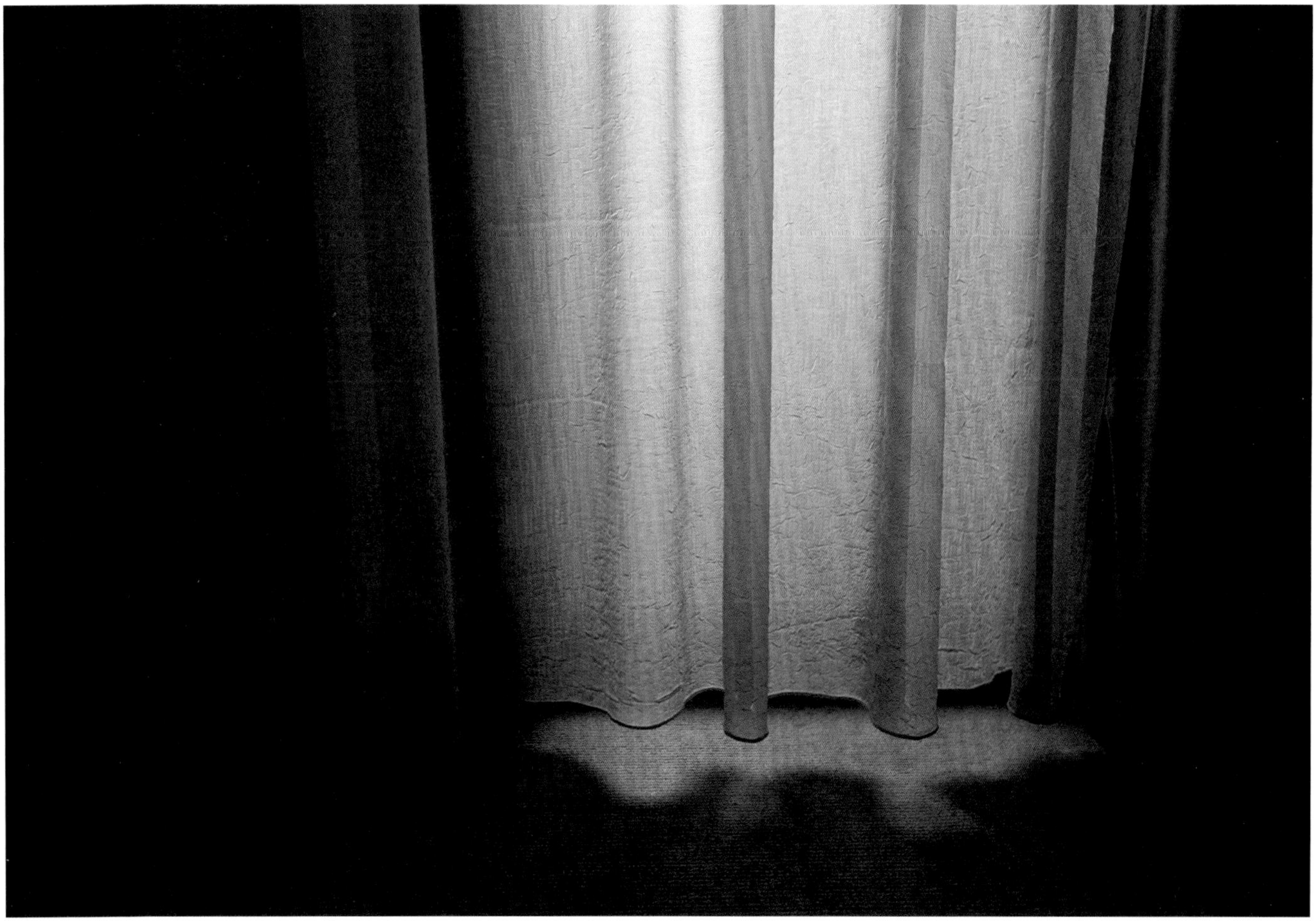

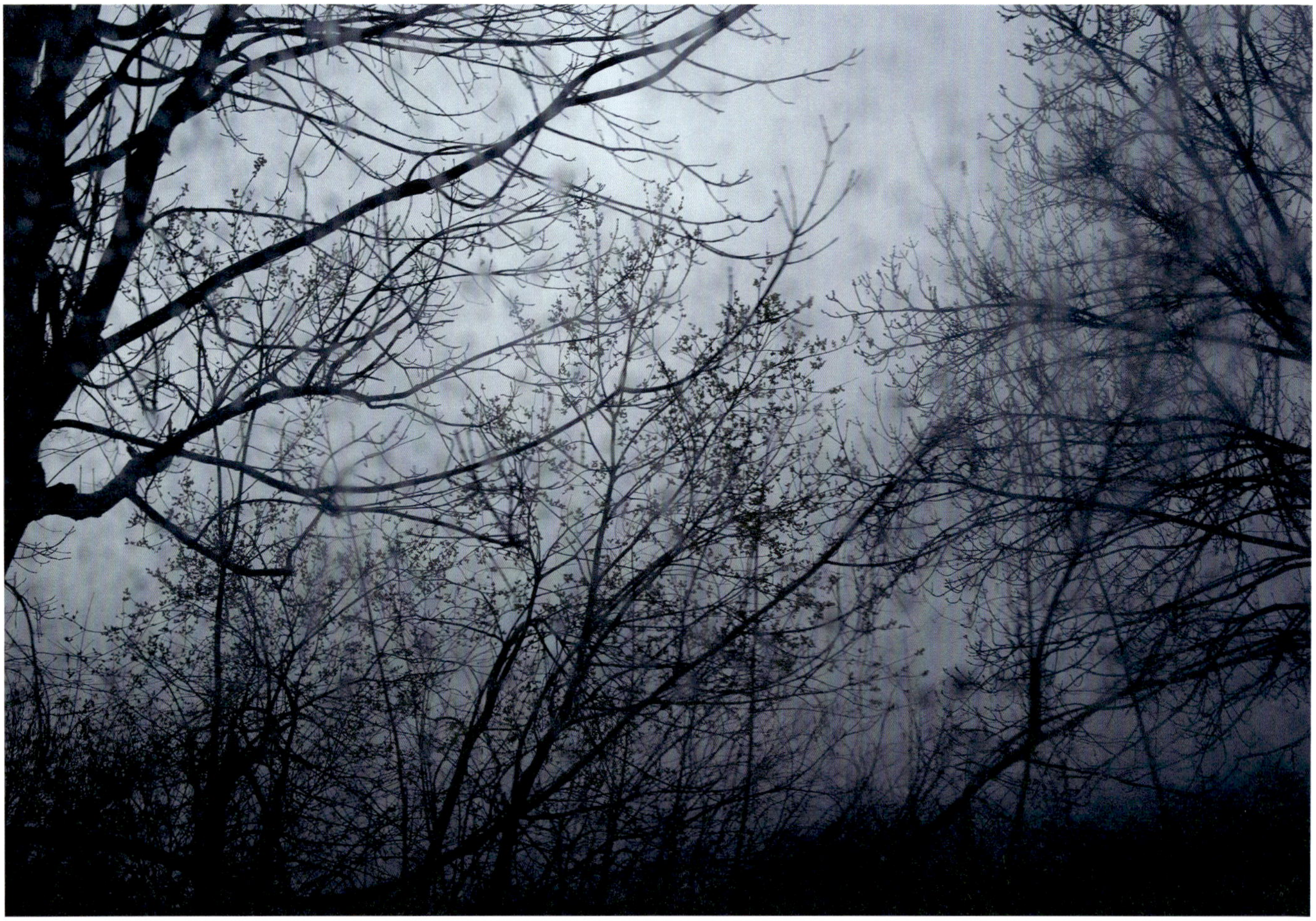

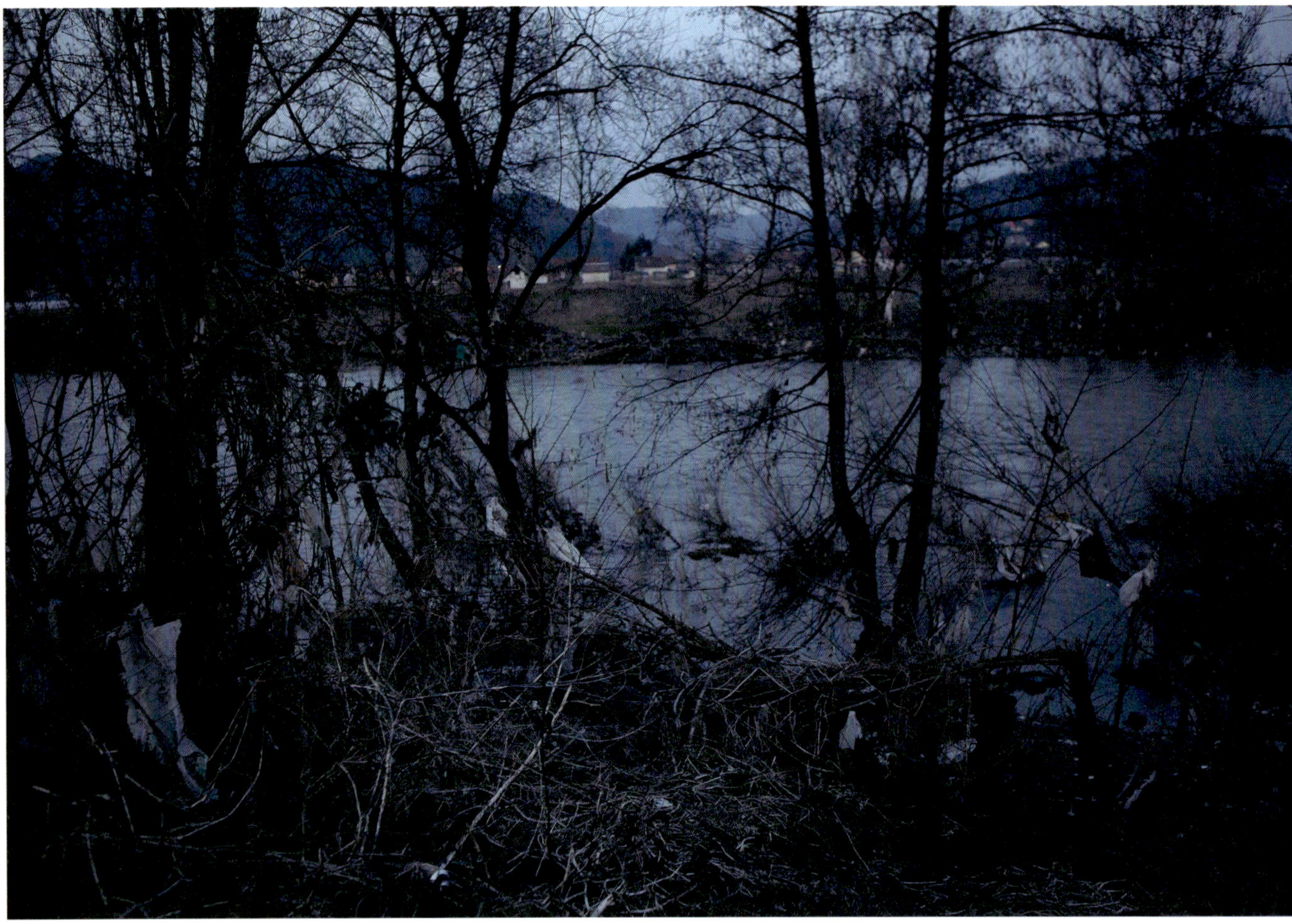

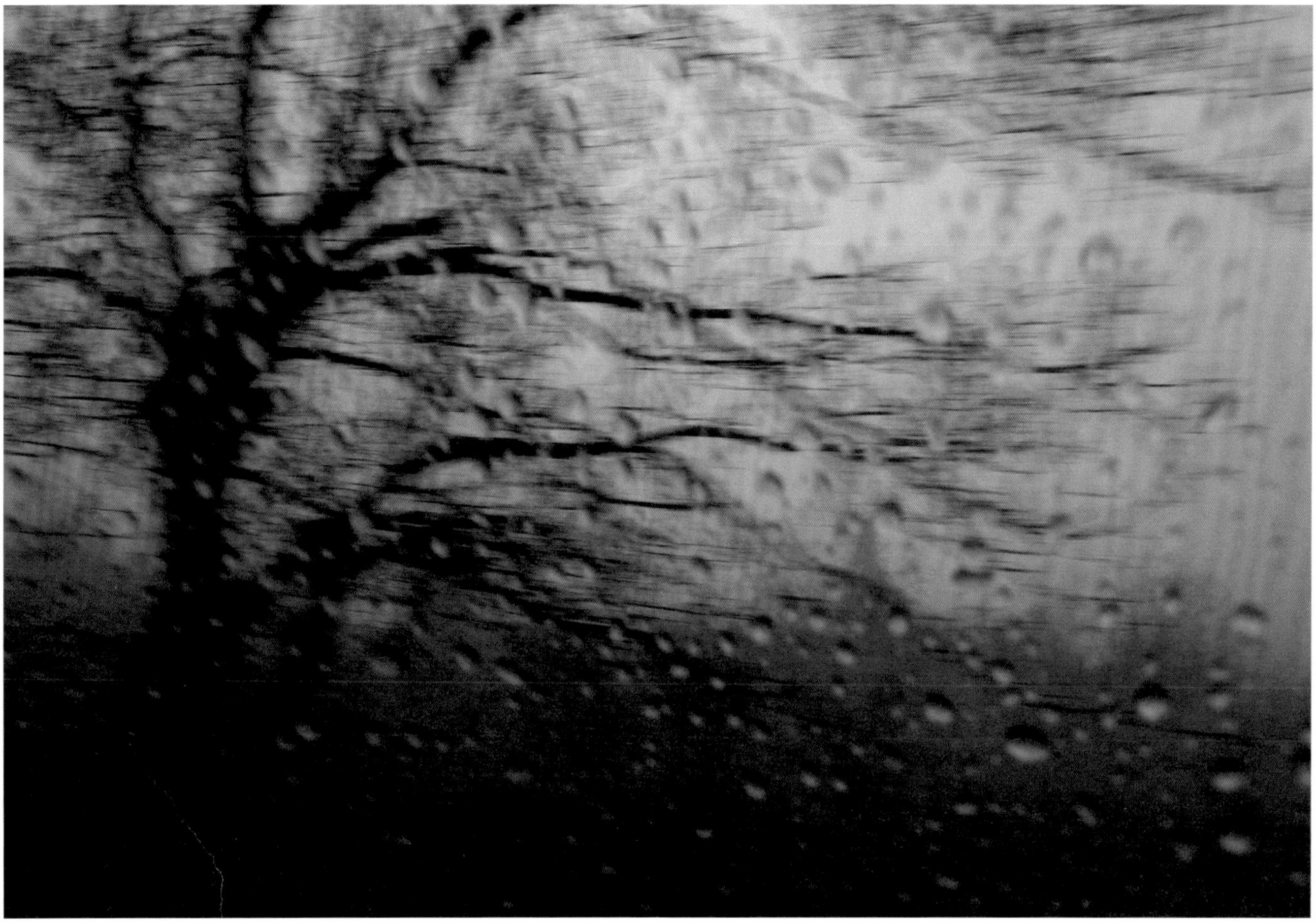

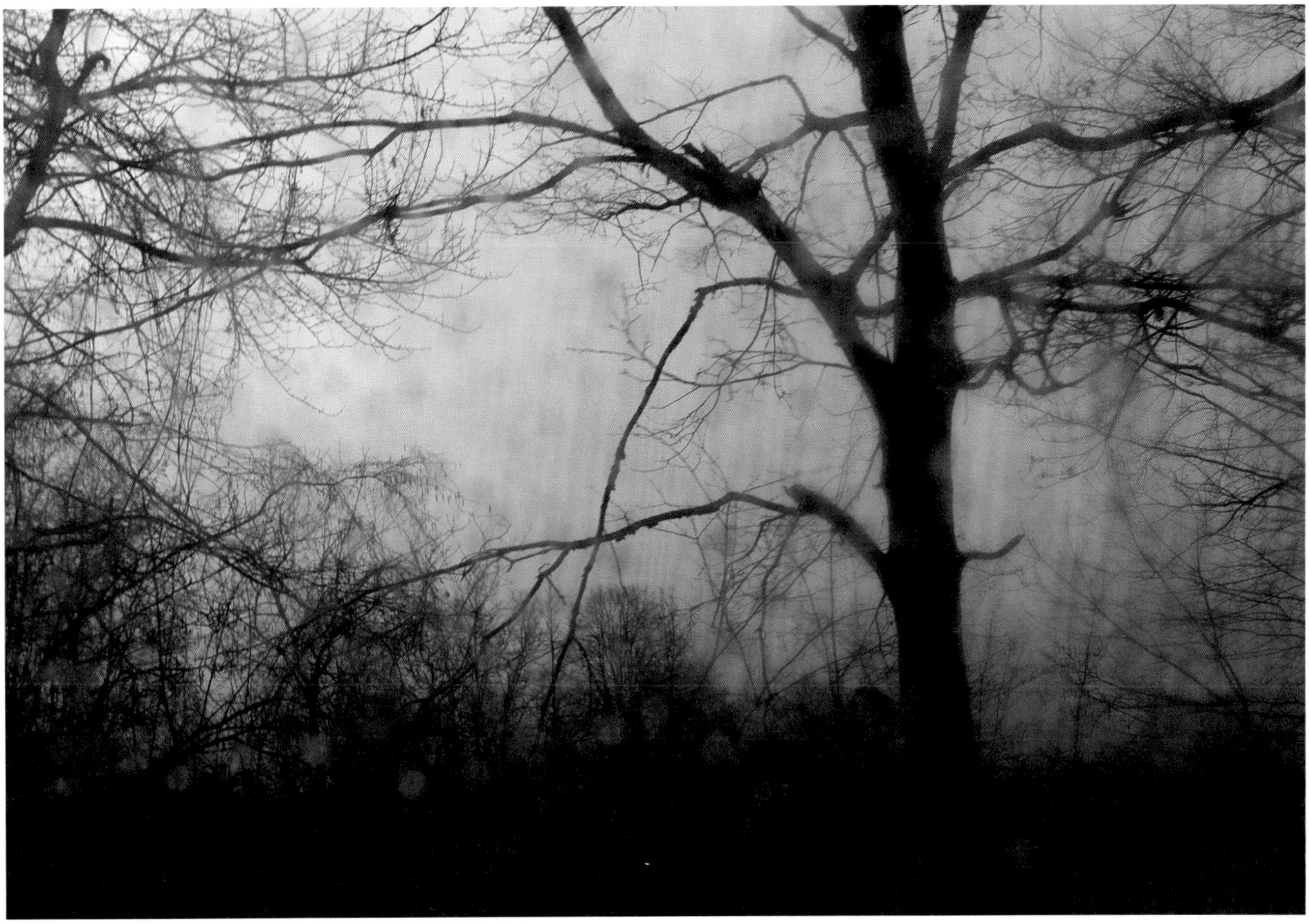

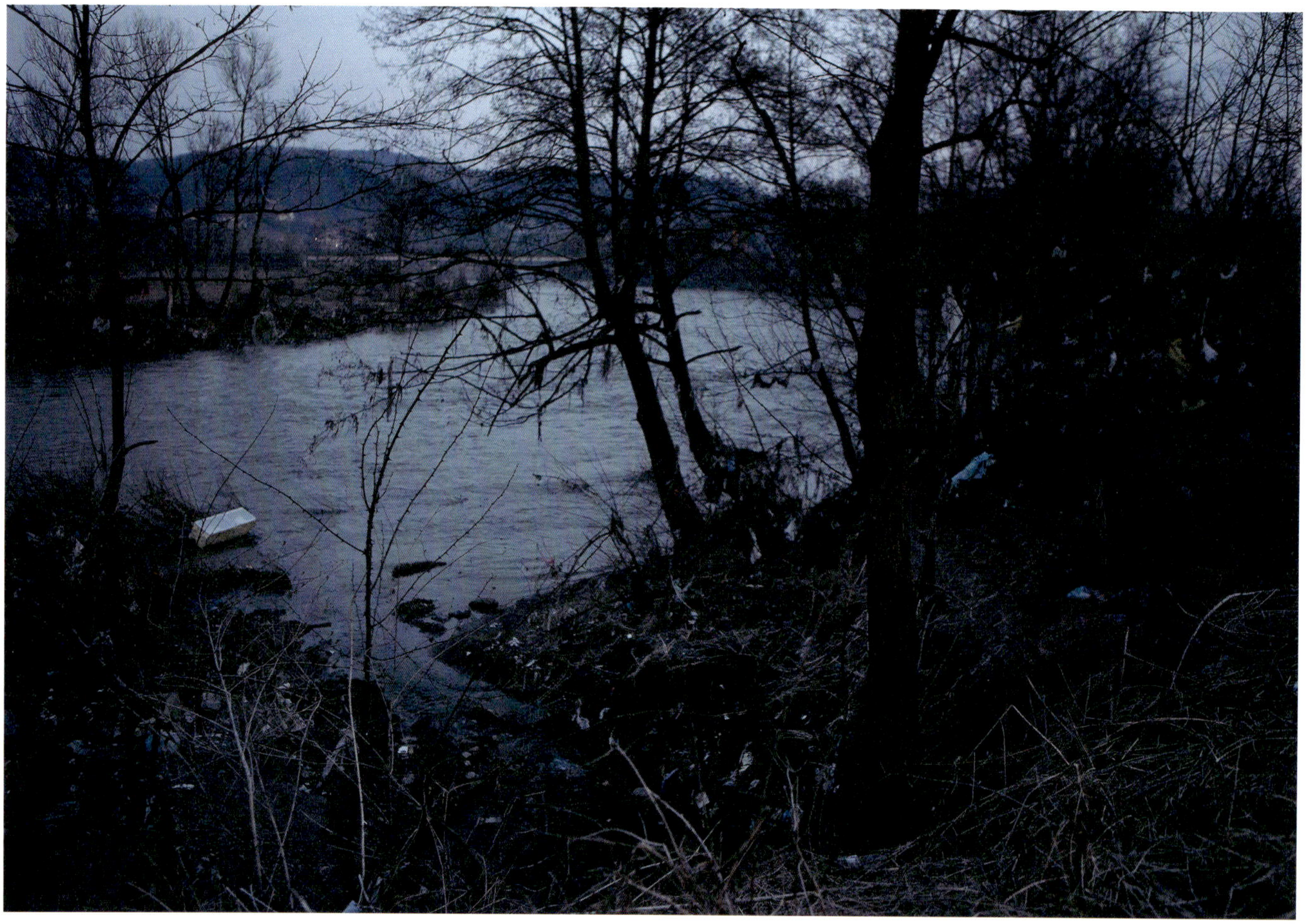

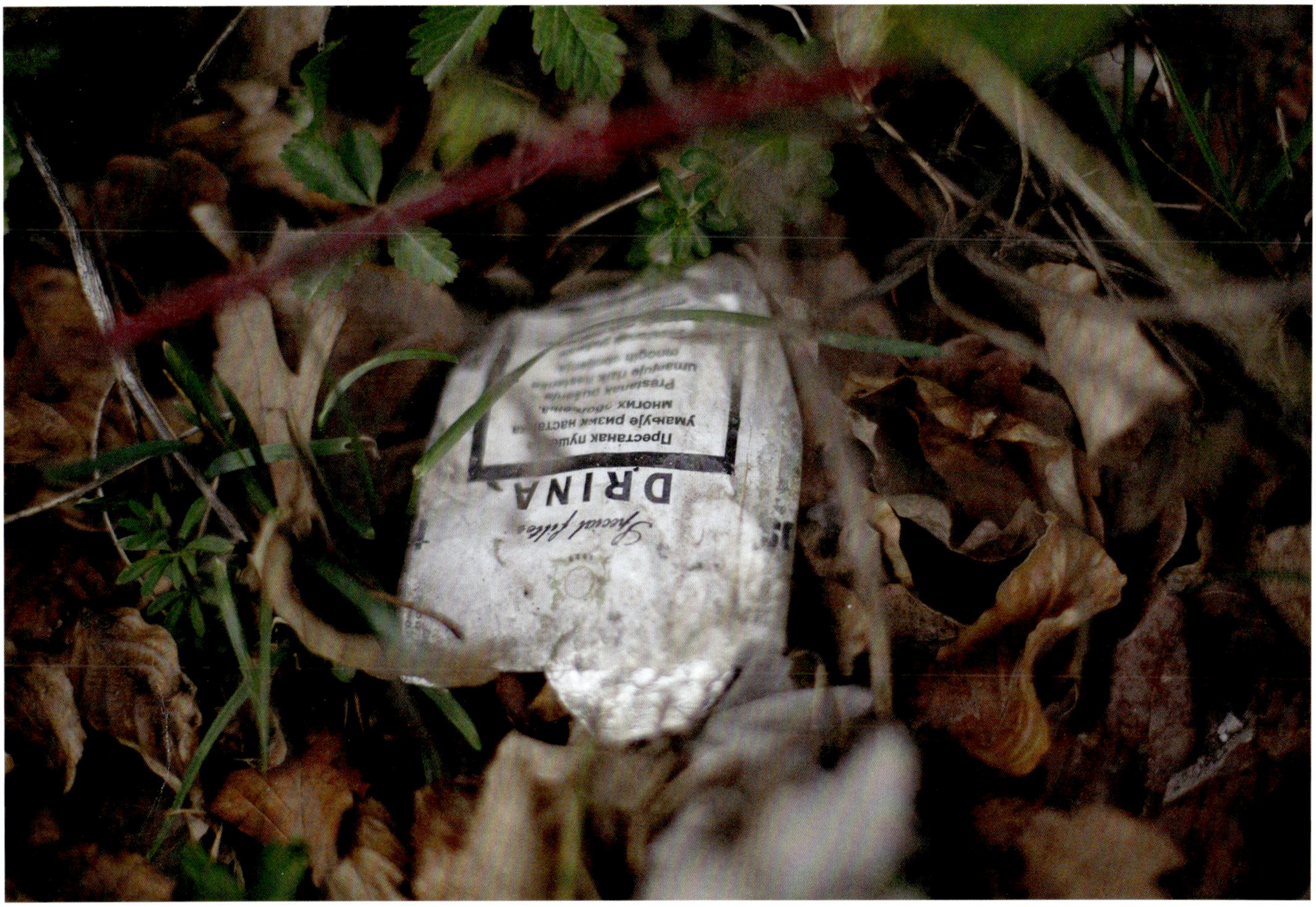
DRINA

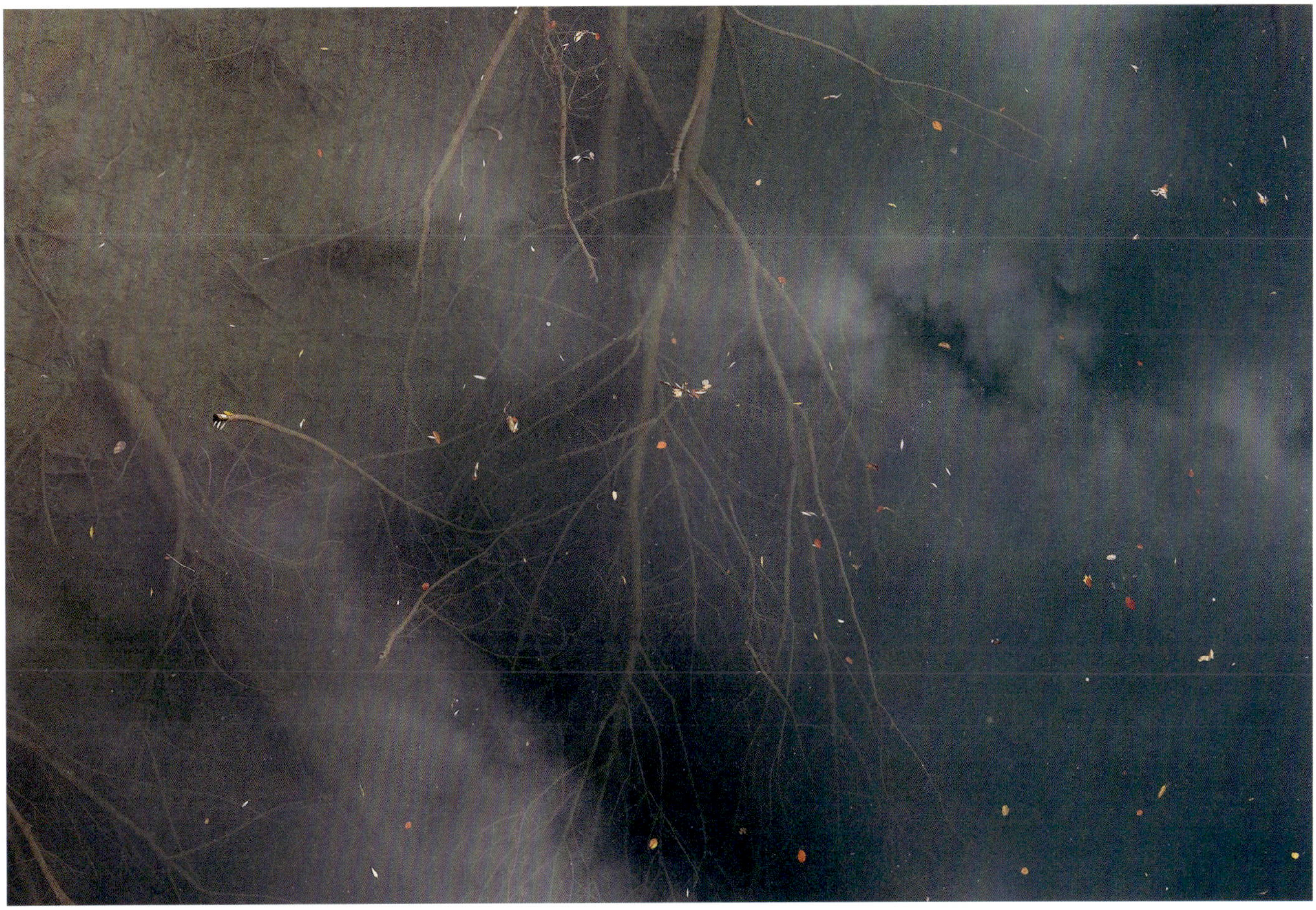

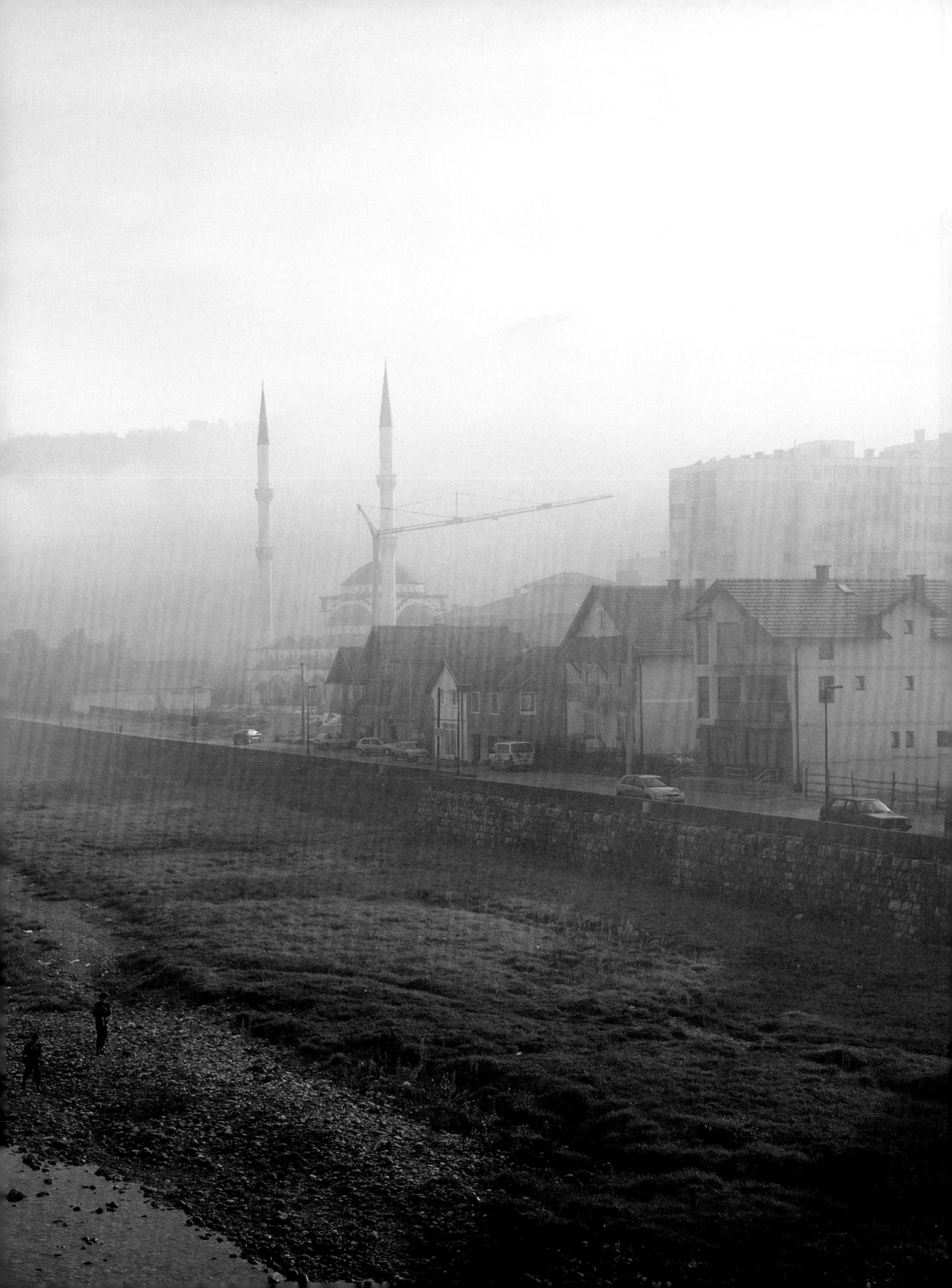

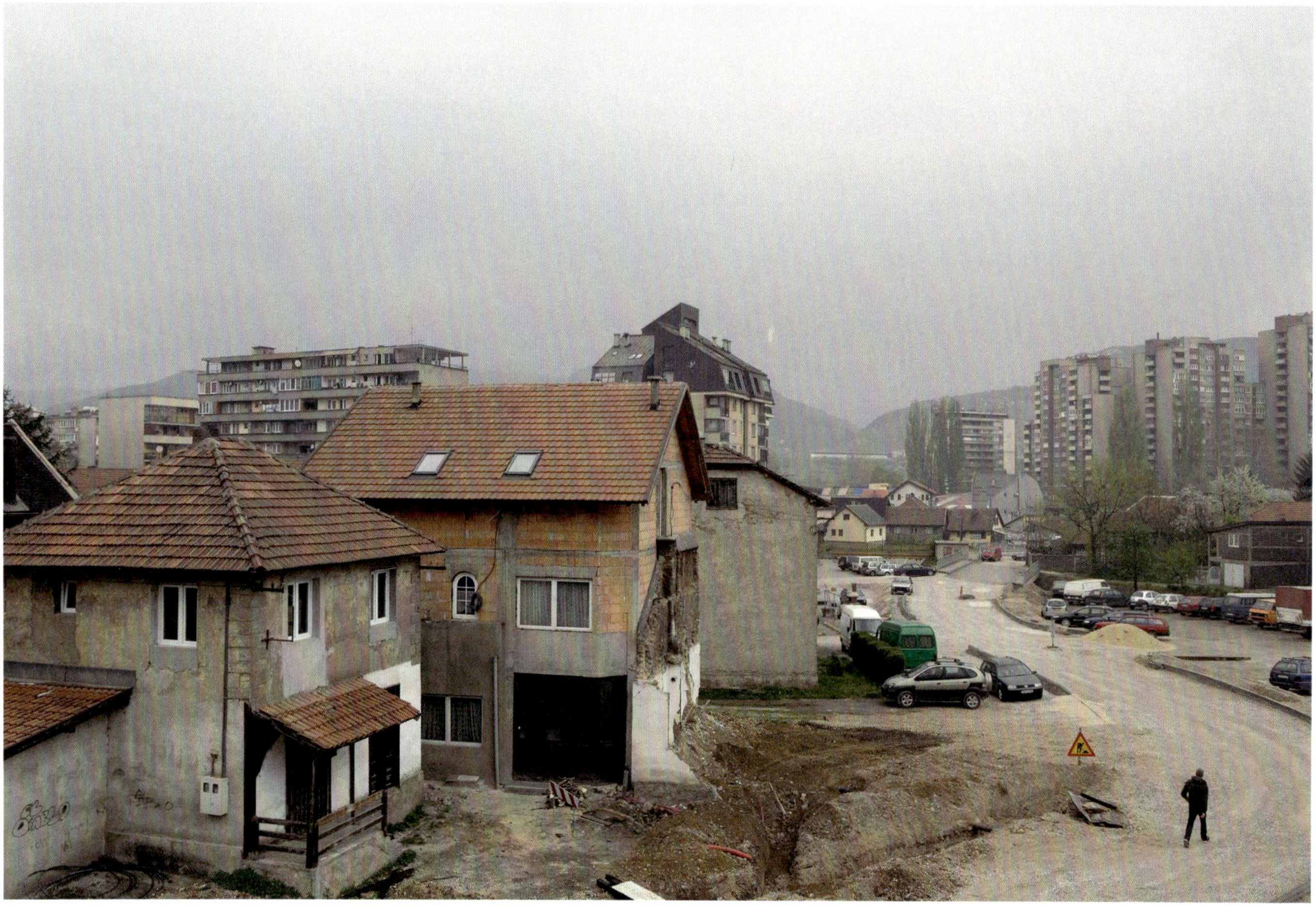

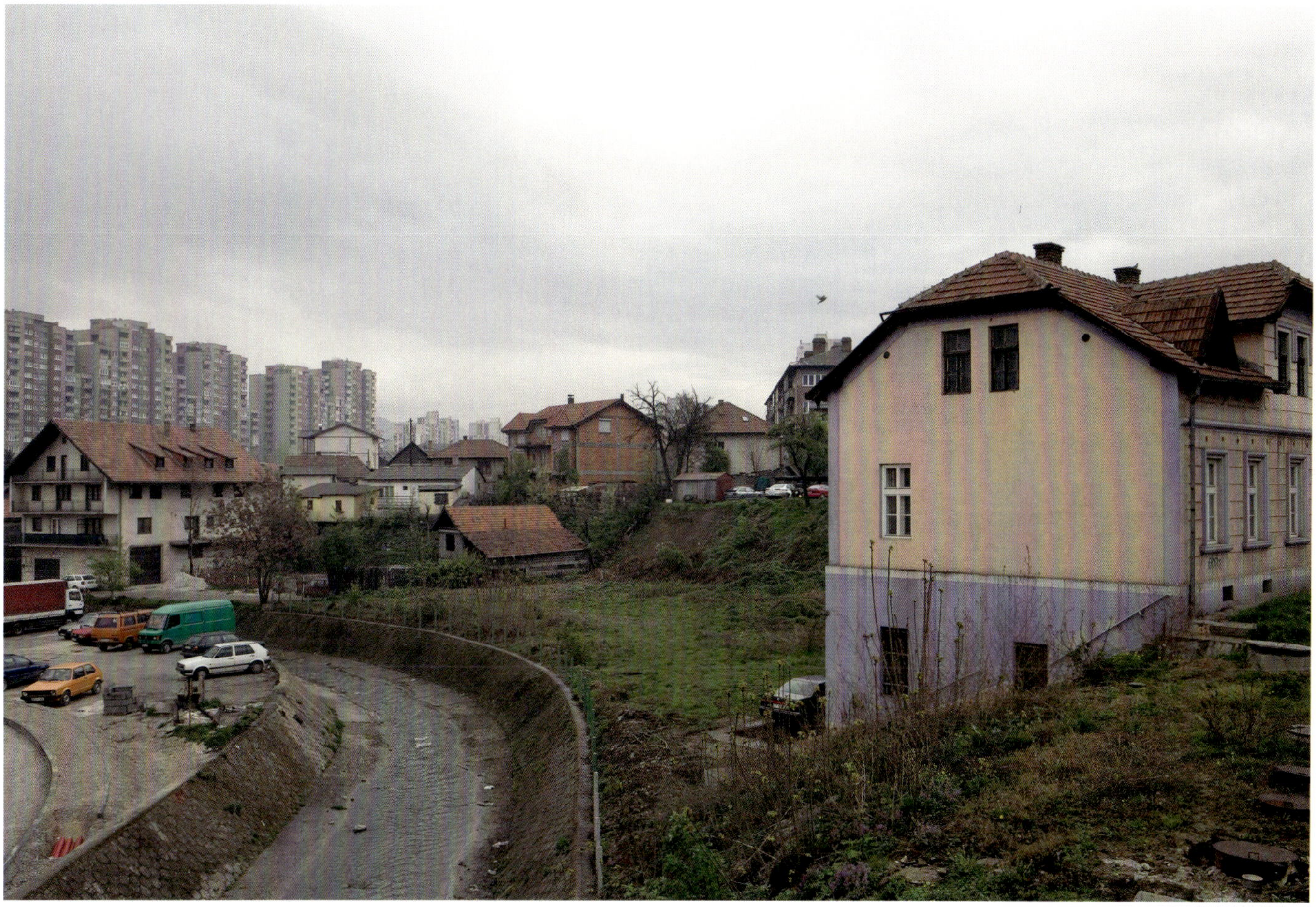

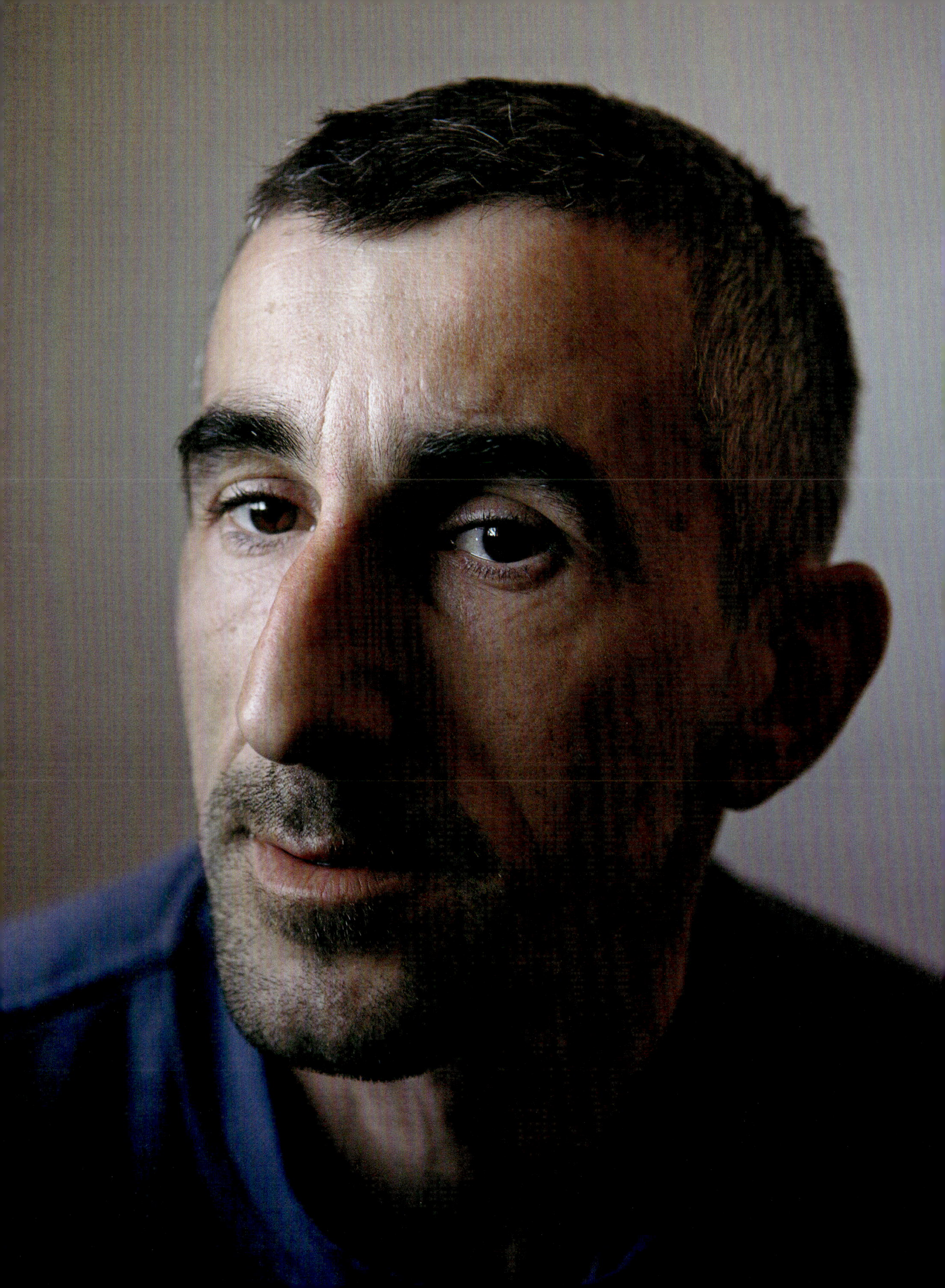

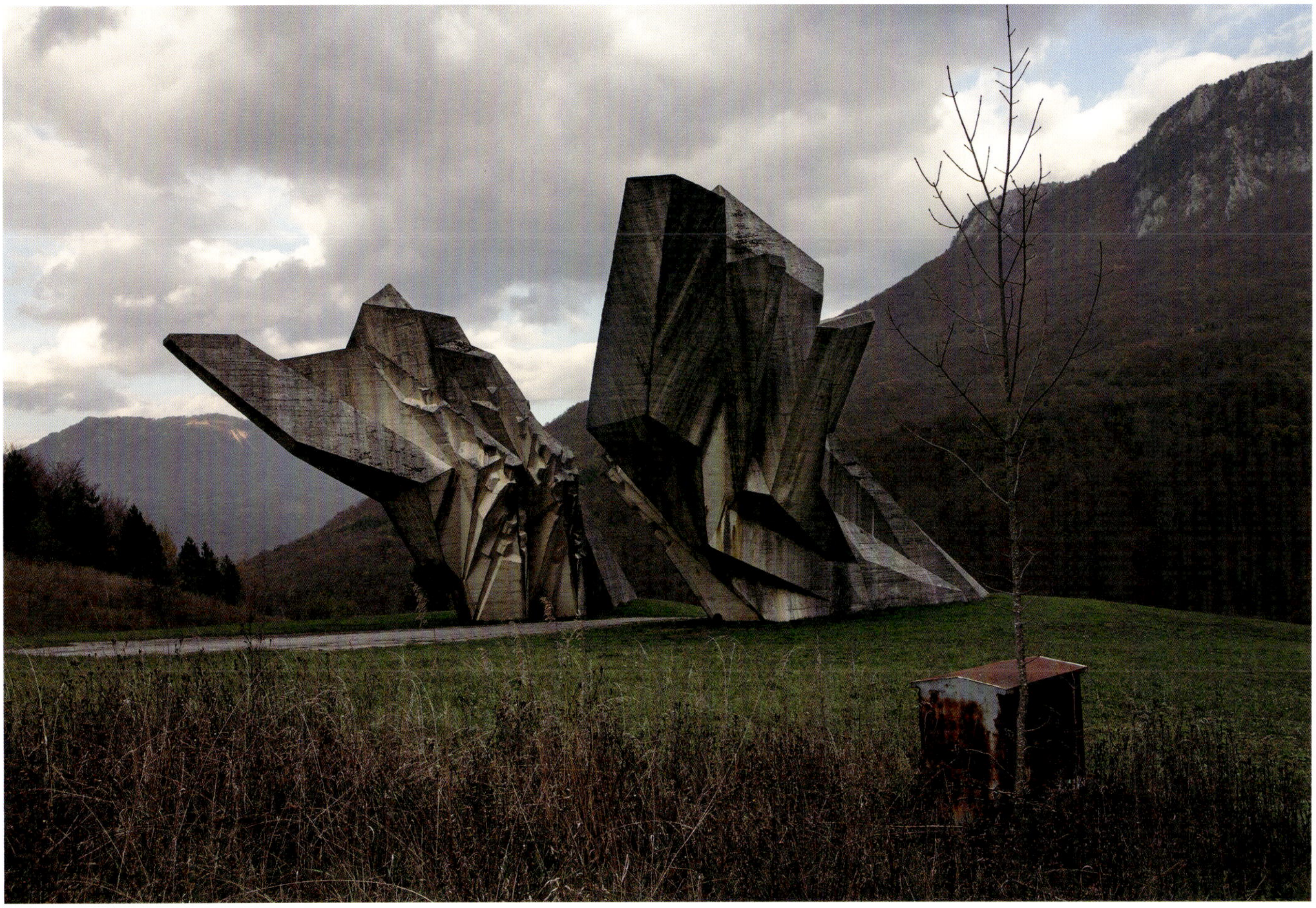

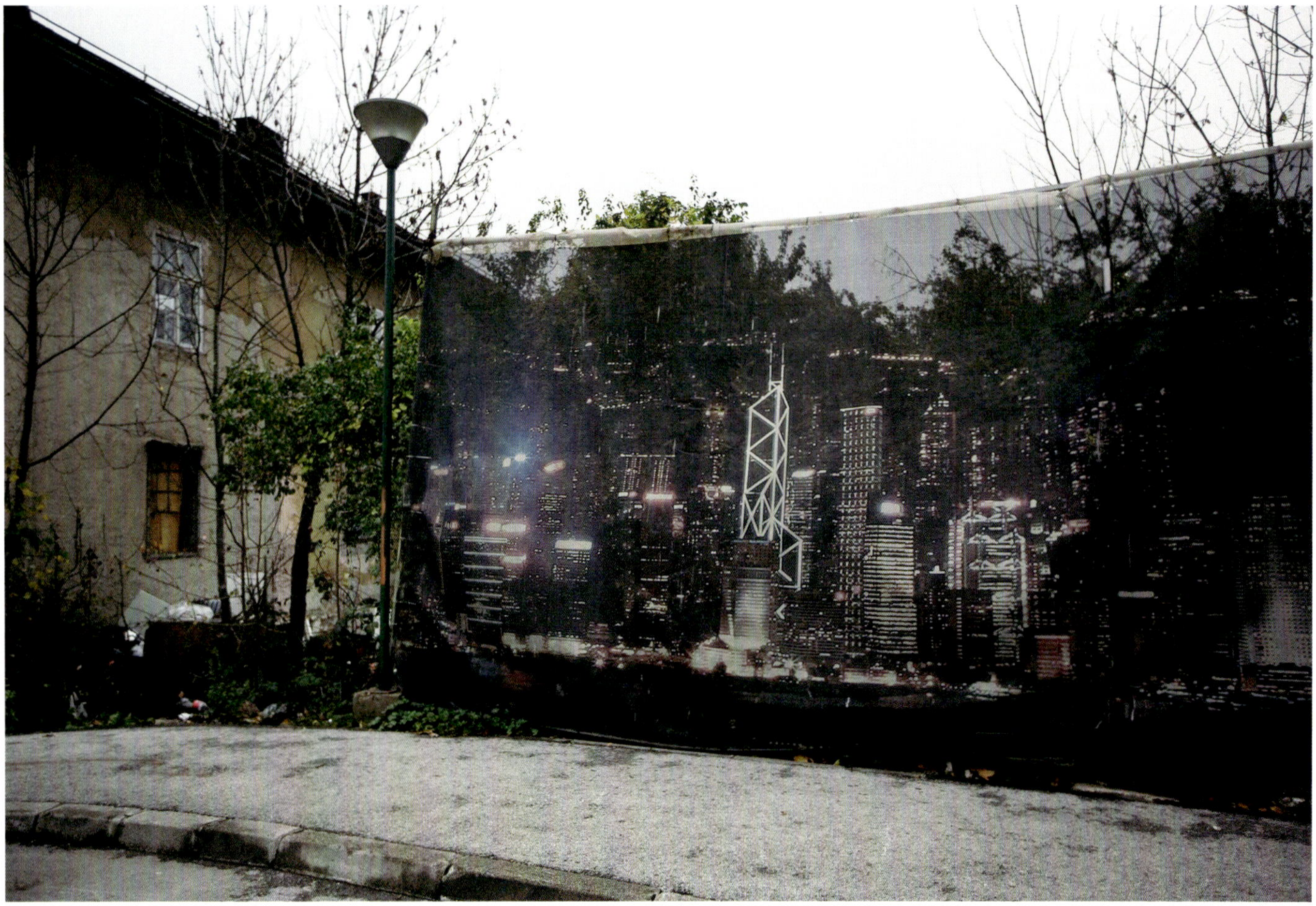

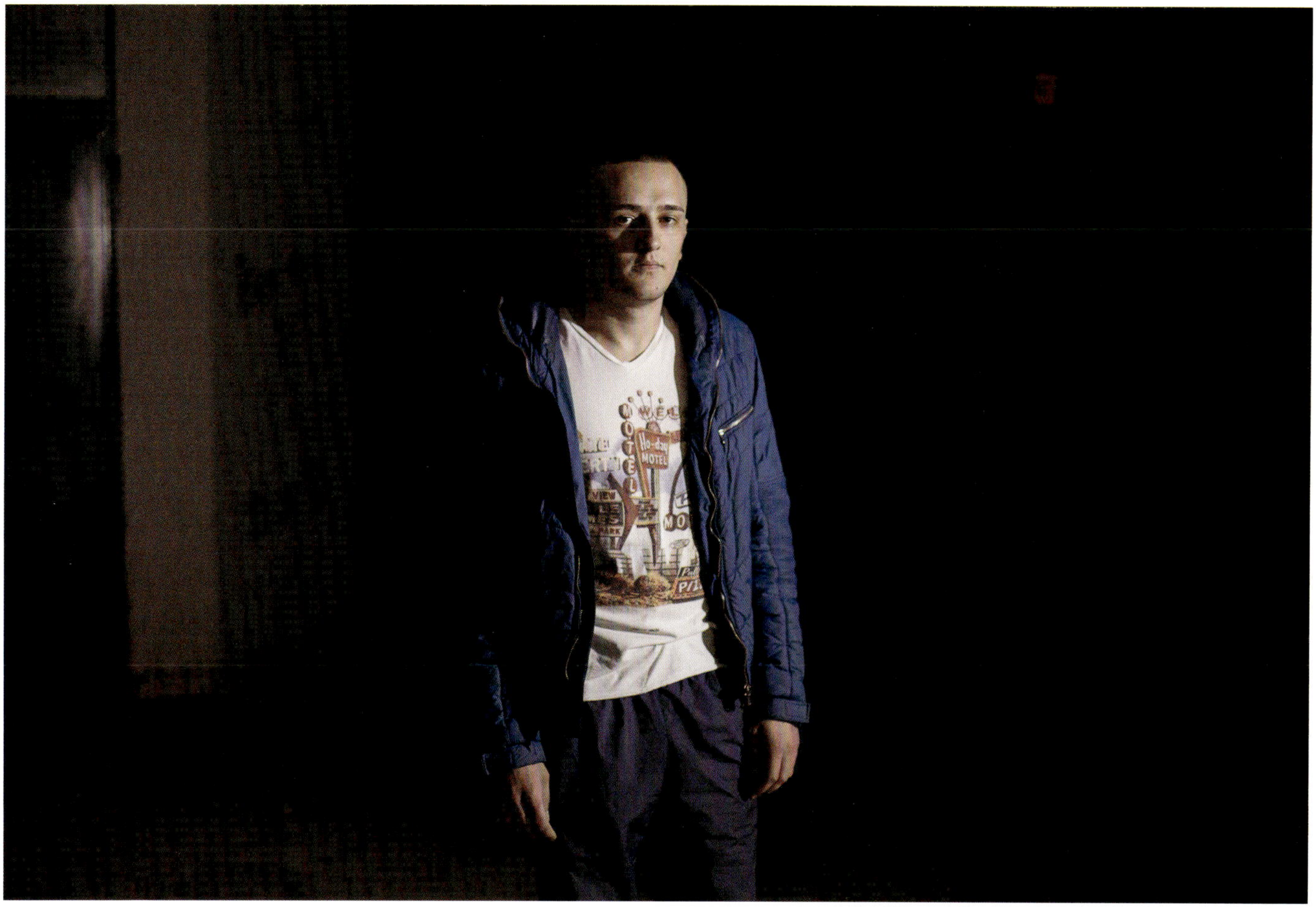

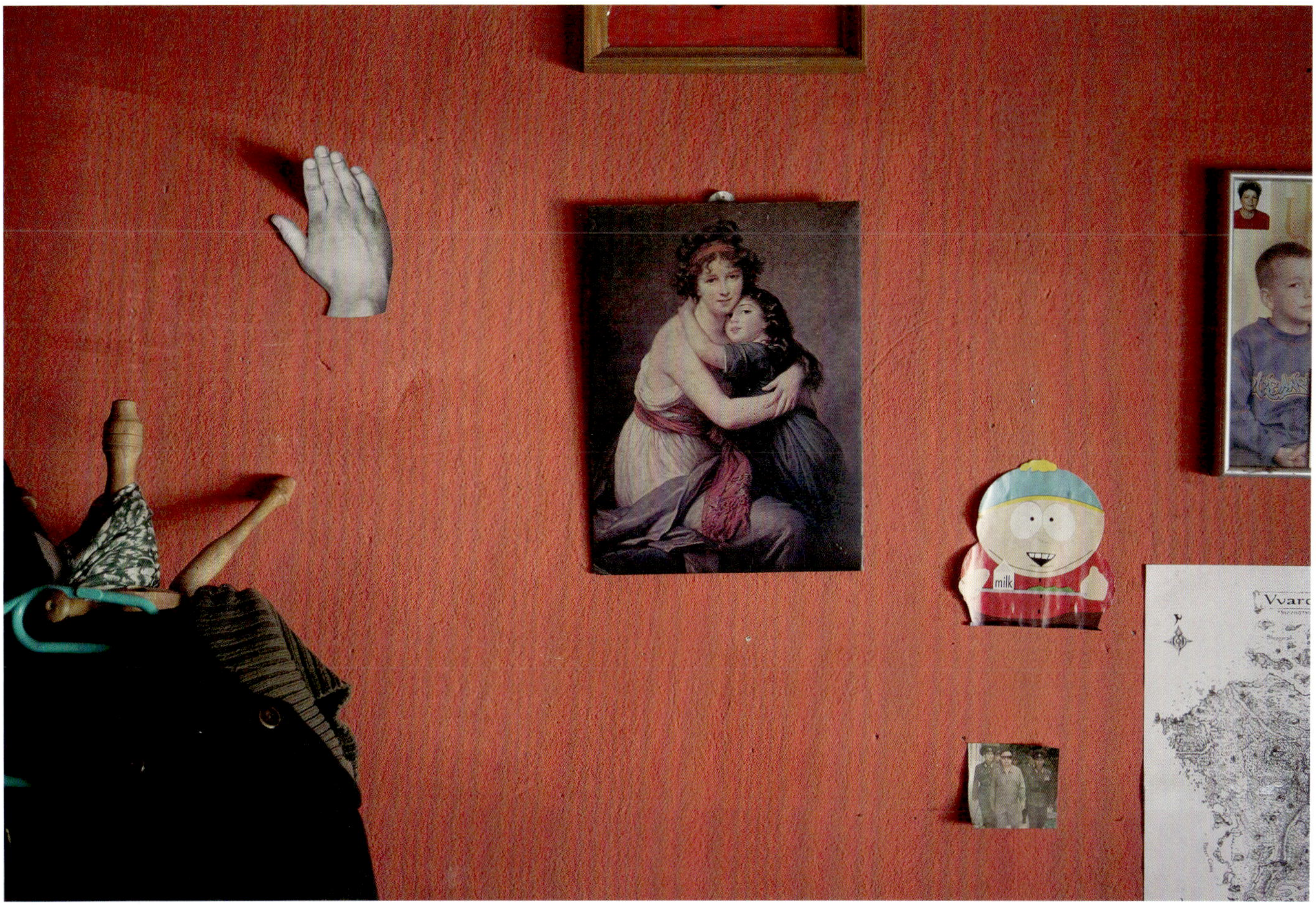
milk

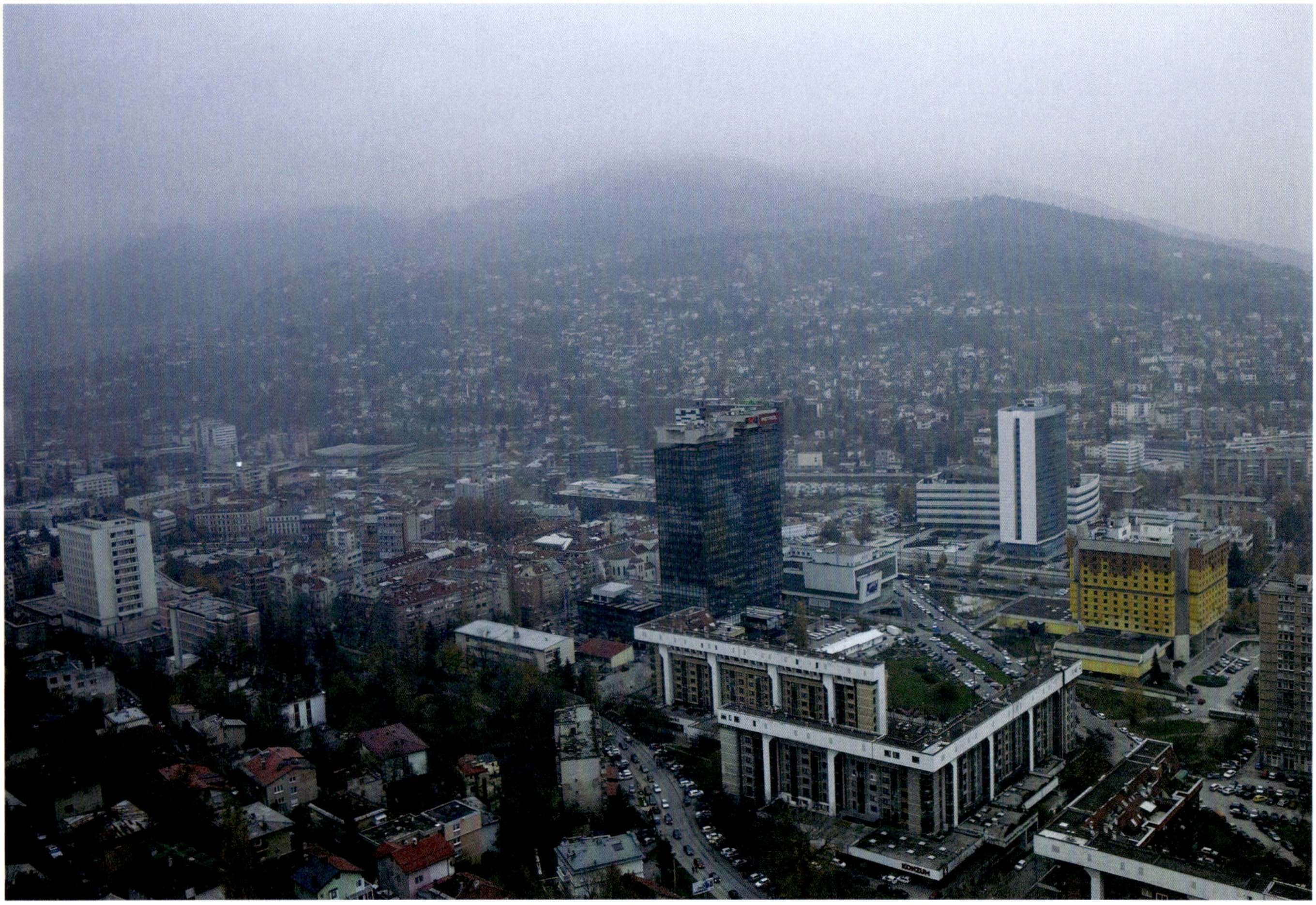

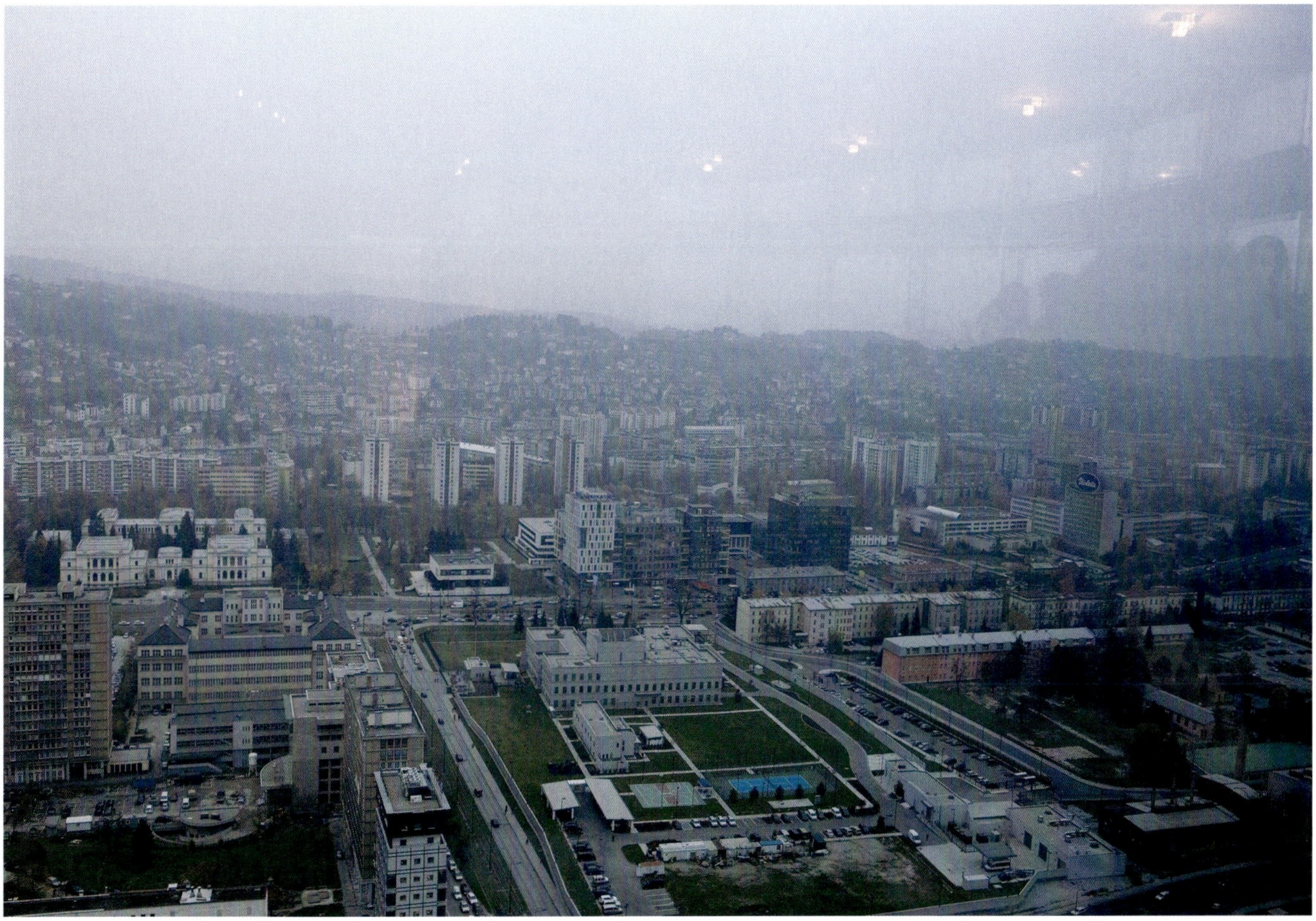

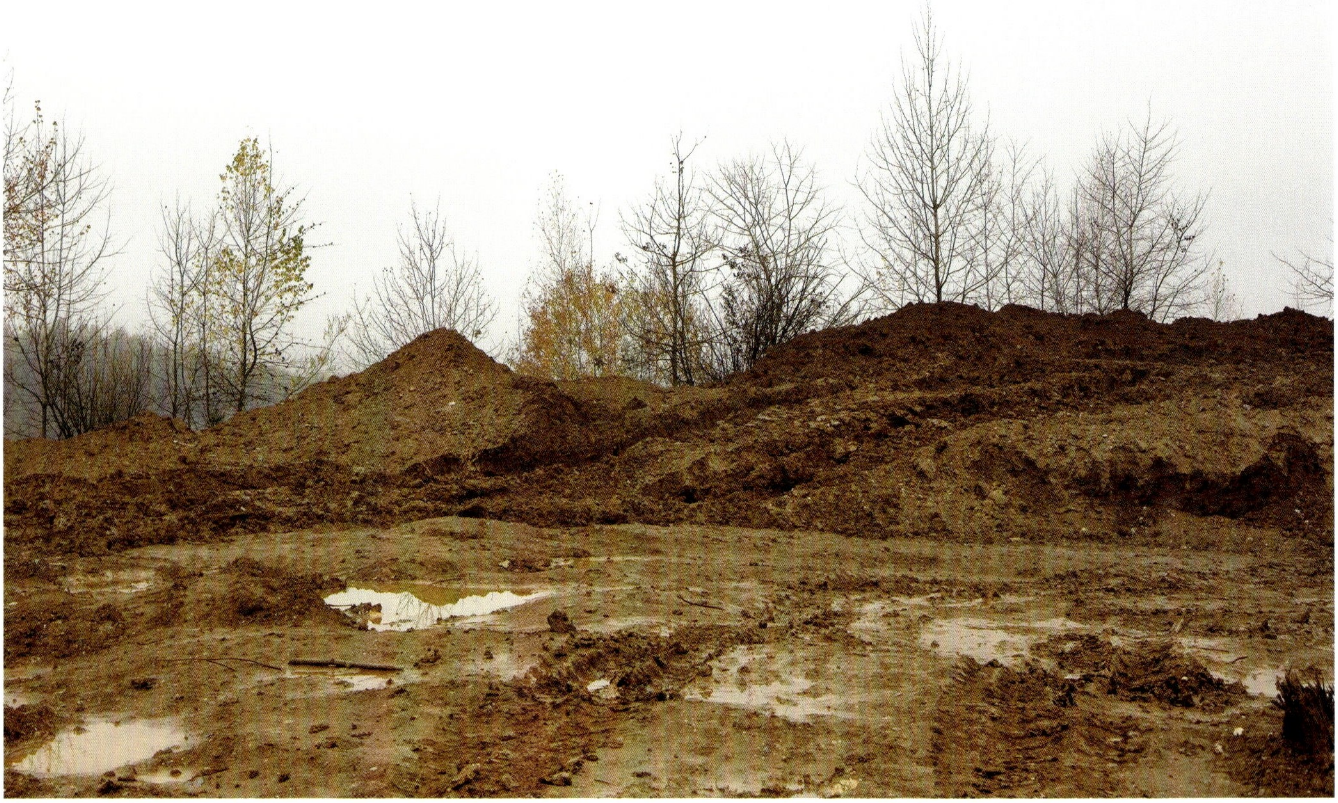

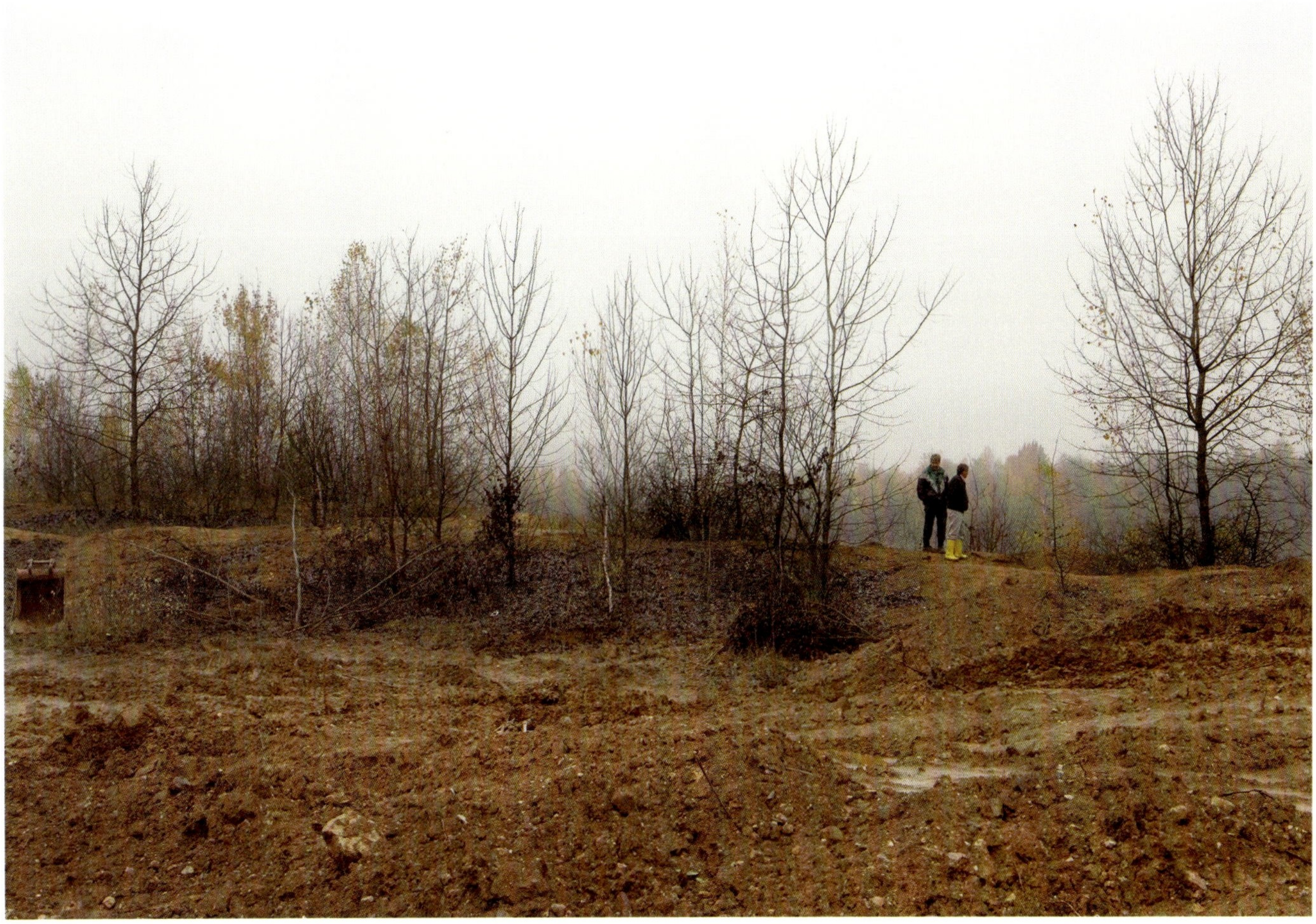

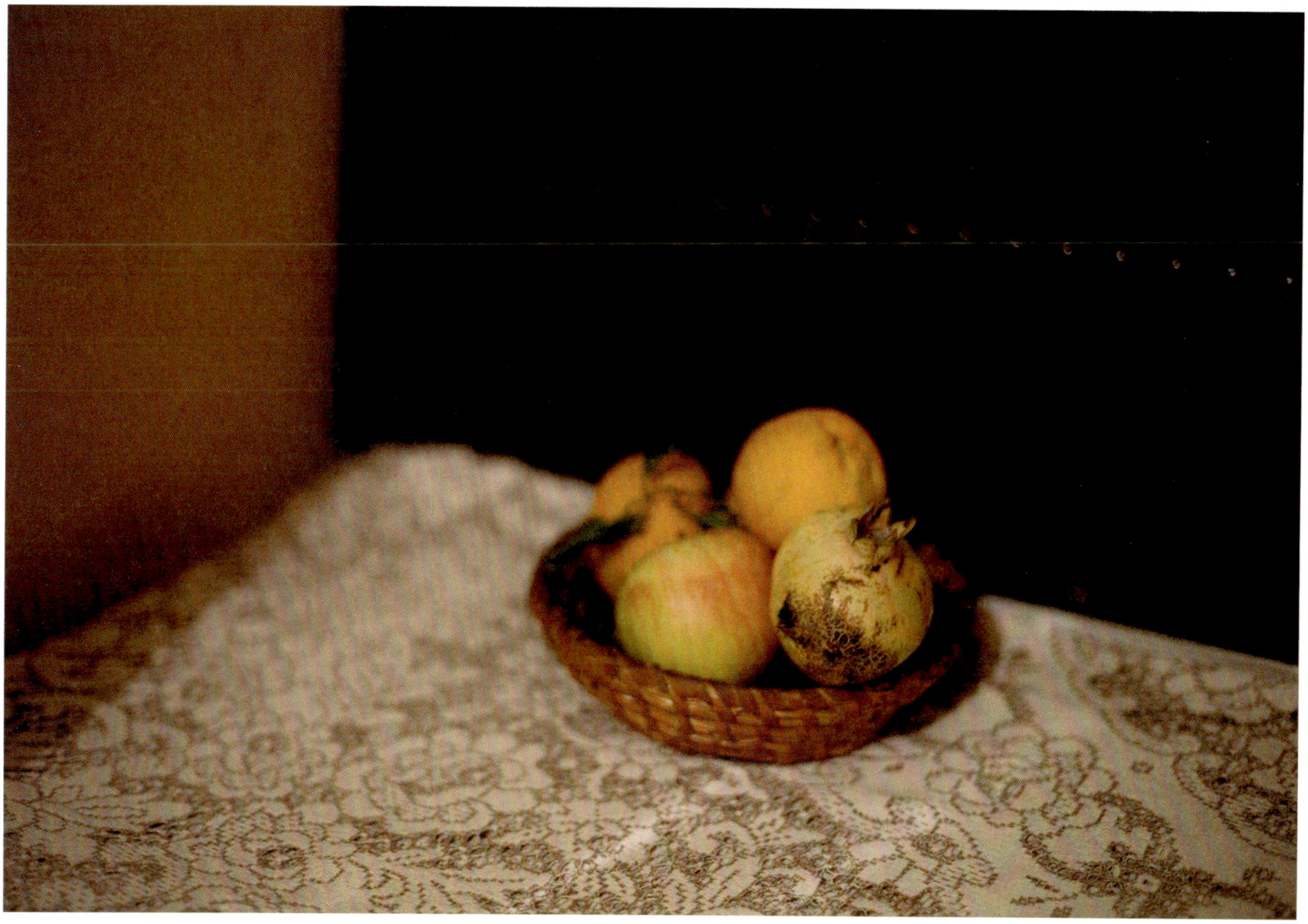

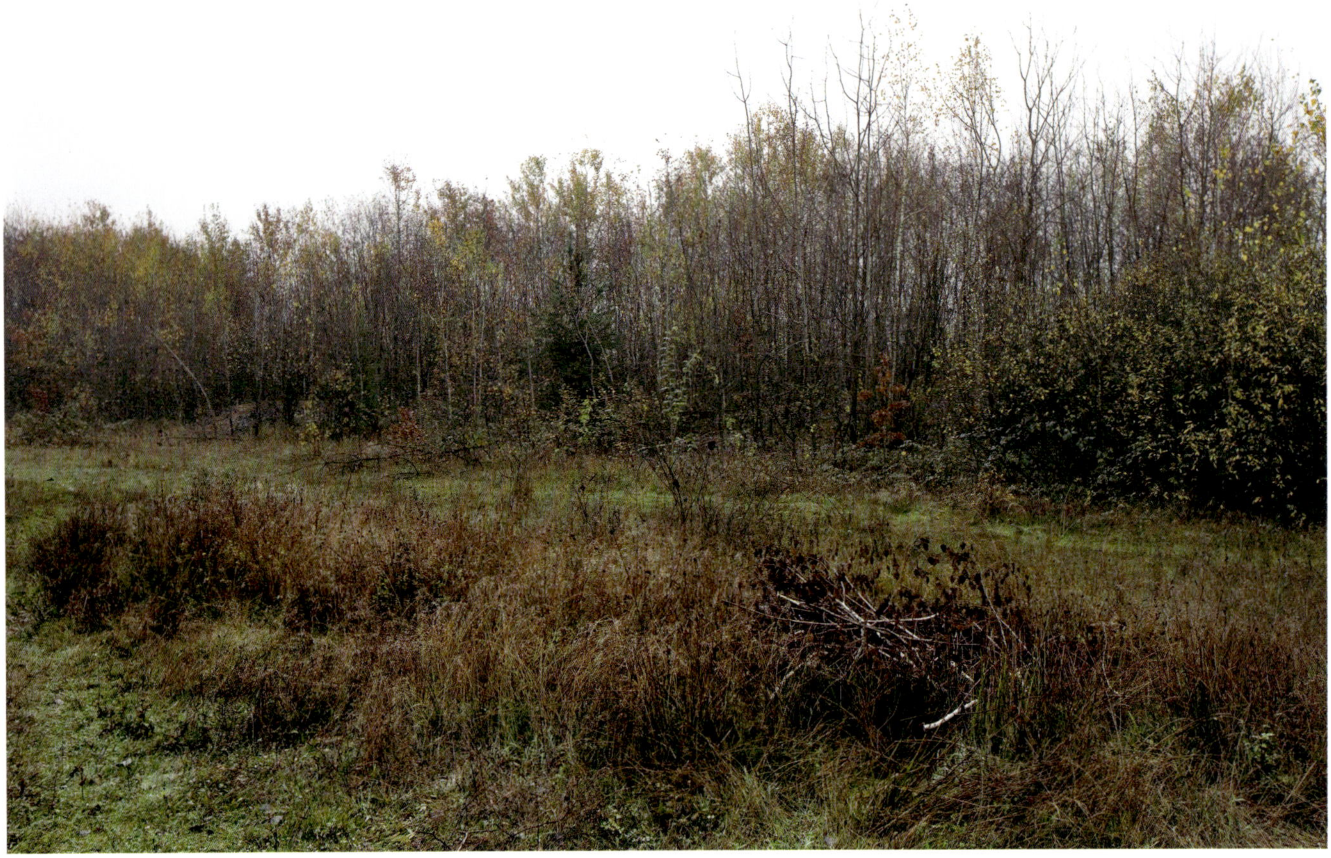

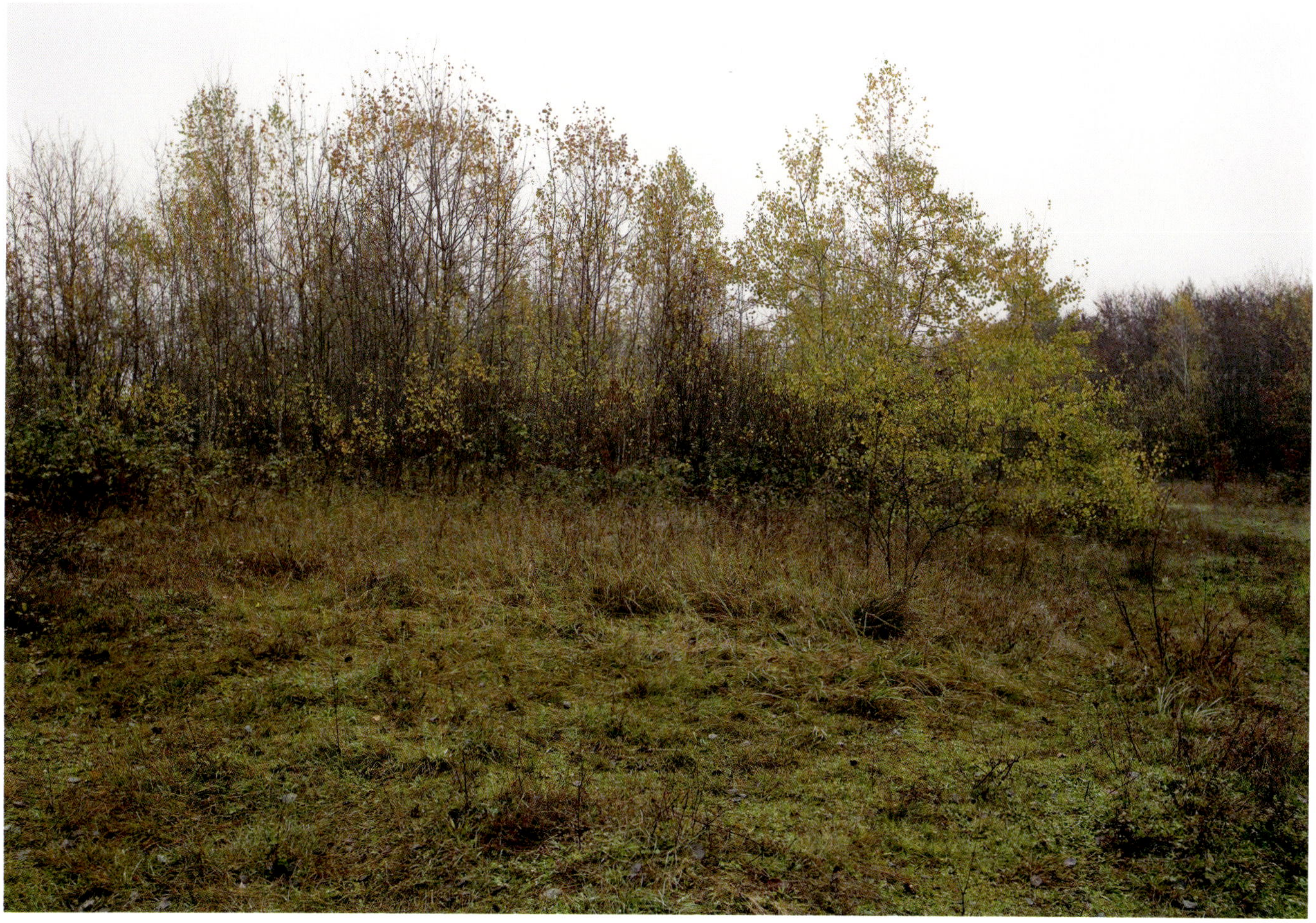

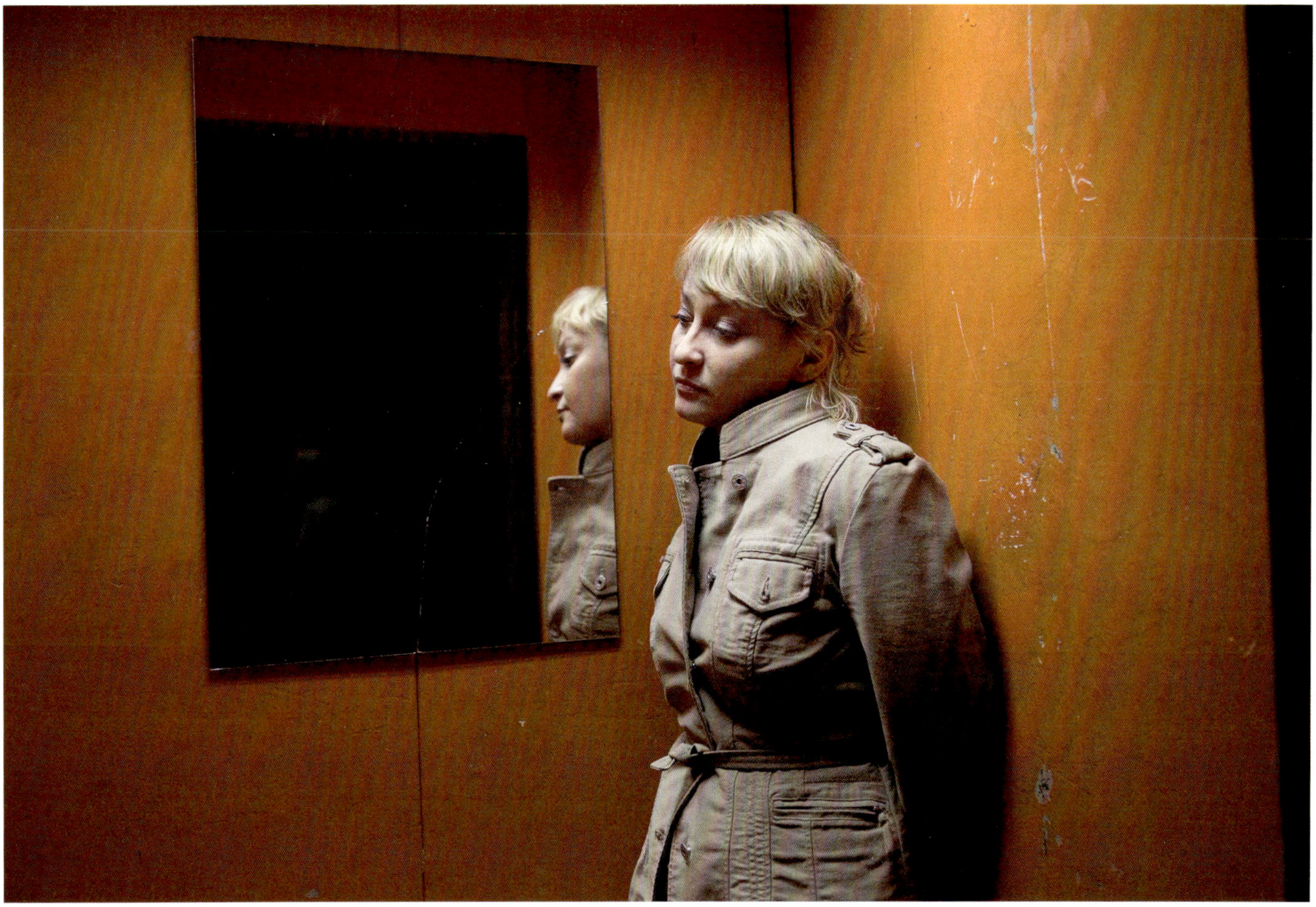

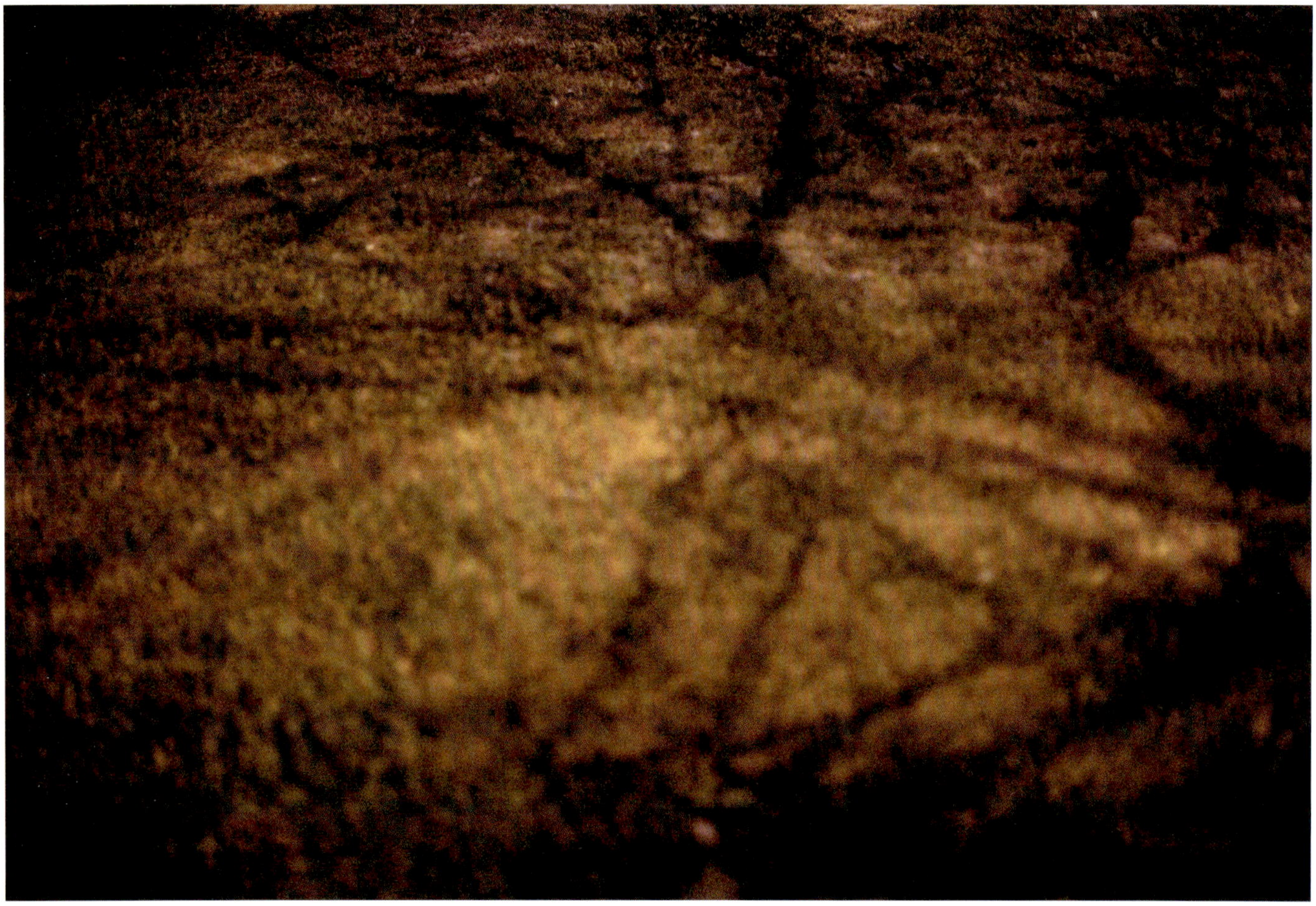

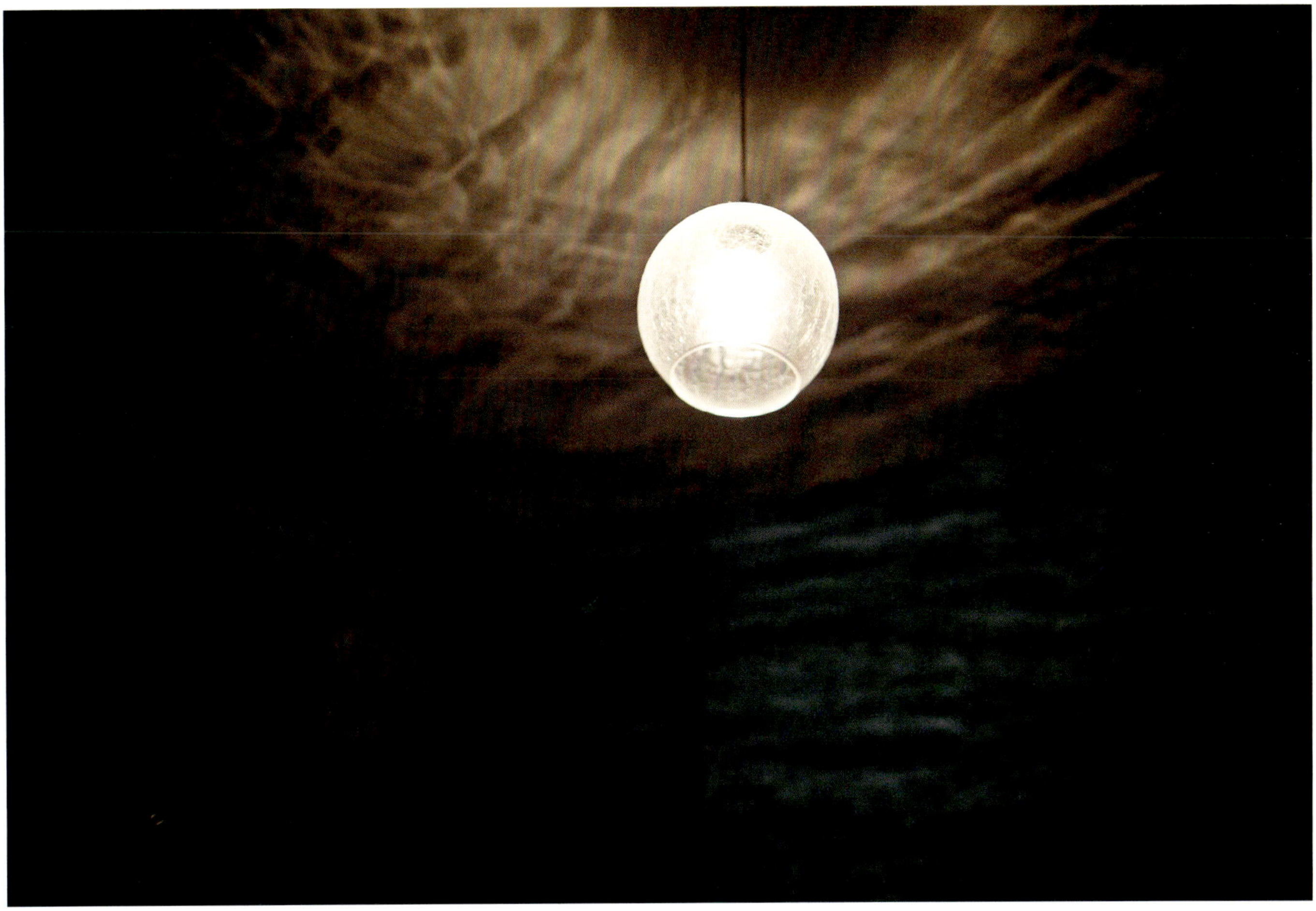

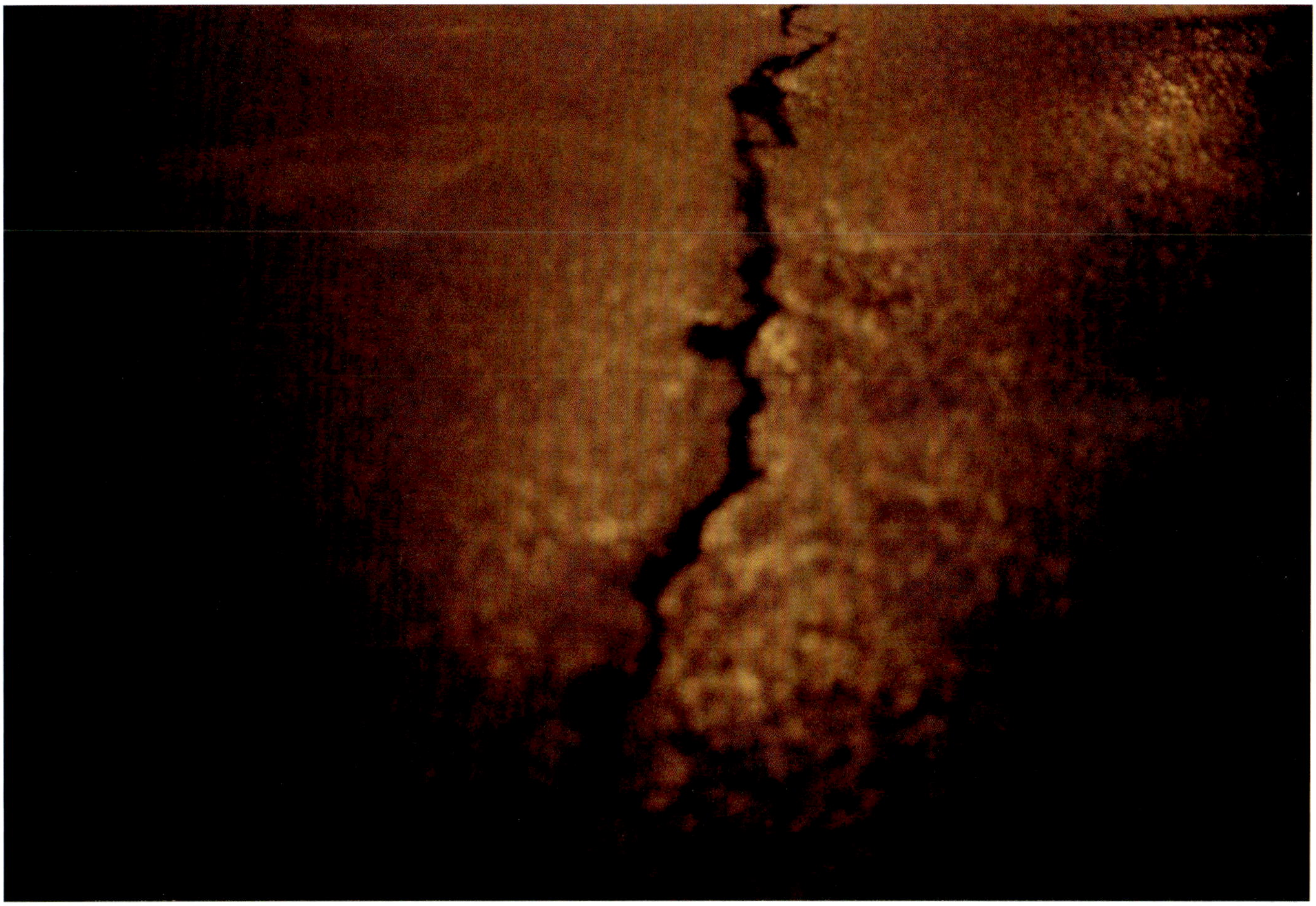

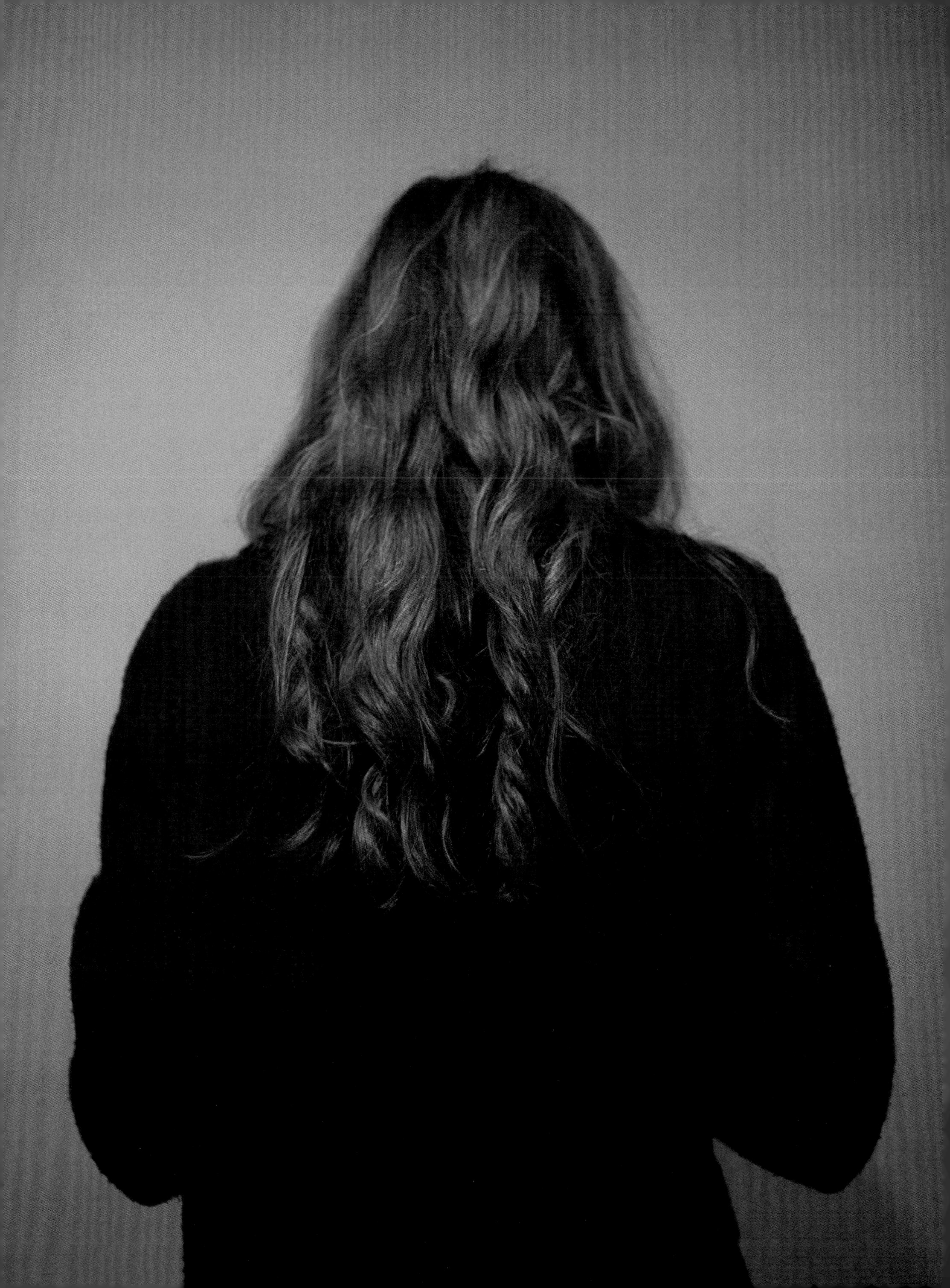

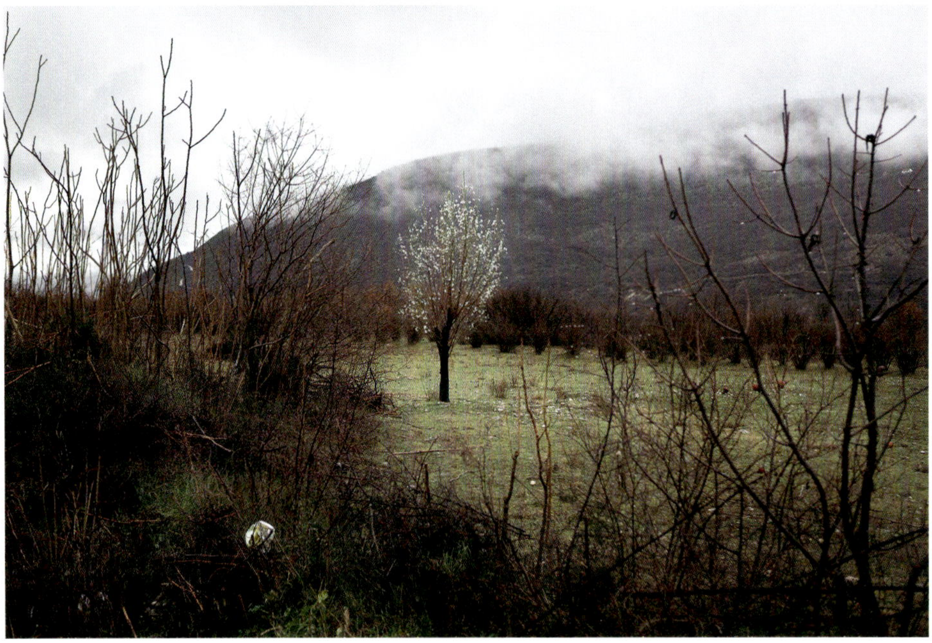

Acknowledgements

Thank you to all of you in Bosnia, who opened your doors and shared so much with us.

Thank you Tima for your hospitality. Jasmina, thank you, your translations and assistance brought the depth and understanding we needed for this project.

Thank you to our families for your infallible support and confidence. Thank you Nutcha Pajareya for your sharp eye and everlasting patience. Working with you is a delight.

Miriam Waldvogel, Patrick Brown and Lek Kiatsirikajorn, you introduced us to the right persons. Thank you so much.

Thanks to the writers. Saša Stanišić, Srećko Latal and Christian Caujolle, your texts completed this book in a magnificent way. We are deeply grateful.

Thanks to our incredible team of translators: Danielle Wagner, Françoise Toraille, Lyn Marven, Sam Pink, Silke Lührmann and Sylvain Gourjaud.

To the very professional and hard working staff at EBS in Verona: thank you! You printed this book majestically.

Thank you to the entire GOST books team. Special thanks to Stuart Smith for your optimism, wit, and dedicated hard work. And thank you to Gordon MacDonald, your thoughts and feedbacks were spot on. Thank you Claudia Palladini, your comments were always coming at the right time. Allon Kaye, Justine Schuster and Eleanor Macnair: thank you!

Thank you to all the external collaborators. You made this project happen.

This project has been supported by: Alexandre Aviolat, Alexandre Milan, Alexis Chappatte, Aline Borcard, Ally Park & Jérôme Métraux, Amina Egger, André Escobar, Annika & Nico Fibbioli, Benjamin Fischer, Benoît Clément, Brigitte Bochud, Bruno Brechet, Camilla Wøldike & Patrick Brown, Caroline Bru & Julien Perriard, Catherine & Christian Baumann, Céline Clénin & Ueli Känzig, Claudia Buess, Cristina Ferraiuolo, David Kramer, David Ruffieux, Dennis Besedic, Evelyne & Stefan Aeby, Fabienne & Ferruccio Gadani, Florence & André Pfyffer Tichelli, François Ingold, Françoise & James Jeanneret, Frederic Rody, Gaëtan Rossier, Geneviève Liaudat, Georges Cabrera, Gilles Mauron, Gisela Knijff-Imark, Isabelle & Pierre Eichenberger, Jean-Luc Gurtner, Jérôme Comment, Jonas Ruh, Josiane Gremaud, Jung-a Jung & Dirk Schlottmann, Lalla Cissé & André Chappatte, Laura Slater & Olivier Dreyfuss, Léa Siffert & Marc Volery, Lucien Bovet, Luis Alberto Ampuero, Madeleine & Pascal Siffert, Madeleine & Peter Häfliger, Magdalena Matus, Malou & Jean-Pierre Métraux, Manfred Rist, Marc-Olivier Paux, Marie-Claude Marmy & Louis Magnin, Michel Waeber, Miriam Waldvogel, Naris Memidzan, Nicolas Coutaz, Nicolas Sperisen, Oam & Guillaume Martin, Patrick Vallélian, Philipp Thalmann, Renato Raimondi, Romano Riedo, Samih Güven, Sébastien Chaperon, Sonya & Lucien Chappatte, Stéphane Arguedas, Sylvain Meyer, Thérèse & François Liaudat, Thérèse & Jean-Pierre Borcard, Thierry Genoud, Vera & Ilya Raskin, Vincent Genoud, Yuri Afanasiev and Yvain Genevay. Thank you so much for your kind contribution!

We acknowledge and thank for the generous support from the Embassy of Switzerland in Bosnia and Herzegovina, SEPT Magazine, Volkart Stiftung, Stiftung Erna und Curt Burgauer and the United Nations in Bosnia and Herzegovina.

Stéphanie Borcard and Nicolas Métraux
info@bm-photo.ch

Schweizerische Eidgenossenschaft
Confédération suisse
Confederazione Svizzera
Confederaziun svizra

This publication is supported by the Embassy of Switzerland in Bosnia and Herzegovina. The content and findings of this publication do not necessarily reflect the views of the Swiss Government.

Saša Stanišić

The Factory

My car pirouettes into the ditch in the driving snow on the high plateau. Small hands are already knocking on the windows, men in wolfskins and Puma tracksuits, they escort me to a farmstead not far from the road, a shack, a modest campfire. They boil water for tea, feed me *Mars* bars, and the tea smells of sheep. We are the shepherds, they say, that's us.

The shepherds' eyes: wide. They don't want to listen anything I have to say.

They don't want to listen, the shepherds, they want to talk: about a building that cleared its throat years in days of yore and then hesitated.

The factory, the shepherds say, behind the fir trees, over there. The shepherds point at the window, the window is all steamed up; the smallest shepherd stands on tiptoe to wipe the glass with his sleeve and the snowstorm obliterates the view.

What does that mean, I ask, it hesitated, and how can buildings clear their throat, is that some kind of joke?

We heard it, say the shepherds, we were there. We were playing cards, sheltering from the wind behind the factory walls. And they eagerly demonstrate what the throat clearing sounded like, gruff and steely, they say, gruff and steely, they rasp through cupped hands, and you can't imagine it.

The shepherds' lifelines: made of earth.

Since then the factory has hesitated, say the shepherds. Since then the plateau has been waiting, the wind and the fog have been waiting, the shepherds wait and so does their snow, waiting for something to come next.

They say: let's pay a visit.

To whom? I ask.

The factory. The shepherds dunk their *Mars* bars in their tea.

I'd rather not, I say.

The shepherds confer behind their hands. The smallest shepherd sits down on my lap. He sings quietly, playing with my collar. It's a children's song, one of the old, brutal ones, with guilt and punishment, and when I join in the chorus he breaks off and bares his eye teeth.

The shepherds have pulled on their hats. Soon we are trudging through the snow, the dogs plough a path ahead, the sheep trot behind us, what are sheep doing out in the snow, the jingling of their bells is warming.

Wind, wind, wind. I lean into it, brow to brow with the snowflakes. I am the only one who seems to be bothered by the weather, the shepherds simply shield their eyes with their hands like saluting soldiers. Wind is always blowing across this desolate plateau, they lie, every breath ever taken by every Serb, Bosniak and Croat who sighed, loved or mourned on the Romanija plateau is interwoven in the wind for all eternity.

The shepherds don't put it quite like that.

The going is easier in the forest, the trees comb the wind back to front, fir trees, black and untouchable like in the children's song. I ask the shepherds if there are mines here, and one throws a snowball at my chest so hard it makes my heart pound.

The shepherds' beards: fir needles.

On the Romanija a building cleared its throat and since then it has hesitated. A large, rectangular building on the edge of the forest, bare concrete walls, two or three bags spilling out gravel, a rusty saw, a hole in a bucket, blocks of wood, a wire fence. A small, weather-beaten radio says nothing among the rubble. The smallest shepherd runs across the snow as if no snow was there, whooping for joy and fear along with the howling sheepdogs, and disappears behind the walls.

The shepherds' heads swaying on thin necks.

The shepherds explain: water was going to be bottled and packaged here. The sheriff had apparently found two springs nearby, had applied for and been granted EU funding, for the plots of land, for the wells, for the bottling plant and and and. Sheriff – because he always wore one of those hats and those jeans, American, they say, a Serb, they say.

A woman, one says, breasts.

The shepherds' grins: full of decay.

It was just after the war or maybe in 2000. The construction contract went to a local company, the sheriff personally recruited workers from the neighbouring villages. Jobs, income, revival of the economy, the shepherds recite in chorus and spit in the snow. For every comma one of them coughs. For every full stop one sits down in the grass by the walls. There is no snow lying near the factory. Snow falls like punctuation in the improbable green.

Then one morning the site manager doesn't turn up on site. And the workers don't get paid any more. And the farmers don't get the promised rent for the use of the land. No further payments for the suppliers of the building materials, who had consigned their goods for a pathetic advance. The sheriff stops taking calls. Soon the line went dead.

The shepherds' eyebrows: ice crystals.

Six months after he disappeared the EU came in person to see what was going on. The shepherds spit.

The shepherds' spittle: brown from the chocolate.

The shepherds had rearranged the factory to play cards in, the sheep ate their fill of the greenery which grew in such abundance here, as if a benevolent god had fertilised the earth while their god had cursed their lands with stony ground. The shepherds welcomed the EU in a fitting manner – their sheep blocked the access road for hours. The EU politely declined the offer of a *Mars* bar and returned, appalled, to the EU.

The shepherds have heard that the EU had transferred four out of six instalments to the sheriff before the payments were stopped. The shepherds don't mention the sum involved, they simply stroke their chins with index finger and thumb.

The smallest shepherd peels a *Mars* bar, his hands and face are furrowed like the bark of the fir trees. He beckons me over and leads me through no gate into the factory. We step into the summery hum of warm air, flies buzzing around.

Absences where there ought to be windows. Earth where there should be floors. Clouds where half the roof is missing. Plants creeping where pipes should snake; a factory standing unfinished on the Romanija, hesitating. Unfinished and bare, used only by the shepherds and their beasts, a shelter when storms hound them, a plastic table where they play rummy.

The shepherds' eyes wide: look around you, stranger.

Migratory birds have constructed nests in the brickwork. One lizard circles another. In the middle of the factory two shepherds are piling up stones into little towers, giggling like lovers. Or are they crying? I ask and they say, the first settlers who looked down on the barren earth from the tops of our mountains were Illyrians, shepherds like us, tough and serious.

The shepherds don't put it quite like that. And they don't elaborate, they give me no story.

The smallest shepherd is by my side again. We know every spring on the Romanija, he whispers. You need to be powerful water to fight your way up and out through our rock – he drops to one knee – and cunning, too, for us not to have found you a long time ago.

He smells so strongly of chocolate that I have to turn away. The others have taken off their wolfskins, some are playing rummy. The factory looks on and manufactures hesitation.

Perhaps the shepherds have cleared the snow away here?

The sheep's bells jangle softly in the trees.

I speak the shepherds' language but I don't understand the things they understand.

One is tending to the dogs, loosening their paws from the ice with udder cream.

One is watering potatoes in the corner. 73 years ago today, he shouts, my grandfather and the 1st Proletarian Brigade were surrounded by Germans on the Romanija. So the Brigade set off across the high plateau, marching through the snow and ice and then crossed cruel Mount Igman in temperatures reaching -30C. A column of partisans, singing, says the shepherd, and one of the others asks how he knows that they were singing.

The shepherds' mobile phones: home-made antennae of aluminium foil and full reception where I have none at all.

And the smallest shepherd climbs up a ladder, singing, he sings louder than before, an old woman's voice, hoarse and gentle:

On a cold winter's night, on a hill up high
The stream has frozen over, under snow it does lie
A bunny searches for the stream, where oh where did it go
Is it lost forever? The poor bunny doesn't know

The bunny cries with all his heart, he misses his stream so
He cries and starts to wonder, where did the water go
The bunny feels confused, did the stream exist at all?
Or maybe it flew south with the swallows in the fall

The shepherds' swift dogs slit each other's throats playfighting, I have to get out of their way, it's like I'm completely surplus to requirements.

The shepherds' teeth: summery yellow.

The smallest shepherd sits on the highest rung and prunes the rambling roses. I have been abandoned.

I have heard tell that on the lump of karst which they call Romanija, between bleak seams of limestone and burial mounds built of stones, the graves of Illyrian shepherds and Yugoslav partisans, there stands a factory. It manufactured a few humble dreams. The shepherds heard it clearing its throat, and watch over its hesitating.

Saša Stanišić, born in 1978, in Višegrad, Yugoslavia, is a writer, essayist and journalist and is the author of two novels. The first one "How the Soldier Repairs the Gramophone" (2006), has been translated into 32 languages, his second one "Vor dem Fest" has been awarded the 2014 Leipzig Book fair prize.

Translated by Lyn Marven

Srećko Latal

The Un-transcending of Bosnia and Herzegovina

Bosnia and Herzegovina (BiH) spent the two decades after its devastating war transcending from a post-conflict country into a modern, EU-oriented society. Somewhere along the way, this process became botched and the country today hangs close to becoming a failed state or breaking apart. The deepening of local political conflicts, hardening of positions across the region and new tensions on the global scene set a difficult and dangerous scene for the resolution of BiH's fate, which will determine not only the future of this troubled country, but have major impact on the fate of the entire Balkan region.

The Dayton Peace Accord, which stopped the war in 1995 and established BiH's new constitutional framework, divided the country among three main ethnic groups – Bosniaks (who are mostly Muslims), Croats (predominantly Catholic) and Serbs (mostly of Orthodox religion) – and into two entities: the predominantly Bosniak and Croat BiH Federation and the predominantly Serb Republika Srpska. The country has also been a home for a number of ethnic minorities, such as Italians, Czechs and Poles, as well as 'Others' – people of a civic orientation or those who, for different reasons, refuse to be identified with any of the three main ethnic groups. Yet many BiH citizens still have conflicting views on country's past, present and future.

For many years, the effects of the diverging goals of BiH's three ethno-political blocks have been neutralised by a strong international military, diplomatic and financial presence. It stabilised the country and enabled swift and successful post-war reconstruction. Over the years, Westerns diplomats and international organisations ventured deeper and deeper into BiH's legal structures, initiating and supporting reforms in security, political, economic, social, cultural and all other sectors. Many of these reforms proved to be a major success, like the unification of BiH's armed forces, or fiscal and taxation systems. But many others – such as police, judicial and media reforms – were troubled from the onset by local obstacles and international mistakes. The West eventually grew weary and started contemplating an exit strategy. In 2006, a US initiative tried and failed to overhaul Dayton's complex and expensive constitutional framework, but the American administration nevertheless decided to reduce their presence and hand over babysitting duties to the EU. Ignoring signs of renewed radicalisation among local politicians, the West decided it was time to stop meddling with the region's daily politics and place the country's fate in the hands of local leaders. Removing external supervision and pressure, while local society was still underdeveloped and unprepared to take over that duty, enabled local politicians to revert to their autocratic, self-centered and hard-line practices. Since then, Bosnia and Herzegovina has been gradually sinking back into political, economic and social crisis.

Today, leaders of the three ethno-political blocks pursue the same nationalist goals and insist on the same maximalist demands as their predecessors did, during and immediately after the war. Bosnian Serb leaders still threaten to separate Republika Srpska from the rest of the country, Bosnian Croat politicians remain focused on creation of a separate Bosnian Croat entity, and Bosniaks keep insisting on centralising the country while, at the same time, inching closer to Turkish and Saudi political and business circles. The country is still regulated by the same cumbersome constitution but, in the absence of the Office of the High Representative's executive powers – which have been rendered useless because of the lack of international support for the OHR – more and more of the Dayton constitution is being ignored and despoiled by political elites, contributing to the growing dysfunctionality of the system.

A Political Pyramid

While hiding behind calls for the protection of their respective ethnic, ideological or political interests, the main focus of politicians has become the distribution of the 'election cake'. This includes the allocation of government seats at different levels, and the positioning of party members in public companies, agencies and other institutions. These companies are then used as cash cows for parties and their selected members, while political appointees in the institutions and their families become a loyal power base that is used by leaders to reinforce their position in the parties.

By reproducing and widening this system from one election cycle to the next, BiH's political scene has, over the years, evolved into a broad and complex pyramidal scheme, which is using ethnic fears and the complicated constitutional and legal framework to perpetuate itself without providing even the minimum of efficient services to its population. Opposition parties strongly criticise ruling parties for corruption and misuse of the system but, if and when they come to power, they assume similar stands and behaviour until they themselves are replaced. Then they wait for the electorate to grow weary of their political opponents, forget their own sins and put them back in power. This behaviour, by almost all political parties, has created a bad political *perpetuum mobile* – a vicious political circle which neither local nor international bodies know how to stop and change.

A Country That Deserves Its Politicians

While much of the blame for this situation belongs to its political elites, their behaviour is merely a reflection of the overall atmosphere in the country. Most of the local media is equally divided and playing along ethnic, political or self-interest lines. Their sensationalist, biased and unprofessional work is frequently a reflection of their political affiliations and is used as a weapon of choice by political elites in their public quarrels.

Meanwhile, non-governmental organisations and academia are focused on their own narrow interests that are usually linked to international or government-funded projects, regardless of their effect – or the lack of it – on the population. In the absence of different viewpoints and positive initiatives, BiH citizens have grown – or have remained – lethargic and disillusioned to the point of being more willing to adjust to the failing state, leave the country or vegetate in the system rather than change it.

The Violent Uprising of 2014

Politicians' zero-sum games, widespread corruption, as well as the worsening economic and social situation created an incendiary combination of popular dissatisfaction, frustration and anger, which eventually exploded in a series of violent protests in February 2014. Burning government buildings, overturned cars and clashes between opportunistic hooligans and police brought scenes of violence unseen since the end of the war. This shocked the country and the rest of the world, but it also triggered hopes of greater citizens' activism and prompted the launch of a new EU initiative for the country. Plenums, which came out of the February protests as a form of BiH's street democracy, withered away over time due to internal divisions and differences. However, social protests have continued across the country throughout the year and their number and intensity seem to have increased since the end of 2014. Being spread all over the country and lacking common organisation or focus, these protests are mostly perceived as separate daily events and remain generally ignored by local politicians and the general public alike. Yet, given the continuation of economic and social misery, these protests represent a time bomb that could explode at any moment in yet another forceful or even violent uprising.

The Catastrophic Floods of 2014

Amidst all its other problems, BiH was, in 2014, hit by a series of massive floods and landslides caused by torrential rains that persisted throughout spring and summer. What soon became regarded as the single biggest natural disaster in the country's modern history damaged or destroyed apartment buildings and private houses, industrial plants and farms, as well as road, rail, water and electricity networks. Estimates of the cost of the damage rose to over two billion euros – more than ten per cent of BiH's GDP.

Yet this disaster unexpectedly revealed a brighter side of the devastated country. As swollen rivers and torrents of mud flooded the land, the people of Bosnia and Herzegovina sprang to help their neighbours, regardless of their ethnic, religious or political background. While most government institutions idly watched as the catastrophe unfolded, towns and villages sought help from their immediate neighbours – often located on the other side of the inter-entity boundary line. Neighbours brought rubber boats, heavy machinery and construction materials to stop the floods, and then provided food, water and temporary shelter to those who were forced to flee their homes. This way, the citizens of Bosnia and Herzegovina showed their humane side – dare I say, their real nature – providing a glimpse of hope that one day this country will find true peace and prosperity.

An Ageing Nation

The political crisis and economic and social downturn have also led to the mass depopulation of BiH in recent years. Surveys show that as many as 60 per cent of the country's population, and a staggering 80 per cent of its youth, would leave the country immediately if they could. Many of them have found the means to implement these plans in recent years and, in many areas, entire villages are being abandoned as whole families leave, seeking a better future in the region or further abroad. With the steadily declining birth rate and increasing mortality, as well as a dwindling number of marriages and a growing number of divorces, BiH's demographic trends have become some of the worst in the area. According to the preliminary results of the 2013 census, BiH's population decreased from 3.84 million in 2009 to 3.83 million in 2012 and currently stands at 3.79 million.

A survey conducted by the Red Cross reveals that BiH could, over the next 35 years, become the country in the region with the oldest population. This dire demographic prospect also has a very negative impact on the economic future of Bosnia, especially bearing in mind that the number of pensioners in Bosnia has already almost caught up with the number of workers.

A Deepening Political Crisis

The absence of international supervision and local scrutiny enabled a steady radicalisation of the political scene, which continues until the present. BiH's political crisis deepened further during the government mandate of 2010-2014, when the political scene effectively collapsed to intensified political battles within and between the three ethno-political blocks. In this period, the political parties established and broke alliances, sometimes on a daily or weekly basis. This almost completely blocked the work of executive and legislative bodies on different administrative levels, and also weakened democratic and pluralistic principles in all main parties, which became fully controlled by party leaders and a handful of their closest lieutenants.

Hopes that the collapsed political system would be restored after the 2014 October general elections have eventually faded away as procedural problems and continued political power games once again slowed down the formation of new governments. The formation of new ruling coalitions on some administrative levels took almost six months, but most of these coalitions soon weakened or collapsed due to the usual political power-plays and self-centred tactics.

By mid-2015, BiH appeared to be entering the critical stage of its crisis. Republika Srpska President Milorad Dodik launched another initiative for a referendum to be held by the end 2015 to challenge the authority of the state judiciary and the Office of the High Representative. This, it was feared, might lead the way for further political and ethnic destabilisation of the country and the entire region. Meanwhile, economic and social reforms initially agreed with the EU and the International Monetary Fund (IMF) remain blocked. Having missed the end-of-June deadline agreed with the IMF, the country has been left without any international financial support. Without this, almost all administrative levels are about to run out of money and the country is facing a critical liquidity crisis. The international community is observing this spreading problem, but still remains uncertain whether to intervene, or how.

The Worsening Regional and Global Environment

As if the local situation was not bad enough, BiH has, in recent years, been increasingly troubled by a deteriorating regional and global environment that has also contributed to a renewed radicalisation and hardening of positions in both Croatia and Serbia. At the same time, BiH is struggling with growing influences from Russia, as well as radical Islamic groups. Meanwhile, the West remains divided and mostly ignorant of the ominous signs coming from BiH. The EU still shies away from taking a more political role and continues trying to resolve BiH's deep structural problems through technical processes - an approach that has failed in the past and is showing similar flaws again. Some US officials are becoming increasingly vocal in their concerns, yet American official foreign policy lacks ideas on what to do with BiH, and remains content as long as the EU is taking a leading role, allowing the US to deal with its own priorities.

An Uncertain Future

BiH's prolonged political crisis has stalled and reversed the process of reform, crippling the economic and social structure of the country and blocking its path to European integration. The functioning of the country's institutions, systems and laws has been slowing down or stalling on different administrative levels. At the same time, the worsening regional and global environment threatens to exacerbate internal tensions and divisions. It is this combination of internal and external problems that feeds into BiH's 'perfect storm', which is greater, more difficult and potentially more dangerous than the simple sum of its parts. This storm is expected to intensify even further by the end of 2015. In this situation, it seems that only the international authority has the capacity to arrest BiH's downfall and once again protect the country's territorial and constitutional integrity. However, the international community remains largely ignorant of the growing troubles in the Balkans and, preoccupied with other global issues, is leaving BiH to face an uncertain future.

Srećko Latal is a Sarajevo-born journalist and political analyst; he has covered the conflicts in the Balkans and Afghanistan for the Associated Press (AP). He later worked for the International Crisis Group (ICG) and Balkans Investigative Reporting Network (BIRN). His articles have been published in The New York Times, The Guardian, and other international media.

Christian Caujolle

Afterword

In the 20th century, before we became immersed in a stream of undifferentiated images so numerous that we are no longer capable of perceiving, reading or understanding what they mean, photography was a means of recording memories in salts of silver. A means of remembering moments in family life, as well as faces, landscapes, journeys and anecdotes experienced. And historical facts and events, too.

It was also towards the end of the 20th century that the siege of Sarajevo took place, the longest siege in the history of modern warfare, resulting in the death of at least 10,000 people. During the siege, not only photographers, but also local inhabitants, took photographs, circulated and exchanged them. Some were published, in the press and in books, and some were even shown in exhibitions. But do we still remember them? It's difficult to say for sure, as so many images of other tragic current events keep on coming, ever more quickly, chasing away the old ones and taking their place. For that is the central question today. Faced with so many images, all jostling for position and moving at an increasingly fast rate as they replace those that preceded them in a spectacle which it is hard to call information – are we heading towards a world in which memories are being wiped out at the very moment they should be formed? And, to take that thought yet further, are we heading for a world in which memory will no longer be valued or needed?

Human memory is a fragile thing, often partial in the stance it adopts and dependent on the emotions upon which it is founded. It varies over time, changes and fades away. It has to face up to nostalgia and to the temptation to fictionalise as the holder of the memory gradually becomes more distant from the instant in which it was formed. There is nothing objective about memory. In this respect, it is hardly any different from photography which – because it cannot exist without the reality which goes before it and which will expire once the image has been taken – gives an impression of realism which serves as the foundation for a collective belief in its supposed 'truth'. What memory and photography have in common is that they are both forms of testimony – documentary fragments – which, except when those who give such testimony choose to confabulate or go down the path of fiction, serve as triggers for the reconstitution of that which was, of a prior moment from their own existence. They are subjective forms of testimony. Totally dependent on how the conditions which led to their formation were experienced.

The history of photography offers no shortage of approaches to the theme of memory, of initiatives, spread over several different moments in time, intended to reactivate memories or question how things have changed, based on the emotion experienced at the time of the events or because images of them have become engraved upon our memories. Going back to the site of a conflict every year, or every ten years, to mark an anniversary, to look for the traces which gradually disappear as they are overtaken by nature and human activity, and to see what is no longer there, or what remains visible, is both an experience and an attempt to fight against things being forgotten.

However, at a time when we are increasingly aware of the limitations of the image - both in terms of its impact and its central role in our society - what approach should we adopt? One which consists of accumulating documentary materials to be brought together in support of a particular belief or a thesis is destined to fail in the same way as all approaches which seek to prove or demonstrate something by way of photography. It thus becomes essential for us to go back to the very fundamental nature of this category of images invented in the 19th century in order to - behold, what an illusion! - *reproduce in the most exact and most precise way possible*, that which is experienced on the ground. Capable of recording, then reproducing and conveying a point of view, photography first and foremost allows us to enter into a relationship with the memory of what the authors of the images experienced. Once they are able to find the right form to allow us to feel what they want to share with us, photographers allow us to see that what we are looking at no longer exists. Such memory is, *by its very nature*, necessarily accompanied by a sense of moments in time which interact, overlap, interlock and allow us to swing back and forth - whilst forgetting the ticking of the clock - between a prior moment in time and the instant, not when the photo was taken, but when I perform the action of looking. I look at a photograph and I make it part of the present whilst, implicitly, I know that it also takes me back to the past.

On the scale of history, the siege of Sarajevo is something which happened just yesterday; not a very long time ago. This tragic episode is part of our history. A part of our history which has already been partially erased from the memories of most of our contemporaries. And yet it is enough to set eyes on a few images and words for us, by some strange process, to reactivate the images of yesterday. The emotion we experience today when we find ourselves face to face with skies, trees, landscapes and faces that we are told have been seen in Bosnia and Herzegovina now serve as a form of memory. Simply because the point is not to describe, demonstrate, explain or make things understood, but simply to place before our eyes some scenes encountered - even fleetingly - then organised. Evocative scenes, which, in the subtle musicality of their colours, put us in a relation with temporality where things stand still for an instant, while everything around us continues to move around and disappear.

Still images but ones which are nevertheless suffused with vibrations which serve to feed our memories. They are themselves a new memory, one of today, in that what they allow us to see is no longer there. Yesterday, today and perhaps tomorrow all brought together in a single instant of shared looks.

Christian Caujolle is an emblematic figure in the world of photography. He is a critic, artistic director and curator of many photography festivals. He is also one of the founders of Agence VU' in Paris.

2/3 Bare silhouettes I, II. Srebrenica, March 2013

4/5 Bare silhouettes III, IV. Srebrenica, March 2013

9 Ibro, 22 years old. Near Srebrenica, March 2013

10/11 Night falls over the wooded hills surrounding Srebrenica. Eastern Bosnia, March 2013

12/13 At a pass and former strategic point, on the road from Sarajevo to Goražde. Eastern Bosnia, March 2015

15 The role of the UN forces during the conflict (1992–1995) remains a very controversial issue for the local population. Zenica, March 2013

16/17 A break in the snow reveals a small track in the forest. One cannot help thinking of the columns of displaced people who walked those paths trying to escape the Serb forces during the events of July 1995. Srebrenica, March 2013

19/20 During the war, this area was used as the head-quarters of General Ratko Mladić. Han Pijesak, March 2013

21 On their way home. Near Šipovo, March 2015

23 Meša, 23 years old. Srebrenica, March 2013

24/25 Kolakovići had 271 inhabitants in 1991. Today, there are only 21 left. Eastern Bosnia, March 2015

27 It has been a long time, yet still no one returned. Near Srebrenica, March 2013

29 Salim, 23 years old. Brakovći, March 2013

31 To guard against long, freezing winters, mattresses and blankets are neatly stacked. Brakovći, March 2013

32/33 Woodland stretches as far as the eye can see. Dense forest covers almost half of the country. Eastern Bosnia, March 2013

34 Myths and legends are still very entrenched in the minds of the rural population. Somedays, the location of a mass grave is revealed to the people through mysterious whispers during the night. Near Pale, March 2015

35 Two decades have passed since the end of the conflict, yet thousands of missing people are still being sought by their relatives. Near Srebrenica, March 2013

37/38 It took almost ten years for the inhabitants of the small village of Brakovci to return. The Srebrenica area now belongs to Republika Srpska. Eastern Bosnia, March 2013

39 Devastated houses alongside newly built housing. Sarajevo, March 2015

41 Samra, 23 years old. Tuzla, March 2015

42/43 Dark clouds above. A flock of birds fly overhead. Sarajevo, March 2015

45 Anida, 18 years old. Travnik, April 2014

46 Graffiti on the walls of a classroom. In the schoolyard, a high fence divides the Bosniak students from the Croatian ones. Travnik, April 2014

47 Adis, 28 years old. Tuzla, November 2013

49 Firewood collected and weighed down in the snow. Kupres, March 2015

50/51 Religious billboard at the entrance to the town. “I did everything for you: I suffered, I was crucified and died on the cross, why do you curse me?” Novi Travnik, March 2013

53 Wintry scene on the banks of the Klinje Lake. Gacko, March 2015

54/55 The small town of Gacko covered by snow. Eastern Bosnia, March 2015

57 It is cold and all feels melancholy. Near Trnovo, March 2015

58/59 A plaque commemorates the construction of the Brčko-Banovići railway during Tito’s regime in 1946. Živinice, March 2015

61 Emil, 32 years old. Banovići, March 2015

63/64 Small mining town at dusk. Banovići, March 2015

65 Coal dust covers the ground. The pride of the country under Tito was in the iron, copper, and brown coal mines. But, their value in the current economy has been heavily diminished. Banovići, March 2015

66 In a room of the Hotel Internacional. Zenica, March 2015

67 Elma, 23 years old. Tešanj, March 2015

69 Due to a serious lack of opportunity, many young people chose to leave their country and start a new life abroad. Živinice, March 2015

70 Deep in the forest I. Han Pijesak, March 2014

71 Deep in the forest II. Han Pijesak, March 2014

72/73 Deep in the forest III. Han Pijesak, March 2014

75 Azra, 25 years old. Osmaci, March 2015

77 Twigs piercing the last of the winter’s snow. Kupres, March 2015

79 In the silent immensity of the plains. Once raging battles took place here. Kupres, March 2015

80/81 Wild horses on the mountain plateau of Livno. In the 70s, they were replaced by agricultural machinery and driven into the wilderness by the villagers. Near Livno, March 2015

83 After a long winter. Near Livno, March 2015

84+89 A barren tract of scrub-land to the south of the country. Southern Bosnia, March 2013

85/88 The presence of landmines disrupts the beauty of the landscape making it inaccessible to the people.

Near Trebinje, March 2013
91 Many Muslim countries finance the construction of new mosques. Turbe, April 2014
92 Metal factories are a legacy of the previous era: under they were promoted throughout Yugoslavia. Lukavac. March 2013
93 According to the interpretation of dreams in Balkan culture, dreaming of birds means that one will soon hear some news. Near Travnik, April 2014
94/95 The country's industry has still not fully recovered from the effects of the devastating war of the 1990s. Vitkovići, March 2015
96/97 Construction of an Orthodox church and new buildings in the city centre. Pale, March 2015
99 Ahmo, 20 years old. Srebrenica, March 2013
101 Giant portrait of General Ratko Mladić painted on a building. Considered as a hero by some, Mladić is now being tried for war crimes at The International Criminal Tribunal for the former Yugoslavia in The Hague, Netherlands. Gacko, November 2013
103 Bojan, 30 years old. Banja Luka, November 2013
104/5 Travnik at dusk. Travnik, April 2014
106 Elma, 20 years old. Tuzla, March 2015
107 The country's youth are under immense pressure to fit in to the established ethnic and religious models of the country. Zenica, March 2015
108+113 Waste hanging from the branches indicates the level reached by the Bosna river during the floods that struck the country in spring 2015. Maglaj, March 2015
109/12 Driving through a landscape of bare trees. Near Srebrenica, March 2013
115 A pack of Drina cigarettes with a health notice in three languages. Since the conflict, the Serbo-Croatian language has become Bosnian, Croatian and Serbian. Travnik, October 2014
117 Branches floating in the deep waters of the Drina. The river defines much of the border between Bosnia and Serbia. Near Goražde, November 2013
118/19 A new dawns along the banks of the Drina River. Goražde, November 2013
120/21 Zenica, an industrial town with brown coal and steel industries. Zenica, April 2014
123 Nedim, 28 years old. Near Srebrenica, March 2013
125 Monument commemorating the Battle of Sutjeska, which took place during World War II. Many Bosnians still feel nostalgic towards Tito's reign. Tjentište, November 2013
126 A photographic cityscape of Hong Kong printed on a tarapaulin is an aspirational note in the city. Sarajevo, November 2013
127 Eldar, 26 years old. Tuzla, March 2015
129 *Madame Vigée-Lebrun and Her Daughter.* Printed on a chocolate box, the reproduction has been carefully cut out for display. Srebrenik, November 2013
130/31 Cityscape from the roof terrace of the Awaz tower, the tallest building in the country. Sarajevo, November 2013
137 Still life with apple, oranges and pomegranate. Mostar, in November 2013
133/34 In October 2013, one of the largest mass graves of the Bosnian War was discovered by the ICMP (International Commission of Missing Persons) near the village of Tomašica. In November 2013, 430 human remains had been exhumed from the site. Western Bosnia, November 2013
135/36 This photograph cannot convey the incessant noise of the digging machines. The mass grave is located just behind us. Near Tomašica, November 2013
139 Jasmina, 32 years old. Tuzla, November 2013
140 Nightwalk. Mostar, November 2014
141 "When you have political repression, then the only place left is your private sphere. People don't feel comfortable in public spaces. They live locked inside, side by side." - Selma, 31 years old. Tuzla October 2013
143 Split in the Road. Mostar, November 2014
145 Anita, 22 years old. Mostar, November 2013
146 Tree in blossom in the Neretva valley. Near Mostar, March 2013

Stéphanie Borcard and **Nicolas Métraux** are two Swiss photographers based in Bangkok, Thailand. Their personal projects are often influenced by both their travels and the relationship between individuals and societies. Their practice is fuelled by a desire for a better understanding and continual questioning of the world.

These photographs are the result of four trips to Bosnia and Herzegovina between Spring 2013 and Spring 2015. The images were taken all across the country, from vast open spaces to very small rooms. *Grey Skies Black Birds* would never have seen the light of day if, during a typically cold and wet winter afternoon, so familiar to the Swiss, a stranger in a café hadn't struck up a conversation.

Thank you Šaban for having invited us to discover your country.

Saša Stanišić

Die Fabrik

Mein Wagen dreht im Schneetreiben auf der Hochebene eine Pirouette in den Graben, schon klopfen kleine Hände gegen die Scheiben, Männer in Wolfsfellen und Pumatrainingsanzügen, sie geleiten mich zu einem Gehöft unweit der Straße, eine Baracke, das offene Feuer brav, sie kochen Wasser für den Tee, sie füttern mich mit *Mars*-Riegeln, und der Tee riecht nach Schaf. Wir sind die Hirten, sagen sie, wir sind es.

Der Hirten Augen groß, wollen nichts von mir wissen.

Wollen nichts wissen, die Hirten, wollen erzählen von einem Gebäude, das sich geräuspert hat vorzeiten und zögert.

Die Fabrik, sagen die Hirten, hinter den Tannen, dort. Die Hirten zeigen zum Fenster, das Fenster ist beschlagen, und der kleinste Hirte steigt auf Zehenspitzen und reibt mit dem Ärmel über das Glas, und alles, was zu sehen wäre, verweht der Schneesturm.

Was heißt das, frage ich, zögern, und wie räuspern sich Gebäude, ist das ein Witz?

Wir haben es gehört, sagen die Hirten, wir waren da. Im Windschatten der Fabrikmauern haben wir Karten gespielt. Und sie machen dir gern vor, wie das Räuspern geklungen hat, schroff und stahl, sagen sie, schroff und stahl, sie schnarren durch den Trichter ihrer Hände, und nichts kannst du dir dabei vorstellen.

Der Hirten Lebenslinien aus Erde.

Seitdem zögert die Fabrik, sagen die Hirten. Seitdem wartet die Hochebene, warten der Nebel und der Wind, warten die Hirten und ihr Schnee, dass etwas hinterherkommt.

Sie sagen: Wir bringen dich zu ihr.

Zu wem? frage ich.

Zu unserer Fabrik. Die Hirten tunken *Mars* in den Tee.

Ich will lieber nicht, sage ich.

Die Hirten beraten hinter vorgehaltener Hand. Der kleinste Hirte setzt sich auf meinen Schoß. Er singt leise, er spielt mit meinem Kragen. Ein Kinderlied ist es, eines von den alten, den brutalen, mit Schuld und Strafe, und als ich in den Refrain einstimme, bricht er ab und zeigt mir seine Eckzähne.

Die Hirten haben ihre Mützen aufgesetzt, schon stapfen wir durch den Schnee, die Hunde pflügen voraus, die Schafe trotten hinterher, was sollen Schafe im Schnee, das Gebimmel ihrer Glocken wärmt.

Wind, Wind, Wind, ich stemme mich schräg gegen seine Stirn aus Schneeflocken, die Witterung scheint nur mir etwas auszumachen, die Hirten legen bloß die Hände vor die Augen wie grüßende Soldaten. Über das karge Hochland gehe immer Wind, lügen sie, darin seien alle Atemzüge aller Serben und Bosniaken und Kroaten, die je auf der Romanija geseufzt, geliebt, getrauert hätten, verwoben in alle Ewigkeit.

Die sagen das nicht ganz so, die Hirten.

Im Wald geht es leichter, die Bäume kämmen den Wind gegen den Strich,

Tannen, schwarz und unverwundbar wie das Kinderlied. Ich frage die Hirten, ob es hier Minen gibt, und einer wirft mir einen Schneeball gegen die Brust, dass ich mein Herz spüre.

Der Hirten Bärte aus Tannennadeln.

Auf der Romanija hat sich ein Gebäude geräuspert und zögert seitdem, ein großes, rechteckiges Gebäude am Waldrand, nackte Betonmauern, zwei, drei aufgeplatzte Säcke mit Splitt, eine verrostete Säge, ein Loch in einem Eimer, Holzblöcke, Drahtzaun. Ein verwittertes kleines Radio schweigt im Schutt. Der kleinste Hirte rennt über Schnee, als läge kein Schnee, jauchzt aus Freude und Angst mit den heulenden Schäferhunden, verschwindet hinter den Mauern.

Der Hirten Köpfe wiegen auf dürren Hälsen.

Die Hirten erzählen: Wasser sollte hier abgefüllt und abgepackt werden. Der Sheriff hätte in der Nähe zwei Quellen gefunden, hätte EU-Gelder beantragt und bekommen, für die Grundstücke, für die Brunnen, für die Abfüllanlage, und, und, und. Der Sheriff, weil er immer solchen Hut und solche Jeans trug, ein Ami, sagen sie, ein Serbe, sagen sie.

Eine Frau, sagt einer, Brüste.

Der Hirten Grinsen aus Karies.

Kurz nach dem Krieg oder 2000 war das. Der Bauauftrag ging an eine Firma aus der Region, der Sheriff persönlich stellte Handwerker aus den umliegenden Dörfern ein. Arbeitsplätze, Kapital, Wiederbelebung der Wirtschaft, zählen die Hirten im Chor auf und spucken in den Schnee. Für jedes Komma hustet einer. Für jeden Punkt setzt sich einer in das Gras bei den Mauern. Es liegt kein Schnee in der Nähe der Fabrik. Satzzeichen schneit es ins unwahrscheinliche Grün.

Und eines Morgens erscheint der Bauleiter nicht auf der Baustelle. Und die Handwerker kriegen keinen Lohn mehr. Und die Landwirte nicht die versprochene Miete für die Grundstücknutzung. Die Baustofflieferanten, die ihre Waren einem mageren Vorschuss anvertraut hatten, keine weiteren Zahlungen. Anrufe nahm der Sheriff nicht mehr entgegen, bald war der Anschluss tot.

Der Hirten Augenbrauen aus Eiskristallen.

Ein halbes Jahr nach seinem Verschwinden kam die EU persönlich vorbei, um sich ein Bild zu machen. Die Hirten spucken.

Der Hirten Spucke braun von Schokolade.

Die Hirten hatten die Fabrik für ihre Kartenspiele hergerichtet, die Schafe labten sich an dem Grünzeug, das hier so reichlich gedieh, als hätte den Boden ein gütiger Gott gedüngt, wo ihr Gott alles Land mit Geröll verletzt. Die EU empfingen die Hirten gebührend – ihre Schafe blockierten die Zufahrtstrasse über Stunden. Die EU lehnte *Mars* dankend ab und fuhr erschüttert zurück in die EU.

Die Hirten haben gehört, vier von sechs Raten hätte die EU an den Sheriff überwiesen, bevor die Zahlungen gestoppt wurden. Die Hirten nennen die Summe nicht, sie streichen sich bloß mit Zeigefinger und Daumen über das Kinn.

Der kleinste Hirte schält ein *Mars*, seine Hände, sein Gesicht zerfurcht wie die Rinde von Tannen. Er winkt mich zu sich und führt mich durch kein Tor in die Fabrik. Wir betreten sommerliches Summen warmer Luft, Fliegen schwirren umher. Wo Fenster sein müssten, Abwesenheiten. Wo Fußböden sein müssten, Erde. Wolken, wo das halbe Dach fehlt. Kletterpflanzen, wo Rohre sich schlängeln sollten; eine Fabrik steht unfertig auf der Romanija und zögert. Unfertig und nackt, gebraucht nur von den Hirten und ihren Tieren, ein Versteck, wenn der Sturm sie jagt, ein Plastiktisch, auf dem sie Rommé spielen.

Der Hirten große Augen: Schau dich, Fremder, um.

Ins Gemäuer haben Zugvögel ihre Nester gestrickt. Eine Eidechse umzirkelt eine Eidechse. In der Mitte der Fabrik stapeln zwei Hirten Steine zu kleinen Türmen und kichern dabei wie Verliebte. Oder weinen sie? Ich frage und sie sagen, die ersten Siedler, die vom Gipfel unserer Berge auf die öde Welt darunter blickten, waren Illyrer, Hirten wie wir, zäh und ernst.

Die sagen das nicht ganz so, die Hirten. Und sie sagen auch nichts weiter, sie geben mir keine Geschichte.

Der kleinste Hirte ist wieder bei mir. Wir kennen, flüstert er, alle Quellen auf der Romanija. Ein kräftiges Wasser musst du sein, dass du dich durch unseren Stein nach oben prügeln kannst – er geht auf ein Knie – und ein schlaues dazu, dass wir dich nicht schon längst gefunden haben.

Er riecht so stark nach Schokolade, dass ich mich abwenden muss. Die anderen haben ihre Felle ausgezogen und spielen Rommé, die Fabrik sieht zu und fabriziert Zögern.

Vielleicht haben die Hirten hier den Schnee geräumt?

Sachte bimmeln die Schafsglöckchen im Wald.

Ich spreche die Sprache der Hirten, aber ich verstehe nicht, was sie verstehen.

Einer kümmert sich um die Hunde, befreit ihre Pfoten mit Melkfett vom Eis.

Einer wässert in der Ecke Kartoffeln. Heute vor 73 Jahren, ruft er, ist mein Großvater mit der Ersten Proletarischen Brigade auf der Romanija von den Deutschen umzingelt gewesen. Also ist die Brigade losmarschiert durch Schnee und Eis über die Hochebene und weiter über den grausamen Igman bei Minus 30. Eine singende Partisanenkolonne, sagt der Hirte, und ein anderer fragt, woher er wisse, dass gesungen wurde.

Der Hirten Mobiltelefone mit selbstgebastelten Alu-Antennen und vollem Empfang, wo ich gar keinen habe.

Und der kleinste Hirte klettert singend auf eine Leiter, er singt lauter als zuvor, die Stimme einer alten Frau, rau und mild:

In einer kalten Winternacht hoch oben auf der Höh
das Bächlein ist gefroren, es liegt verdeckt im Schnee
Ein Hase sucht das Bächlein, er sucht es überall
Ist es denn verloren? Das wäre ja fatal.

Es weint der gute Hase um sein Bächlein sehr
er weint aus ganzem Herzen, zweifelt immer mehr:
Gab's das Bächlein je? Er fühlt sich so betrogen
Oder ist es mit den Vögeln gen Süden weggeflogen.

Der Hirten schnelle Hunde schlitzen einander die Kehlen im Spiel auf, ich muss ihnen ausweichen, es ist als sei ich gar nicht nötig.

Der Hirten Zähne sommergelb.

Der kleinste Hirte sitzt auf der obersten Sprosse und stutzt Kletterrosen. Man hat mich aufgegeben.

Ich habe gehört, auf dem Karstklotz namens Romanija, zwischen öden Kalkschollen und Hügelgräbern aus Klaubsteinen, Gräbern für illyrische Hirten und jugoslawische Partisanen, steht eine Fabrik. Sie hat ein paar bescheidene Träume hergestellt. Die Hirten haben ihrem Räuspern gelauscht und hüten ihr Zögern.

Saša Stanišić, geboren in 1978 in Višegrad, Jugoslawien, Schriftsteller, Essayist und Journalist, ist Autor zweier Romane. Der erste, "Wie der Soldat das Grammofon repariert" (2006), wurde in 32 Sprachen übersetzt. Der zweite, "Vor dem Fest", wurde 2014 mit dem Preis der Leipziger Buchmesse ausgezeichnet.

Srećko Latal

Bosnien und Herzegowina: ein Land im Rückschritt

Seit dem verheerenden Balkankrieg vor zwanzig Jahren befindet sich Bosnien und Herzegowina (BiH) im Übergang von einem Post-Konflikt-Staat zu einer modernen, in Richtung EU ausgerichteten Gesellschaft. Irgendwann geriet diese Entwicklung ins Straucheln und heute steht das Land kurz davor, entweder als gescheiterter Staat zu enden oder auseinanderzubrechen. Die Verschärfung lokaler politischer Konflikte, die Verhärtung der Positionen in der gesamten Region sowie die Entstehung neuer weltpolitischer Spannungen schaffen schwierige und riskante Rahmenbedingungen für die Klärung des Schicksals von BiH: eine Lösungsfindung, an der sich nicht nur die Zukunft dieses zerrissenen Landes entscheiden wird, sondern die auch schwerwiegende Folgen für die gesamte Region zeitigen wird.

Das Friedensabkommen von Dayton, das 1995 den Krieg beendete und den neuen verfassungsrechtlichen Rahmen für BiH schuf, teilte das Land zwischen den drei größten ethnischen Gruppen – den mehrheitlich muslimischen Bosniaken, den mehrheitlich katholischen Kroaten und den mehrheitlich orthodoxen Serben – in zwei Entitäten, die hauptsächlich von Bosniaken bevölkerte Föderation Bosnien und Herzegowina und die hauptsächlich von Serben bevölkerte Republika Srpska. Darüber hinaus leben in BiH Angehörige verschiedener ethnischer Minderheiten, darunter Italiener, Tschechen und Polen sowie „Sonstige", die sich aus unterschiedlichen Gründen mit keiner der drei größten ethnischen Gruppen identifizieren wollen. Jedoch können sich die Bürger BiHs bis heute nicht auf eine einheitliche Sicht auf die Vergangenheit, Gegenwart und Zukunft ihres Landes verständigen.

Dass die auseinandergehenden Vorstellungen der drei ethnisch-politischen Blöcke über viele Jahre so gut wie keine politische Wirkung entfalteten, lag an der starken militärischen, diplomatischen und finanziellen Präsenz ausländischer Mächte, die das Land stabilisierte und einen schnellen und erfolgreichen Wiederaufbau möglich machte. Westliche Diplomaten und internationale Organisationen griffen tief in die Rechtsstrukturen BiHs ein, indem sie Reformen in sämtlichen Sektoren anstießen und förderten – Sicherheit, Politik, Wirtschaft, Gesellschaft, Kultur. Viele dieser Reformen erwiesen sich als große Erfolge, so etwa die Zusammenlegung der Streitkräfte und die Vereinheitlichung des Finanz- und Steuerwesens. Andere wiederum – Reformen des Polizei- und Rechtswesens und der Medien – wurden von Anfang an durch Unkenntnis der Verhältnisse vor Ort und Fehler der ausländischen Initiatoren behindert. Der Westen wurde der Sache schließlich überdrüssig und begann sich ernsthafte Gedanken über eine Exit-Strategie zu machen. Nach dem Scheitern eines amerikanischen Versuchs, den komplizierten und teuren verfassungsrechtlichen Rahmen des Abkommens von Dayton zu revidieren, reduzierte die US-Regierung 2006 ihre Verpflichtungen und trat die Aufpasserrolle an die EU ab. Anzeichen einer erneuten Radikalisierung in der politischen Führungsschicht BiHs wurden ignoriert, als der Westen beschloss, zukünftig von weiteren Einmischungen in die Tagespolitik abzusehen und das

Schicksal des Landes in die Hände ebendieser Führungsschicht zu legen. Der Wegfall der externen Kontrollen zu einem Zeitpunkt, als die gesellschaftlichen Strukturen vor Ort noch unterentwickelt und unzureichend auf die Übernahme dieser Verantwortung vorbereitet waren, führte zum Rückfall der politischen Elite in die autokratischen Praktiken einer kompromisslosen Durchsetzung eigener Interessen. Seither ist BiH immer tiefer in eine politische, wirtschaftliche und gesellschaftliche Krise gestürzt.

Die politischen Führer der drei ethnisch-politischen Blöcke verfolgen heute die gleichen nationalistischen Ziele wie ihre Vorgänger vor, während und unmittelbar nach dem Krieg und rücken kaum von deren überzogenen Forderungen ab: Die bosnischen Serben drohen nach wie vor mit der Sezession der Republika Srpska, die bosnischen Kroaten mit der Gründung eines eigenen Staats, während die Bosniaken die Zentralisierung des Landes fordern, gleichzeitig jedoch stetig näher an Kreise aus der türkischen und saudiarabischen Politik und Wirtschaft heranrücken. Die umständliche, in Dayton aus der Taufe gehobene Landesverfassung hat nach wie vor Gültigkeit, wird jedoch von den politischen Eliten zunehmend ignoriert und korrumpiert, seit die Exekutivgewalt des Büros des Hohen Repräsentanten mangels internationaler Unterstützung quasi nur noch auf dem Papier besteht. Auch dadurch wird die Funktionstauglichkeit des Systems weiter untergraben.

Eine politische Spekulationspyramide

Politiker nutzen Forderungen nach dem Schutz ihrer jeweiligen ethnischen, ideologischen oder politischen Interessen, um sich auf ihr eigentliches Ziel zu fokussieren: die Verteilung des „Wahlkuchens". Darunter fällt die Zuteilung von Parlamentssitzen auf den verschiedenen Regierungsebenen ebenso wie die Positionierung von Parteimitgliedern in staatlichen Unternehmen, Behörden und anderen Institutionen. Diese Unternehmen dienen den Parteien und ihren auserwählten Mitgliedern dann als Goldesel, während die politischen Amtsträger und ihre Familien in den Institutionen eine loyale Machtbasis bilden, mit deren Hilfe die politischen Führer ihre eigene Position innerhalb der Partei stärken.

Dieses System wird von einem Wahlzyklus zum nächsten reproduziert und ausgebaut, sodass es sich im Laufe der Jahre zu einer komplexen und breit aufgestellten Spekulationspyramide entwickelt hat, die sich durch die geschickte Nutzung ethnischer Vorurteile einerseits und der komplizierten verfassungsrechtlichen Strukturen andererseits perpetuieren lässt, ohne auch nur ein Mindestmaß an effizienten Leistungen für die Bevölkerung zu erbringen. Bei aller vehementen Kritik der Oppositionsparteien an der Korruption und dem Missbrauch des Systems verhalten diese sich nicht anders, wenn sie selber an die Macht kommen, sondern nutzen die vorhandenen Möglichkeiten nach Kräften aus, bis sie wieder abgewählt werden. Dann warten sie einfach ab, bis die Wähler ihrer politischen Gegner überdrüssig geworden und ihre eigenen Sünden in

Vergessenheit geraten sind. Dieses Verhalten so gut wie aller politischen Parteien hat eine üble politische Endlosschleife entstehen lassen – einen Teufelskreis, den weder in- noch ausländische Akteure zu durchbrechen vermögen.

Die Politiker, die das Land verdient

Es stimmt zwar, dass ein Großteil der Schuld an diesen Zuständen die politische Elite trifft, jedoch reflektiert deren Verhalten lediglich die Stimmung in der Gesellschaft insgesamt. Die Mehrheit der Medien ist ebenfalls entlang ethnischen und politischen Linien bzw. wirtschaftlichen Interessen gespalten. Entsprechend sensationsgierig, voreingenommen, unseriös und von politischen Loyalitäten geprägt ist ihre Berichterstattung, die den politischen Eliten bei ihren öffentlichen Streitereien immer wieder als Munition dient.

Die nichtstaatlichen Organisationen und wissenschaftlichen Institutionen des Landes konzentrieren sich derweil auf ihre eigenen schmalspurigen Interessen, die in der Regel im Zusammenhang mit internationalen oder staatlich finanzierten Projekten stehen, unabhängig davon, wie viel – oder wie wenig – Nutzen diese der einheimischen Bevölkerung bringen. Mangels alternativer Standpunkte und positiver Initiativen machten sich die Bürger BiHs eine lethargische und desillusionierte Grundhaltung zu Eigen bzw. sahen keinen Grund, diese Haltung aufzugeben. So schienen viele Menschen eher gewillt, in einem gescheiterten Staat vor sich hin zu vegetieren oder das Land zu verlassen, anstatt etwas zu verändern.

Die Unruhen von 2014

Die Nullsummenspiele der Politiker im Verbund mit der weitverbreiteten Korruption und den sich verschlimmernden wirtschaftlichen und sozialen Zuständen haben ein explosives Gemisch aus Unzufriedenheit, Überdruss und Wut erzeugt, das sich schließlich im Februar 2014 in einer Reihe gewalttätiger Ausschreitungen entlud. Brennende Regierungsgebäude, umgestoßene Autos und Zusammenstöße zwischen opportunistischen Rowdys und der Polizei sorgten für Szenen, wie man sie seit dem Ende des Krieges nicht mehr gesehen hatte. Diese Bilder lösten im In- und Ausland Entsetzen aus, ließen aber auch Hoffnungen auf einen verstärkten bürgerlichen Aktivismus wach werden und veranlassten die EU zu einer neuen Reforminitiative für BiH. Die Bürgerplena, die im Zuge der Unruhen als ein Versuch entstanden, der Straßendemokratie in BiH eine Stimme zu geben, welkten aufgrund interner Differenzen und Spaltungen dahin. Die Proteste setzten sich jedoch landesweit fort und scheinen seit Ende 2014 noch an Intensität zugenommen zu haben. Da sie über das ganze Land verstreut stattfinden und ihnen eine zentrale Organisation ebenso fehlt wie eine einheitliche Stoßrichtung haben, werden diese Demonstrationen zumeist als Einzelvorfälle wahrgenommen und von der politischen Elite und der Allgemeinheit gleichermaßen ignoriert. Angesichts des sich verschlimmernden wirtschaftlichen und sozialen Elends stellen sie indes eine Zeitbombe dar, die jederzeit in erneuten gewaltsamen Unruhen explodieren kann.

Die Überschwemmungen von 2014

Zu allem Überfluss wurde BiH im Frühjahr und Sommer 2014 von einer Reihe massiver Überschwemmungen und Erdrutsche getroffen. Die bislang schlimmste Naturkatastrophe in der jüngeren Geschichte des Landes beschädigte oder zerstörte Wohnhäuser und Eigenheime, Fabriken und landwirtschaftliche Betriebe, Straßen, Schienen, Wasser- und Stromleitungen. Der Gesamtschaden belief sich Schätzungen zufolge auf mehr als zwei Milliarden Euro – über zehn Prozent des BIP.

Jedoch brachte die Katastrophe ganz unerwartet eine positive Seite des verwüsteten Landes zum Vorschein. Als geschwollene Flüsse und Schlammfluten das Land überschwemmten, eilten die Bürger von Bosnien und Herzegowina ihren Nachbarn zu Hilfe, ohne nach deren ethnischem, religiösem oder politischem Hintergrund zu fragen. Während die meisten staatlichen Institutionen untätig zusahen, baten Städte und Dörfer ihre unmittelbaren Nachbarn um Hilfe – die oftmals jenseits der Grenze zwischen den einzelnen Landesteilen lagen. Die Nachbarn kamen mit Gummibooten, Schwermaschinen und Baustoffen, um der Überschwemmungen Herr zu werden, und stellten Lebensmittel, Trinkwasser und Notunterkünfte für die Menschen zur Verfügung, die ihre Häuser verlassen mussten. Auf diese Weise zeigten die Bürger von Bosnien und Herzegowina ihre menschliche Seite, womöglich gar ihre wahre Natur, und ließen einen Hoffnungsschimmer aufkommen, dass dieses Land eines Tages doch noch zu echtem Frieden und Wohlstand finden wird.

Alternde Bevölkerung

Die politische Krise, Konjunkturschwäche und der soziale Abschwung haben in den letzten Jahren zudem zu einer massiven Entvölkerung geführt. Verschiedene Meinungsumfragen haben gezeigt, dass ganze 60 Prozent der Bevölkerung – unter den Jugendlichen liegt diese Zahl sogar bei 80 Prozent – das Land sofort verlassen würden, wenn sie könnten. Viele andere haben bereits die Mittel dazu gefunden, sodass in manchen Gegenden ganze Dörfer zu Geisterorten geworden sind, deren Einwohner auf der Suche nach einer besseren Zukunft die Region oder gar das Land verlassen haben. Im Verbund mit der stetig fallenden Geburten- und ansteigenden Sterblichkeitsrate sowie der rückläufigen Anzahl der Eheschließungen bei gleichzeitiger Zunahme der Scheidungsfälle weist BiH mittlerweile eine demographische Entwicklung auf, die zu den schlechtesten in der Region zählt. Zwischen 2009 und 2012 ging die Bevölkerung von 3,84 Millionen auf 3,83 Millionen zurück, den vorläufigen Ergebnissen der Volkszählung von 2013 zufolge liegt sie derzeit nur noch bei 3,79 Millionen.

Das Rote Kreuz hat Zahlen vorgelegt, denen zufolge BiH in den nächsten 35 Jahren die älteste Bevölkerung in der Region aufweisen wird. Diese trübe demographische Perspektive hat sehr konkrete negative Auswirkungen auf die wirtschaftliche Zukunft des Landes, zumal sich die Anzahl der Rentner und die der Erwerbstätigen bereits heute die Waage halten.

Die politische Krise verschärft sich

Die fehlende Kontrolle durch die internationale Gemeinschaft und die Aufsichtsbehörden vor Ort ermöglichte eine bis heute anhaltende Radikalisierung der politischen Stimmung. In der Regierungsperiode 2010 bis 2014 verschärfte sich die politische Krise weiter und es kam effektiv zu einem Zusammenbruch der politischen Strukturen im Zeichen sich intensivierender Auseinandersetzungen sowohl innerhalb der drei ethnisch-politischen Blöcke als zwischen ihnen. Neue Bündnisse zwischen den politischen Parteien entstanden und zerbrachen manchmal täglich oder wöchentlich. Die Arbeit der gesetzgebenden Organe und der Exekutive auf den unterschiedlichen Verwaltungsebenen wurde dadurch mehr oder weniger komplett blockiert und die Grundsätze von Demokratie und Pluralismus soweit geschwächt, dass die Macht in allen großen Parteien bei den Vorsitzenden und einer Handvoll ihrer engsten Vertrauten lag.

Hoffnungen auf eine Wiederherstellung des kollabierten politischen Systems infolge der Parlamentswahlen im Oktober 2014 verblassten angesichts der verfahrensrechtlichen Probleme und anhaltenden politischen Machtspiele, die erneut auf allen Ebenen die Regierungsbildung verlangsamten. So nahm die Bildung neuer arbeitsfähiger Koalitionen teilweise knapp ein halbes Jahr in Anspruch, und die Mehrzahl dieser Koalitionen hielt dem Druck der egoistischen Taktiken zur Durchsetzung eigener Interessen nicht lange statt.

Mitte 2015 sah es ganz so aus, als trete BiH in die kritische Phase der derzeitigen Krise ein. Der Präsident der Republika Srpska, Milorad Dodik, setzte für Ende 2015 eine Volksabstimmung zur Einschränkung der Befugnisse der Justiz und des Hohen Repräsentanten für Bosnien und Herzegowina (Englisch Office of the High Representative, OHR) an. Es steht zu befürchten, dass dies zur weiteren politischen Destabilisierung des Landes und der gesamten Region führen wird. Die mit der EU und dem Internationalen Währungsfonds (IWF) vereinbarten wirtschafts- und sozialpolitischen Reformen werden weiterhin blockiert. Die mit dem IWF ausgehandelte Frist bis Ende Juni ließ die Regierung verstreichen, sodass BiH nun ohne finanzielle Unterstützung aus dem Ausland dasteht. Auf fast allen Verwaltungsebenen geht das Geld aus, und das Land steht vor einer kritischen Liquiditätskrise. Die internationale Gemeinschaft beobachtet die sich ausweiten de Krise, bleibt jedoch weiterhin unentschlossen, ob und wenn ja in welcher Form eine Intervention erforderlich ist.

Verschlechterung der Lage auf regionaler und globaler Ebene

Als wäre die Lage im eigenen Land nicht schlimm genug, sieht sich BiH seit einigen Jahren zunehmend mit Problemen auf regionaler und globaler Ebene konfrontiert, die wiederum zur erneuten Radikalisierung und Verhärtung der

Positionen sowohl im kroatischen als auch im serbischen Landesteil beitragen. Zudem hat BiH mit dem wachsenden Einfluss Russlands sowie radikal-islamischer Gruppen zu kämpfen. Die westlichen Länder können sich derweil auf keinen einheitlichen Kurs verständigen und verschließen weitgehend die Augen vor den unheilvollen Vorzeichen aus BiH. Die EU scheut bislang vor einem verstärkten politischen Eingreifen zurück und versucht stattdessen, die tiefen strukturellen Probleme durch technische Lösungsansätze zu beheben - aus den Fehlern der Vergangenheit hat man anscheinend wenig gelernt. Aus den USA werden zunehmend warnende Stimmen laut, jedoch fehlt auch der amerikanischen Außenpolitik eine klare Linie gegenüber BiH, stattdessen überlässt man der EU die Führungsrolle, um sich anderen Prioritäten widmen zu können.

Ungewisse Aussichten

Die anhaltende politische Krise in BiH hat die Reformen abgewürgt, die wirtschaftliche und soziale Struktur des Landes gelähmt und den Weg in die europäische Integration versperrt. Die Funktionsfähigkeit seiner Institutionen, Systeme und Gesetze ist auf verschiedenen Verwaltungsebenen beeinträchtigt. Diese Verkettung unglücklicher Umstände, interner und externer Probleme, hat eine Situation herbeigeführt, die komplizierter und potentiell gefährlicher ist als die Summe ihrer Teile. In der zweiten Jahreshälfte ist mit einer weiteren Verschärfung zu rechnen. Angesichts dieser Zustände verfügen höchstens die internationalen Institutionen über die erforderliche Kompetenz, um den Untergang BiHs aufzuhalten und die territoriale und verfassungsrechtliche Integrität des Landes zu retten. Leider weiß die internationale Gemeinschaft viel zu wenig über die weiter schwelenden Krisenherde auf dem Balkan, sondern ist auf andere globale Herausforderungen fokussiert und überlässt BiH seinem ungewissen Schicksal.

Srećko Latal, in Sarajevo geboren, Journalist und politischer Analyst, war Berichterstatter der Balkan- und Afghanistan-Konflikte für die Associated Press (AP). Danach arbeitete er für die International Crisis Group (ICG) und dem Balkans Investigative Reporting Network (BIRN). Seine Artikel erschienen im New York Times, im Guardian und anderen internationalen Medien.

Übersetzt von Silke Lührmann

Christian Caujolle

Nachwort

Im 20. Jahrhundert - bevor ein Strom beliebiger Bilder mit solcher Wucht über uns hereinbrach, dass wir nicht mehr in der Lage sind, sie wahrzunehmen, zu entschlüsseln, zu verstehen, so zahlreich sind sie - hielt Fotografie Erinnerung in Silbersalzen fest. Erinnerung an Momente des Familienlebens, an Gesichter, Landschaften, Reisen, Anekdoten, aber auch an historische Handlungen und Ereignisse.

Ebenfalls im - ausgehenden - 20. Jahrhundert fand die Belagerung von Sarajevo statt, die längste in der modernen Kriegsgeschichte, die mindestens 10 000 Todesopfer forderte. Während dieser Belagerung machten Fotografen, aber auch Einwohner, Aufnahmen, die sie verbreiteten, unter sich tauschten, manche wurden in der Presse, in Büchern veröffentlicht, bisweilen gab es dazu Ausstellungen. Sind uns diese Bilder noch präsent? Nicht sicher - wo so viele andere Bilder von anderen tragischen Ereignissen in einem immer schnelleren Rhythmus die älteren verdrängen und überlagern. Denn heute lautet die Kernfrage: angesichts der Fülle von aufeinander prallenden, sich immer schneller verbreitenden Bildern, die die vorherigen ersetzen in einer Show, die sich nunmehr schwerlich als Information bezeichnen lässt, sind wir womöglich auf dem Weg zu einer Welt, in der die Erinnerung in dem Augenblick schwindet, in dem sie entstehen sollte? Und sind wir darüber hinaus etwa auf dem Weg zu einer Welt, für die Erinnerung weder als Wert noch als Notwendigkeit gilt?

Die menschliche Erinnerung ist empfindlich, oft bruchstückhaft und abhängig von den Emotionen, die ihr zugrunde liegen. Sie wechselt mit der Zeit, verändert sich, schwächt sich ab, sieht sich immer mehr den Sehnsüchten und Versuchungen der Fiktion gegenübergestellt, je weiter derjenige, der sie in sich trägt, sich vom Augenblick ihrer Entstehung entfernt. Sie ist überhaupt nicht objektiv. Und unterscheidet sich dabei kaum von der Fotografie, die sich, weil sie nicht existieren kann ohne das Reale, das ihr vorausgeht und doch gleich nach der Bildaufnahme überholt sein wird, einen Anschein von Realismus gibt, auf dem eine kollektive Leichtgläubigkeit fußt in der Annahme ihrer „Wahrhaftigkeit". Erinnerung und Fotografie vereint die gemeinsame Eigenschaft, Zeugnisse zu sein - Teile von Belegstücken - die, außer wenn deren Träger fabulieren oder sich bewusst ins Reich der Fiktion begeben, als Auslöser von Rekonstruktionen wirken von dem, was einmal war, in einer Vorzeit ihres eigenen Daseins. Subjektive Zeugnisse. Gänzlich abhängig von den bei ihrer Entstehung erlebten Bedingungen.

Die Geschichte der Fotografie ist reich an Bemühungen, Erinnerung zu bewahren, an aufeinander folgenden Ansätzen, um die Entwicklung der Dinge wiederzubeleben oder in Frage zu stellen, auf der Grundlage der zur Zeit der Ereignisse erlebten Emotion oder weil Bilder sie in unser Gedächtnis eingebrannt haben. Jedes Jahr, alle zehn Jahre, anlässlich eines Jahrestages an den Ort eines Konflikts zurückzukehren, auf der Suche nach Spuren, die die Natur und die Tätigkeit des Menschen nach und nach verwischen; festzustellen, dass was einmal war, nicht mehr vorhanden ist oder aber sichtbar bleibt: Dies ist gleichzeitig eine Erfahrung und der Versuch, gegen das Vergessen anzukämpfen.

Im Moment jedoch, da wir uns der Grenzen des Bildes – ebenso wie seiner Wirkung und zentraler Stellung in unserer Gesellschaft - immer bewusster werden, für welche Vorgehensweise sollen wir uns entscheiden? Diejenige, die darin besteht, Dokumente anzuhäufen, um sie in Beziehung zu setzen im Dienste einer Überzeugung oder einer Theorie, ist zum Scheitern verurteilt, wie alle Versuche, Fotografien als Nachweis, zur Beweisführung einzusetzen.

Als unabdingbar erweist sich dann die Rückbesinnung auf den eigentlichen Kern dieser Art von Bildern, die im 19 Jahrhundert erfunden wurden, um – welche Täuschung! – *eins zu eins bis ins letzte Detail zu reproduzieren*: die Erfahrung vor Ort. Weil sie einen Standpunkt festzuhalten vermag, um ihn dann wiederzugeben und zu überliefern, setzt uns die Fotografie zunächst in Verbindung mit der Erinnerung der Schöpfer der Bilder an das Erlebte.

Dadurch dass sie fähig waren, die geeignete Form zu finden, um uns nachempfinden zu lassen, was sie mit uns teilen wollen, vermitteln uns die Fotografen, dass es das, was wir anschauen, nicht mehr gibt. Diese Erinnerung drängt *per se* unterschwellig ein Gefühl auf von sich kreuzenden, überlappenden, in einander verstrickenden Zeitebenen, die außerhalb des Uhrentaktes zwischen einem Vorher und dem Moment nicht der Bildaufnahme, sondern meines tätigen Blicks hin- und her pendeln. Ich betrachte ein Foto und verleihe ihm Gegenwart, implizit wohlwissend, dass es mich auf die Vergangenheit verweist.

Im geschichtlichen Maßstab fand die Belagerung Sarajevos gestern statt, vor sehr kurzer Zeit, diese tragische Episode gehört zu unserer Geschichte. Zu unserer aus dem Gedächtnis der meisten unserer Zeitgenossen schon ausgelöschten Geschichte. Und doch genügt es, dass Bilder und einige Worte uns ins Auge fallen, um uns – seltsamer Prozess – Bilder von gestern reaktivieren zu lassen. Die heutige Emotion angesichts von Darstellungen des Himmels, Bäumen, Landschaften, Gesichtern, von denen es heißt, sie wären heute in Bosnien und Herzegowina gesehen worden, dient dem Gedenken. Einfach weil es nicht darum geht, zu beschreiben, zu beweisen, zu verstehen zu geben, zu erklären. Sondern einfach nur darum, zufällig getroffene, flüchtig aufgenommene und später angeordnete Wahrnehmungen in unsere Augen einzuprägen, Erscheinungen, deren musikalisch zarte Schattierungen ein Zeitgefühl durchsetzen, das uns abrupt stillstehen lässt, während alles um uns herum tobt und verschwindet.

Unbewegte Bilder, aber von Vibrationen durchdrungen, die das Gedächtnis nähren. Sie sind selbst eine neue Erinnerung – von heute – während das, was sie uns zu sehen geben, schon nicht mehr ist. Gestern, heute, morgen vielleicht geronnen zu einem einzigen Moment geteilter Blicke.

Christian Caujolle ist eine emblematische Figur in der Welt der Fotografie. Er ist Kritiker, künstlerischer Leiter und Kurator von vielen Fotofestivals. Er ist auch Mitbegründer der Pariser Agence VU'.

Übersetzt von Danielle Wagner

2/3 Kahle Silhouetten I, II. Srebrenica, März 2013

4/5 Kahle Silhouetten III, IV. Srebrenica, März 2013

9 Ibro, 22 Jahre alt. In der Nähe von Srebrenica, März 2013

10/11 Einbruch der Dunkelheit auf den bewaldeten Hügeln rund um Srebrenica. Ostbosnien, März 2013

12/13 An einem Pass - ehemals strategischer Punkt - auf der Straße von Sarajevo nach Goražde. Ostbosnien, März 2015

15 Die Rolle der UN-Truppen während des Konflikts (1992-1995) bleibt ein sehr umstrittenes Thema in der lokalen Bevölkerung. Zenica, März 2013

16/17 Die nur dünne Schneeschicht lässt einen schmalen Waldweg erkennen. Man kommt nicht umhin, an die Flüchtlingskolonnen zu denken, die während der Ereignisse vom Juli 1995 auf diesen Waldwegen flüchteten, beim Versuch, der serbischen Armee zu entkommen. Srebrenica März 2013

19/20 Während des Krieges diente dieses Gebiet als Hauptquartier von General Ratko Mladić. Han Pijesak, März 2013

21 Auf dem Weg nach Hause. In der Nähe von Šipovo, März 2015

23 Meša, 23 Jahre alt. Srebrenica, März 2013

24/25 Kolakovići hatte 271 Einwohner in 1991. Heute sind nur noch 21 übrig. Ostbosnien, März 2015

27 Viel Zeit ist vergangen, doch es kam noch niemand zurück. In der Nähe von Srebrenica, März 2013

29 Salim, 23 Jahre alt. Brakovći, März 2013

31 Um dem langen eiskalten Winter zu trotzen, wurden vorsorglich Matratzen und Decken ordentlich gestapelt. Brakovći, März 2013

32/33 So weit das Auge reicht, bewaldete Hügel. Dichte Wälder bedecken fast die Hälfte des Landes. Ostbosnien März 2013

34 Mythen und Sagen sind im Geiste der ländlichen Bevölkerung noch stark verankert. Es kommt vor, dass die Stelle eines Massengrabes während der Nacht den Bewohnern durch geheimnisvolles Flüstern offenbart wird. In der Nähe von Pale, März 2015

35 Zwei Jahrzehnte sind seit dem Ende des Konflikts vergangen - trotzdem werden noch Tausende von Vermissten von ihren Angehörigen gesucht. In der Nähe von Srebrenica, März 2013

37/38 Es dauerte fast zehn Jahre bis die Einwohner des kleinen Dorfes von Brakovci zurückkamen. Das Gebiet von Srebrenica gehört heute zur Republika Srpska. Ostbosnien, März 2013

39 Verwüstete Häuser stehen neben neuen Gebäuden. Sarajevo, März 2015

41 Samra, 23 Jahre alt. Tuzla, März 2015

42/43 Düstere Wolken am Himmel. Ein Vogelschwarm fliegt empor. Sarajevo, März 2015

45 Anida, 18 Jahre alt. Travnik, April 2014

46 Graffitis auf den Wänden eines Klassenzimmers. Im Schulhof trennt ein hohes Gitter die bosniakischen Schüler von den kroatischen. Travnik, April 2014

47 Adis, 28 Jahre alt. Tuzla November 2013

49 Gesammeltes und beschwertes Brennholz im Schnee. Kupres, März 2015

50/51 Religiöses Plakat am Eingang der Stadt. „Ich habe alles für euch getan: Ich litt, wurde gekreuzigt und starb am Kreuz, warum verflucht ihr mich ?“ Novi Travnik, März 2013

53 Winterliche Szene am Ufer des Klinje Sees. Gacko, März 2015

54/55 Die kleine Stadt Gacko mit Schnee bedeckt. Ostbosnien, März 2015

57 Es ist kalt und alles nichts als Melancholie. In der Nähe von Trnovo, März 2015

58/59 Eine Gedenktafel erinnert an den Bau der Brčko-Banovići Bahn 1946 unter Titos Regime. Živinice, März 2015

61 Emil, 32 Jahre alt. Banovići, März 2015

63/64 Kleine Bergbaustadt in der Dämmerung. Banovići, März 2015

65 Kohlenstaub bedeckt den Boden. Eisen-, Kupfer-, und Braunkohlengruben waren unter Tito des Landes ganzer Stolz. In der heutigen Wirtschaft haben sie aber erheblich an Wert verloren. Banovići, März 2015

66 In einem Zimmer des Hotel Internacional. Zenica, März 2015

67 Elma, 23 Jahre alt. Tešanj, März 2015

69 Mangels Perspektiven entscheiden sich viele junge Leute dafür, ihr Land zu verlassen und ein neues Leben im Ausland zu beginnen. Živinice, März 2015

70 Im tiefen Wald I. Han Pijesak, März 2014

71 Im tiefen Wald II. Han Pijesak, März 2014

72/73 Im tiefen Wald III. Han Pijesak, März 2014

75 Azra, 25 Jahre alt. Osmaci, März 2015

77 Zweige ragen aus dem letzten Schnee des Winters. Kupres, März 2015

79 In der stillen Weite der Ebene. Früher fanden hier schwere Kämpfe statt. Kupres, März 2015

80/81 Wilde Pferde auf der Hochebene von Livno. In den 70er Jahren wurden sie durch landwirtschaftliche

Maschinen ersetzt und von den Dorfbewohnern ausgewildert. In der Nähe von Livno, März 2015

83 Nach einem langen Winter. In der Nähe von Livno, März 2015

84+89 Karge Heidelandschaft im Süden des Landes. Süd Bosnien, März 2013

85/88 Landminen machen die Landschaft unzugänglich und damit ihre Schönheit zunichte. In der Nähe von Trebinje, März 2013

91 Viele muslimische Länder finanzieren den Bau neuer Moscheen. Turbe, April 2014

92 Hüttenwerke sind ein Erbe der früheren Ära: unter Tito waren sie in ganz Jugoslawien verbreitet. Lukavac. März 2013

93 Nach der Traumdeutung in der balkanischen Tradition bedeutet von Vögeln zu träumen, dass man bald Nachrichten bekommen wird. In der Nähe von Travnik, April 2014

94/95 Die Wirtschaft des Landes hat sich immer noch nicht von den Auswirkungen des verheerenden Krieges in den 1990er Jahren erholt. Vitkovići, März 2015

96 97 Bau einer orthodoxen Kirche und neuer Gebäude in der Stadtmitte. Pale, März 2015

99 Ahmo, 20 Jahre alt. Srebrenica, März 2013

101 Riesenporträt vom General Ratko Mladić auf einem Gebäude. Von manchen als Held betrachtet, steht Mladić zurzeit wegen Kriegsverbrechen vor dem Internationalen Strafgerichtshof für das ehemalige Jugoslawien (ICTY) in Den Haag, die Niederlande. Gacko, November 2013

103 Bojan, 30 Jahre alt. Banja Luka, November 2013

104/5 Travnik in der Abenddämmerung. Travnik, April 2014

106 Elma 20 Jahre alt. Tuzla, März 2015

107 Die Jugend des Landes steht unter dem enormen Druck, sich an die ethnischen und religiösen Muster des Landes anpassen zu müssen. Zenica, März 2015

108+113 An Zweigen hängende Abfälle zeigen den Pegel an, den die Bosna während der Überschwemmungen vom Frühjahr 2015 erreichte. Maglaj, März 2015

109/12 Fahrt durch eine Landschaft kahler Bäume. In der Nähe von Srebrenica, März 2013

115 Eine Drina Zigaretten-schachtel mit einer dreisprachigen Warnaufschrift. Seit dem Konflikt wurde die serbokroatische Sprache zu Bosnisch, Kroatisch und Serbisch. Travnik, Oktober 2014

117 Zweige treiben im tiefen Gewässer der Drina, die einen Großteil der Grenze zwischen Bosnien und Serbien bildet. In der Nähe von Goražde, November 2013

118/19 Ein neuer Morgen dämmert am Ufer der Drina. Goražde, November 2013

120/21 Zenica, eine Industriestadt bekannt für ihre Braunkohle und Stahlindustrie. Zenica, April 2014

123 Nedim, 28 Jahre alt. In der Nähe von Srebrenica, März 2013

125 Monument zum Gedenken an die Schlacht von Sutjeska, die im Zweiten Weltkrieg stattfand. Viele Bosnier fühlen eine Sehnsucht nach Titos Regierungszeit. Tjentište, November 2013

126 Ein Bild von Hong Kong auf einer Plane gedruckt oder der Traum von besseren Zeiten. Sarajevo, November 2013

127 Eldar 26 Jahre alt. Tuzla, März 2015

129 *Madame Vigée-Lebrun und ihre Tochter.* Auf einer Schokoladenschachtel gedruckt, wurde die Abbildung sorgfältig passend ausgeschnitten. Srebrenik, in November 2013

130/31 Stadtansicht von der Dachterrasse des Awaz Turms, des höchsten Gebäudes des Landes. Sarajevo, November 2013

137 Stillleben mit Apfel, Orangen und Granatapfel. Mostar, November 2013

133/34 Im Oktober 2013 wurde eines der größten Massengräber des Bosnienkriegs durch das ICMP (International Commission of Missing Persons) in der Nähe des Dorfes Tomašica entdeckt. Im November 2013 wurden bereits 430 sterbliche Überreste exhumiert. Westbosnien, November 2013

135/36 Dieses Bild ist nicht in der Lage, den unaufhörlichen Lärm der Bagger wiederzugeben. Genau hinter uns liegt das Massengrab. In der Nähe von Tomašica, November 2013

139 Jasmina, 32 Jahre alt. Tuzla, November 2013

140 Nachtwanderung. Mostar, November 2014

141 “In einem Regime politischer Repression, bleibt einem nur die Privatsphäre als einziger Rückzugsort. Leute fühlen sich im öffentlichen Raum nicht wohl. Sie bleiben zu Hause eingeschlossen und leben nebeneinander.” - Selma, 31 Jahre alt. Tuzla Oktober 2013

143 Riss in der Straße. Mostar, November 2014

145 Anita, 22 Jahre alt. Mostar, November 2013

146 Blühender Baum im Neretva Tal. In der Nähe von Mostar, März 2013

Stéphanie Borcard und **Nicolas Métraux** sind zwei Schweizer Fotografen die in Bangkok, Thailand leben und arbeiten. Ihre persönlichen Projekten werden oft durch ihre Reisen und zugleich durch die Beziehung zwischen dem Einzelnen und der Gesellschaft beeinflußt. Triebkraft ihres Wirkens ist der Wunsch nach einem besseren Verständnis und einer ständigen Infragestellung der Welt.

Diese Fotografien sind das Ergebnis von vier Reisen nach Bosnien und Herzegowina zwischen Frühjahr 2013 und Frühjahr 2015. Die Bilder wurden im ganzen Land aufgenommen, von der Weite zu engen Zimmer. *Grey Skies Black Birds* wäre nie entstanden, wenn in einem Café an einem typisch kalten und feuchtem Winter-Nachmittag, so bekannt in der Schweiz, ein Fremder nicht ein Gespräch angefangen hätte.

Danke Šaban uns in Dein Land eingeladen zu haben.

Saša Stanišić

L'usine

Dans la tempête de neige, sur le plateau, ma voiture pirouette et se retrouve dans le fossé, déjà des petites mains martèlent les vitres, hommes vêtus de peaux de loups, en survêtements Puma, ils m'escortent jusqu'à une ferme non loin de la route, une baraque, la cheminée docile, ils font chauffer de l'eau pour le thé, ils m'approvisionnent de barres de *Mars* et le breuvage sent le mouton. Nous sommes les bergers, disent-ils, nous voilà.

Grands, les yeux des bergers, ne veulent rien savoir de moi.

Ne veulent rien savoir, ces bergers, mais veulent parler d'une bâtisse, elle s'est, il y a un bout de temps, raclé la gorge, elle hésite.

L'usine, disent les bergers, derrière les sapins, là-bas. Les bergers montrent par la fenêtre, la vitre est couverte de buée, le plus petit d'entre eux se dresse sur la pointe des pieds, il la frotte de sa manche et tout ce que l'on pourrait voir, la tempête de neige l'emporte dans son souffle.

Je demande : Qu'est-ce que cela veut dire, hésiter, et comment des bâtisses font-elles pour se racler la gorge, c'est une blague ?

Nous l'avons entendu, disent les bergers, nous y étions. Abrités du vent derrière les murs de l'usine, nous étions en train de jouer aux cartes. Ils ne se font pas prier pour faire entendre le bruit de gorge que cela a fait, brusque, métal, disent-ils, brusque, métal, ils grondent dans le porte-voix de leurs mains, et cela ne t'aide pas à te représenter quoi que ce soit

Les lignes de vie des bergers faites de terre.

Depuis, l'usine hésite, disent les bergers. Depuis, le haut plateau attend, et attendent aussi le brouillard et le vent, les bergers et leur neige, ils attendent ce qui doit suivre.

Ils disent : nous allons te conduire jusqu'à elle.

Jusqu'à qui, je le leur demande.

Jusqu'à notre usine. Les bergers trempent des *Mars* dans leur thé.

Je n'y tiens pas, réponds-je.

Les bergers se consultent, discutent en se cachant derrière leurs mains. Le plus petit grimpe sur mes genoux. Il chante doucement, il joue avec mon col. C'est une chanson enfantine, une de ces chansons anciennes, violentes, pleines de faute et de châtiment, et au moment où j'entonne moi aussi le refrain, il s'interrompt et me montre les crocs.

Les bergers ont mis leurs bonnets, nous voilà déjà en train d'avancer pas à pas dans la neige, les chiens labourent la neige devant nous, les moutons trottinent derrière nous, des moutons dans la neige, que font-ils donc là, le tintement de leurs cloches nous réchauffe.

Le vent, le vent, le vent, je m'arcboute contre son front de neige, flocons, l'intempérie ne semble affecter que moi, les bergers se contentent de porter leurs mains à hauteur de leurs yeux comme des soldats saluant. Le vent souffle en permanence sur ce plateau élevé et aride, disent-ils, mensonge, les souffles de tous les Serbes, Bosniaques, Croates qui ont un jour sur le Mont Romanija soupiré, aimé, porté leur deuil, s'y entrelacent à tout jamais, ajoutent-ils.

Ils ne le disent pas tout à fait ainsi, les bergers.

Dans la forêt, la marche est plus facile, les arbres contrecarrent la force du vent, sapins, noirs et invincibles comme la chanson enfantine. Je demande aux bergers s'il y a des mines, l'un d'eux me lance une boule de neige, elle me frappe si fort la poitrine que je sens mon cœur.

Les barbes des bergers, aiguilles de pins.

Sur le Mont Romanija, une bâtisse s'est raclé la gorge et depuis, hésite, une grande bâtisse rectangulaire en lisière de forêt, murs de béton nus, deux ou trois sacs de gravats éventrés, une scie rouillée, un trou dans un seau, des billots de bois, du grillage. Un petit poste de radio hors d'âge se tait dans les débris. Le plus petit des bergers court sur la neige comme s'il n'y avait pas de neige, il jubile, joie et peur mêlées, au milieu des chiens hurlants, il disparaît derrière les murs.

Les têtes des bergers se bercent sur leurs cous noueux.

Les bergers racontent : il était prévu qu'ici l'eau soit mise en bouteille et préparée pour être expédiée. Le shérif, dit-on, avait dans les parages découvert deux sources, avait sollicité des aides de l'Europe, les avait obtenues, pour les terrains, pour les fontaines, pour l'usine d'embouteillage, et ainsi de suite. Le shérif, parce qu'il portait toujours un chapeau et des jeans de ce genre, un Amerloque, disent-ils, un Serbe, disent-ils.

Une femme, dit l'un d'eux, des seins.

Le ricanement carieux des bergers.

Peu de temps après la guerre, ou bien en 2000. C'est une entreprise du coin qui avait eu le contrat de construction, le shérif avait embauché lui-même des ouvriers dans les villages avoisinants. Des emplois, du capital, renaissance de l'économie, énumèrent les bergers en chœur et ils crachent dans la neige. A chaque virgule, l'un d'eux tousse. A chaque point, l'un d'eux s'assied dans l'herbe près des murs. Il n'y a pas de neige à proximité de l'usine. Les signes de ponctuation s'abattent comme neige sur ce vert improbable.

Et un beau jour, le chef de chantier ne vient pas sur le chantier. Les ouvriers ne perçoivent plus de salaire. Les agriculteurs ne touchent pas le loyer promis pour la mise à disposition de leur terrain. Les fournisseurs de matériaux de construction qui avaient livré de confiance leurs matériaux après une maigre avance ne voient plus venir aucun autre paiement. Le shérif ne répondait plus au téléphone, et bientôt, la ligne fut muette.

Les sourcils des bergers, cristaux de glace.

Six mois après la disparition du shérif, l'Europe se présenta en personne pour se faire une idée de la situation. Les bergers crachent.

Leur salive couleur chocolat.

Les bergers avaient aménagé l'usine pour leurs parties de cartes, les moutons se régalaient de la verdure qui poussait ici en surabondance, comme si un dieu bienveillant avait engraissé le sol, dans cet endroit où leur dieu afflige le pays tout entier de pierraille. L'Europe, les bergers l'avaient accueillie comme il se doit – leurs moutons avaient des heures durant bloqué les routes menant à l'usine.

L'Europe avait poliment refusé les *Mars* et était repartie vers l'Europe, ébranlée.

Les bergers ont appris que l'Europe avait effectué sur le compte du shérif quatre des six versements prévus avant de suspendre ses paiements. Les bergers ne mentionnent pas la somme, ils se contentent de se caresser le menton du pouce et de l'index.

Le plus petit des bergers dépiaute un *Mars*, ses mains, son visage, ridés comme l'écorce des sapins. Il me fait signe de m'approcher et me fait franchir l'absence de portail pour entrer dans l'usine. Nous pénétrons dans un bruissement estival d'air chaud, les mouches s'affairent et bruissent autour de nous.
A l'endroit où devraient se trouver des fenêtres, béances. A l'endroit où devraient se trouver des planchers, terre. Nuages à l'endroit où manque la moitié du toit. Plantes grimpantes à l'endroit où devraient serpenter des tuyauteries ; une usine se dresse inachevée sur le Mont Romanija, elle hésite. Inachevée et nue, ne servant qu'aux bergers et à leurs bêtes, refuge, quand la tempête les chasse, une table en plastique sur laquelle ils jouent au rami.

Les grands yeux des bergers : Regarde, étranger, autour de toi.

Des oiseaux migrateurs ont serti leurs nids dans les murailles. Un lézard tourne autour d'un lézard. Au milieu de l'usine deux bergers empilent des pierres pour édifier des petites tours, rigolant comme des amoureux. Ou bien pleurent-ils ? Je les interroge et ils me répondent que les premiers habitants des lieux, qui du haut de ces monts regardèrent le monde aride à leurs pieds, étaient des Illyriens, « des bergers comme nous autres, rudes et graves ».

Ils ne le disent pas tout à fait ainsi, les bergers. Ils ne disent d'ailleurs rien de plus, ils ne me donnent pas d'histoire.

Le plus petit des bergers est de nouveau près de moi. Nous connaissons, murmure-t-il, toutes les sources du Mont Romanija. Tu dois, eau, être bien vigoureuse pour réussir à te frayer de haute lutte un chemin au travers de notre roche et pour t'élever – il met un genou à terre – et rusée, en plus, puisque nous ne t'avons pas depuis déjà longtemps découverte.

Il sent si fort le chocolat que je suis obligé de me détourner. Les autres ont enlevé leurs peaux et jouent au rami, l'usine regarde et fabrique le doute.

Ici, les bergers ont peut-être dégagé la neige ?

Les clochettes des moutons tintinnabulent doucement dans le bois.

Je parle la langue des bergers, mais je ne comprends pas ce qu'ils comprennent.

L'un d'eux s'occupe des chiens, il dégage en s'aidant de graisse à traire la glace incrustée dans leurs pattes.

Un autre, dans un coin, arrose des pommes de terre. Il y a soixante-treize ans jour pour jour, s'exclame-t-il, mon grand-père, avec la Première Brigade Prolétarienne, a été encerclé par les Allemands sur le Mont Romanija. Alors, la Brigade s'est mise en route à travers neige et glace, elle a franchi le plateau et a continué, gravissant le cruel Igman par moins trente. Une colonne de partisans, chantant, dit le berger, et un autre lui demande comment il sait qu'ils chantaient.

Les téléphones portables des bergers et leurs antennes en aluminium, qu'ils ont bricolées eux-mêmes ; ils ont plein réseau là où je ne reçois rien du tout.

Le plus petit des bergers grimpe sur une échelle en chantant, il chante plus fort qu'auparavant, voix de vieille femme, rêche et douce à la fois :

Par une froide nuit d'hiver là-haut sur la montagne
Tout caché par la neige, le ruisselet gelé.
Un lièvre cherche l'eau, où s'en est-elle allée ?
Se serait-elle perdue ? Fâcheux assurément !

Et le brave animal mainte larme répand,
Il pleure à chaudes larmes,
Toujours plus indécis, son ruisselet pleurant :
Y eut-il donc jamais un ruisselet ici ? - Lièvre se sent berné.
S'est-il comme les oiseaux vers le Sud envolé ?

Les chiens alertes des bergers jouent à s'entr'égorger, je dois leur laisser place et m'écarter, c'est comme si je n'étais pas du tout nécessaire.

Les dents des bergers, jaunes comme l'été.

Le plus petit des bergers est perché sur l'échelon le plus haut et taille les roses trémières. On m'a abandonné.

J'ai entendu dire que sur le massif karstique qui a nom Romanija, entre d'arides blocs de calcaire et des tumulus de moellons, tombes pour les bergers illyriens et pour les partisans yougoslaves, il y a une usine. Elle a donné naissance à quelques rêves humbles. Les bergers ont prêté l'oreille quand elle s'est raclé la gorge, ils sont les gardiens de son hésitation.

Saša Stanišić, né en 1978 à Višegrad, Yougoslavie, écrivain, essayiste et journaliste, est l'auteur de deux romans. Le premier, "Le soldat et le gramophone" (2006), a été traduit en 32 langues. Le deuxième, "Avant la fête", a remporté le prix du Salon du livre de Leipzig en 2014.

Traduit par Françoise Toraille

Srećko Latal

La stabilisation de la Bosnie-Herzégovine : un processus impossible ?

Deux décennies se sont écoulées depuis la fin de la guerre qui a dévasté la Bosnie-Herzégovine. Deux décennies qui ont fait d'un pays marqué par le conflit dont il sortait un pays moderne et tourné vers l'Europe. Mais cette reconstruction a d'une façon ou d'une autre été entravée et le pays est aujourd'hui sur le point de se démanteler ou de devenir un état en déliquescence. L'intensification des conflits politiques locaux, le durcissement des positions dans la région et les nouvelles tensions à l'échelle mondiale dessinent les contours d'une évolution complexe et pleine de dangers pour le devenir de la Bosnie-Herzégovine. L'enjeu est essentiel : l'avenir de ce pays déstabilisé aura un impact majeur sur l'avenir de l'ensemble de la région des Balkans.

Les accords de paix de Dayton qui ont mis fin à la guerre en 1995 et établi le nouveau cadre constitutionnel de la Bosnie-Herzégovine ont partagé le pays entre trois principaux groupes ethniques - les Bosniaques (pour la plupart musulmans), les Croates (majoritairement catholiques) et les Serbes (principalement de religion orthodoxe) -, créant deux entités politiques autonomes ; la Fédération de Bosnie-et-Herzégovine, peuplée majoritairement de Bosniaques et Croates, et la République serbe (Republika Srpska), territoire principalement serbe. Le pays accueille également un certain nombre de minorités comme des Italiens, des Tchèques ou des Polonais ainsi que d'autres communautés ou encore des populations qui, pour différentes raisons, refusent d'être assimilés à l'un des trois principaux groupes constitutifs du pays. Or, de nombreux citoyens de la Bosnie-Herzégovine affichent encore des points de vue conflictuels sur le passé, l'état actuel et l'avenir de leur pays.

Pendant de nombreuses années, les conséquences des objectifs divergents des trois blocs politico-ethniques ont pu être enrayées par une présence militaire forte des puissances étrangères ainsi que par une pression diplomatique et financière soutenue, ce qui a permis de stabiliser le pays et d'assurer une rapide et efficace reconstruction d'après-guerre. La diplomatie occidentale et les organisations internationales sont intervenues de plus en plus profondément dans les structures légales de la Bosnie-Herzégovine, mettant en place et favorisant des réformes dans l'ensemble des secteurs, qu'il s'agisse de la sécurité ou des domaines politique, économique, social, culturel, etc. Nombre de ces réformes furent une véritable réussite, comme l'unification des forces armées du pays ou celle des systèmes fiscal et d'imposition. Néanmoins, nombre d'autres initiatives, ainsi celles portant sur la réforme de la police, du système judiciaire ou des médias, furent entravées dès le début par les oppositions locales et les maladresses internationales. L'Occident a fini par se lasser et par envisager son désengagement. En 2006, les États-Unis tentèrent - sans succès - de faire réviser le cadre constitutionnel instauré par Dayton, jugé complexe et coûteux, puis finirent par réduire leur présence sur le territoire bosnien, laissant à l'Union européenne le soin d'exercer un rôle de contrôle. Ignorant les signes de regain de radicalisation chez les politiciens locaux, l'Occident décida qu'il était temps de cesser d'intervenir dans la politique intérieure de cette région et de remettre l'avenir du pays entre les mains des dirigeants locaux. Cependant, supprimer la supervision et l'influence de la communauté internationale alors que la société n'avait encore connu qu'une fragile reconstruction et n'était pas encore préparée aux défis qui l'attendaient permit aux politiciens de réaffirmer leurs pratiques autocratiques, intransigeantes et centrées sur leurs propres intérêts. Depuis lors, la Bosnie-Herzégovine sombre progressivement à nouveau dans le marasme économique, politique et social.

Aujourd'hui, les dirigeants des trois communautés politico-ethniques du pays nourrissent les mêmes intentions nationalistes que leurs prédécesseurs pendant et au lendemain de la guerre, affirmant les mêmes prétentions maximalistes. Les dirigeants serbes de Bosnie brandissent toujours la menace de la séparation de la République serbe (Republika Srpska) du reste du pays, les politiciens croates restent focalisés sur la création d'une entité croate de Bosnie propre et les Bosniaques musulmans veulent un pays centralisé tout en se rapprochant progressivement des cercles économiques et politiques turcs et saoudiens. Le pays reste soumis à la constitution complexe mise en place après les accords de paix de Dayton, mais sans les pouvoirs exécutifs accordés au Bureau du Haut-Représentant (BHR), désormais inutile en raison du manque de soutien de la communauté internationale, un nombre croissant d'articles de cette constitution sont ignorés et spoliés de leur valeur par les élites politiques, ce qui contribue au dysfonctionnement croissant du système.

Un système politique pyramidal

Prenant pour prétexte la nécessité de protéger leurs intérêts ethniques, idéologiques ou politiques, les hommes politiques ont en réalité pour principale préoccupation de renforcer la présence de leur parti sur la scène politique et de se partager le gâteau, notamment par l'attribution de sièges à divers niveaux du gouvernement et la nomination de membres de leur parti au sein d'entreprises, agences ou autres institutions publiques. Les partis en question et leurs représentants tirent ainsi un profit maximum des vaches à lait que constituent ces entreprises et les dirigeants peuvent compter sur la loyauté de ces membres (et sur celle de leurs proches) ainsi nommés afin de renforcer leurs positions dans les différents partis.

En reproduisant et en élargissant ce système à chaque cycle électoral, la scène politique du pays est progressivement devenue au fil du temps un vaste et complexe système pyramidal, tirant parti des craintes interethniques et d'un cadre constitutionnel et légal obscur afin de garantir sa pérennité, mais sans atteindre dans les services publics une efficacité répondant aux besoins de la population. Les partis d'opposition ont beau jeu de critiquer de manière véhémente ceux qui sont au pouvoir et de les accuser de corruption et d'abus du système, mais lorsqu'ils accèdent au pouvoir, on observe chez eux les mêmes postures et la même façon d'agir, jusqu'à ce qu'ils soient remplacés à leur tour. Puis ils attendent que l'électorat soit déçu des opposants, oublie les erreurs de leur mandat et leur rende sa faveur lors des élections suivantes. Ce comportement politique, que l'on observe dans presque tous les partis, a contribué à créer une sorte de mouvement perpétuel, cercle politique vicieux qu'aucun acteur de la scène locale ou internationale ne sait comment briser ou changer.

Des politiciens à l'image d'un pays

Si les responsables d'une telle situation sont évidemment les élites politiques, leur attitude est néanmoins le reflet de l'atmosphère générale qui plane sur la société toute entière. La plupart des médias locaux se répartissent également selon des lignes de partage qui suivent des axes ethniques, politiques, ou appuient le jeu des intérêts personnels. Leurs méthodes, guidées par le souci du sensationnel, ignorant l'impartialité et le professionnalisme, reflètent souvent des orientations politiques particulières et les élites politiques s'appuient volontiers dessus pour leurs règlements de comptes publics.

Les ONG et le milieu universitaire quant à eux se concentrent sur leurs intérêts immédiats, souvent liés à des projets financés par l'aide internationale ou par le gouvernement, sans se préoccuper des bénéfices qu'elles apportent - ou non - à la population. Et celle-ci, face à l'absence de perspectives différentes et au manque d'initiatives, est devenue - ou demeure - léthargique et désabusée au point de préférer s'accommoder de l'état actuel d'un pays en faillite, de quitter le pays ou de survivre dans un tel système plutôt que de chercher à y apporter des changements.

Les violences de 2014

En février 2014 éclata une série de manifestations violentes, conséquence de la colère, de la frustration et du sentiment d'insatisfaction générale de la population et résultant de l'accumulation d'éléments explosifs : les jeux politiques à somme nulle, la corruption endémique, la dégradation constante des conditions économiques et sociales. Un tel niveau de violence n'avait pas été atteint depuis la fin de la guerre : bâtiments officiels en flammes, voitures retournées, affrontements entre la police et les casseurs venus se mêler aux manifestants, des scènes qui ont choqué le pays et la communauté internationale, mais ont aussi suscité l'espoir d'un engagement citoyen plus important et encouragé la mise en place d'une nouvelle initiative européenne pour le pays. Les plénums de citoyens, sorte de mouvement de démocratie de rue ayant émergé lors des manifestations de février, s'éteignirent progressivement sous l'effet des divergences et dissensions internes. Néanmoins, le mouvement de contestation s'est poursuivi tout au long de l'année dans l'ensemble du pays et il semble que leur nombre et leur intensité se soient accrus depuis la fin de 2014. En raison de leur caractère épars et de l'absence d'une organisation ou d'objectifs communs, ces manifestations sont pour la plupart perçues comme des évènements isolés, et sont ainsi généralement ignorées par les politiciens ainsi que par la population. Cependant, dans un contexte de misère sociale et économique persistante, ce mouvement de protestation n'en demeure pas moins une bombe à retardement menaçant de conduire à tout moment à de nouvelles explosions de violence.

Les inondations catastrophiques de 2014

S'ajoutant à la somme des problèmes du pays, la Bosnie-Herzégovine connut également en 2014 une série d'inondations et de glissements de terrain d'une ampleur exceptionnelle causés par les pluies diluviennes survenues tout au long du printemps et de l'été. Rapidement qualifiées de catastrophe naturelle majeure de l'histoire récente du pays, ces pluies torrentielles endommagèrent ou détruisirent des immeubles d'habitation, des résidences particulières, des usines et des cultures. Les routes, voies ferroviaires ainsi que les réseaux d'eau et d'électricité ne furent pas épargnés, et les dommages furent estimés à plus de deux milliards d'euros, soit plus de 10 % du PIB du pays.

En revanche, la catastrophe mit à jour de façon inattendue un aspect plus positif du pays dévasté. Alors que les rivières en crue et les torrents de boue ravageaient le pays, les habitants de Bosnie-Herzégovine se précipitèrent pour aider leurs voisins, sans s'arrêter aux différences d'ethnie, de religion ou d'affiliation politique. Pendant que la plupart des institutions gouvernementales observaient sans réagir la catastrophe s'abattant sur le pays, les villes et villages faisaient appel à l'aide de leur voisins les plus proches, qui appartenaient bien souvent aux communautés situées de l'autre côté des lignes de démarcation ethno-nationales. À l'aide de canots pneumatiques, d'engins de chantier et de matériel de construction, les voisins mobilisés entreprirent d'endiguer les inondations puis offrirent nourriture et abris provisoires à ceux qui avaient été forcés de fuir leur domicile. Une façon pour les citoyens de Bosnie-Herzégovine de montrer leur côté humain, et même leur nature profonde, ce qui donne l'espoir qu'un jour le pays puisse enfin connaître paix et prospérité.

Une population vieillissante

La crise politique et le ralentissement économique et social ont également entraîné au cours des dernières années un dépeuplement du pays à grande échelle. Plusieurs études ont révélé que pas moins de 60 % de la population – ainsi qu'un taux spectaculaire de 80 % parmi les jeunes - seraient prêts à quitter le pays immédiatement s'ils le pouvaient. Nombreux sont ceux qui ont trouvé les moyens de mettre en œuvre ce projet ces dernières années, laissant derrière eux des villages entiers abandonnés par les familles parties à la recherche d'un avenir meilleur dans les autres pays des Balkans ou dans d'autres pays étrangers. Avec une baisse du taux de natalité et une hausse du taux de mortalité constantes, auxquelles s'ajoutent une diminution des mariages et un nombre croissant de divorces, la Bosnie-Herzégovine affiche une des tendances démographiques les plus négatives de la région. Entre 2009 et 2012, la population est passée de 3,84 millions d'habitants à 3,83 millions et selon les premiers résultats du recensement de 2013, le pays ne compte plus désormais que 3,79 millions d'habitants.

Une étude menée par la Croix-Rouge affirme que dans les 35 prochaines années, la Bosnie-Herzégovine pourrait bien devenir le pays des Balkans présentant le vieillissement de population le plus marqué. Une tendance démographique aussi extrême implique également des conséquences négatives concrètes en termes d'avenir économique de la Bosnie-Herzégovine, notamment lorsque l'on sait qu'actuellement, le nombre de retraités a presque déjà rattrapé le nombre d'actifs.

Une crise politique qui s'intensifie

L'absence de contrôle de la communauté internationale et d'une surveillance au niveau local ont entraîné une radicalisation progressive de la scène politique qui se poursuit de nos jours. La crise politique s'est encore aggravée lors du mandat gouvernemental de 2010-2014 avec un véritable effondrement du paysage politique sous le coup d'intenses affrontements entre et au sein des trois blocs ethno-politiques. Cette période vit des alliances se faire et se défaire entre les partis politiques parfois du jour au lendemain ou d'une semaine à l'autre. Une telle instabilité a provoqué un blocage pour ainsi dire complet des corps exécutif et législatif à différents niveaux de l'administration, affaiblissant en parallèle les principes de la démocratie et du pluralisme au sein des principaux partis. Ceux-ci se retrouvèrent alors sous le contrôle exclusif de leurs dirigeants et de leurs plus proches lieutenants.

Les espoirs qu'un système politique stable soit rétabli à la suite des élections générales d'octobre 2014 se sont finalement évanouis face aux problèmes procéduraux et à la persistance des jeux de pouvoir politiques qui ont une fois de plus retardé la formation de nouveaux gouvernements. La formation de nouvelles coalitions gouvernementales a nécessité presque six mois à certains échelons administratifs, mais la plupart se sont affaiblies ou effondrées en raison des éternels jeux de pouvoir politiques et de tactiques centrées sur les intérêts personnels.

Au milieu de l'année 2015, la Bosnie-Herzégovine semblait avoir atteint le seuil critique de la crise qui la touche. Le président de la Republika Srpska, Milorad Dodik, a proposé à nouveau la mise en place d'un référendum qui se tiendra à la fin de l'année afin de remettre en question l'autorité de l'appareil judiciaire de l'État et du Bureau du Haut-Représentant. On craint que ce référendum puisse ouvrir la voie à une nouvelle déstabilisation politique et interethnique du pays et de la région toute entière. En attendant, les réformes économiques et sociales initialement approuvées par l'Union européenne et le Fond monétaire international (FMI) demeurent bloquées. Faute d'avoir respecté la date limite de la fin juin accordée par le FMI, le pays se trouve désormais privé de toute aide internationale. La plupart des échelons administratifs vont par conséquent se retrouver devant des caisses vides, entraînant le pays dans une crise de liquidités certaine. Face à cette propagation de la crise, la communauté internationale observe, sans savoir s'il faut intervenir ni comment.

Une situation qui s'aggrave à l'échelle régionale et mondiale

Comme si l'état de la situation à l'échelle du pays n'était pas suffisamment grave, la Bosnie-Herzégovine est depuis ces dernières années de plus en plus touchée par le contexte régional et international qui se détériore, contribuant ainsi à un renouveau de la radicalisation et un durcissement des positions à la fois en Croatie et en Serbie. Le pays lutte également contre l'influence grandissante de la Russie et de groupes islamistes radicaux pendant que l'Occident reste divisé sans prendre conscience des signes inquiétants émanant de la Bosnie-Herzégovine. L'Union européenne marque peu d'empressement à assumer la responsabilité d'un rôle politique plus important et persiste à tenter d'apporter des solutions techniques aux problèmes structuraux du pays – approche qui avait déjà échoué dans le passé et présente les mêmes faiblesses qu'auparavant. Certains représentants américains dénoncent de plus en plus fermement ces signes inquiétants, néanmoins, la politique extérieure des États-Unis n'affiche aucune solution quant à la situation en Bosnie-Herzégovine et continue à se satisfaire de voir l'Union européenne assumer le rôle clef, ce qui lui permet de se concentrer sur ses propres priorités.

Des perspectives incertaines

La crise politique qui se prolonge en Bosnie-Herzégovine a retardé et inversé les processus de réformes, paralysant les structures économiques et sociales du pays et bloquant son engagement sur la voie de l'intégration européenne. Le fonctionnement des lois, des systèmes et des institutions du pays a été ralenti ou suspendu à divers niveaux administratifs. En parallèle, le contexte régional et international qui se détériore menace de multiplier les tensions et divisions internes dans le pays. Cet enchevêtrement de difficultés internes et internationales débouche sur une situation de crise d'une ampleur extrême et qui se révèle plus importante, plus difficile à résoudre et potentiellement plus dangereuse que la simple somme de ses éléments constitutifs. Cette situation réellement inquiétante pourrait encore s'aggraver d'ici la fin 2015 et il semble que seule l'autorité internationale ait la capacité de mettre fin au démantèlement de la Bosnie-Herzégovine et de protéger une fois encore l'intégrité territoriale et constitutionnelle du pays. Cependant, la communauté internationale ignore encore largement les dangers croissants qui agitent la région des Balkans et demeure préoccupée par d'autres problèmes d'ordre international, abandonnant ainsi la Bosnie-Herzégovine à une perspective incertaine.

Srećko Latal, né à Sarajevo, est un journaliste et analyste politique qui a couvert les conflits dans les Balkans et en Afghanistan pour l'Associated Press (AP). Il a ensuite travaillé pour l'International Crisis Group (ICG) et le Balkans Investigative Reporting Network (BIRN). Ses articles ont été publiés dans le New York Times, le Guardian, et dans d'autres médias internationaux.

Traduit par Sylvain Gourjaud

Christian Caujolle

Postface

Au XXème siècle, avant notre immersion dans un flux d'images indifférenciées que nous ne sommes plus capables de percevoir, de lire, de comprendre tant elles sont nombreuses, la photographie inscrivit de la mémoire dans les sels d'argent. Mémoire de moments familiaux, de visages, de paysages, de voyages, d'anecdotes mais également de faits et d'événements historiques.

C'est également au XXème siècle, sur sa fin, qu'eut lieu le siège de Sarajevo, le plus long de l'histoire de la guerre moderne, qui fit au moins 10 000 morts. Durant ce siège des photographes, mais aussi des habitants, prirent des photographies, les diffusèrent, les échangèrent, certaines furent publiées, dans la presse, dans des livres, elles donnèrent parfois lieu à des expositions. En avons-nous encore le souvenir ? Pas certain, tant d'autres images d'autres actualités tragiques, à un rythme de plus en plus rapide, viennent chasser les anciennes et se substituer à elles. Car telle est, aujourd'hui, la question centrale : face à l'abondance des images qui se heurtent, circulent de plus en plus vite, remplacent les précédentes dans un spectacle de ce qu'il devient difficile de qualifier d'information, allons-nous vers un monde dans lequel la mémoire s'efface au moment où elle devrait se constituer ? Et, au-delà, irions-nous vers un monde pour lequel la mémoire ne serait plus ni une valeur ni une nécessité ?

La mémoire humaine est fragile, souvent partielle et dépendante des émotions qui la fondent. Elle varie avec le temps, se modifie, s'estompe, se confronte aux nostalgies et aux tentations de la fiction au fur et à mesure que celui qui la porte s'éloigne de l'instant qui la constitua. Elle n'a rien d'objectif. Elle n'est, en cela, guère différente de la photographie qui se donne, parce qu'elle ne saurait exister sans le réel qui la précède et qui sera caduc dès la fin de la prise de vue, une apparence de réalisme sur lequel s'est constituée une crédulité collective en sa supposée « vérité ». Mémoire et photographie ont en commun d'être des témoignages – des bribes documentaires – qui, sauf lorsque ceux qui les portent affabulent ou ont choisi le champ de la fiction, opèrent comme les déclencheurs de reconstitutions de ce qui fut, d'un avant de leur propre existence. Des témoignages subjectifs. Totalement dépendants des conditions vécues de leur constitution.

L'histoire de la photographie est riche des démarches mémorielles, des dispositifs, en plusieurs temps, destinés à réactiver ou questionner, sur la base de l'émotion vécue au moment des événements ou parce que des images les ont gravés dans nos souvenirs, l'évolution des choses. Retourner sur le site d'un conflit chaque année,
tous les dix ans, à l'occasion d'un anniversaire, rechercher les traces que la nature et l'activité humaine font peu à peu disparaître, constater que ce qui fut n'est plus ou reste visible est à la fois une expérience et la tentative de lutter contre l'oubli.

Cependant, au moment où nous sommes de plus en plus conscients des limites de l'image – tout autant que de son impact et de sa place centrale dans notre société – quelle démarche adopter ? Celle qui consiste à accumuler des documents pour les mettre en relation au service d'une conviction ou d'une thèse est vouée à l'échec de toutes les approches qui cherchent à prouver, à démontrer avec la photographie. Il s'avère alors indispensable de retourner à ce qui fonde la nature même de cette catégorie d'images inventées au XIXème siècle pour – quelle illusion ! – *reproduire de la façon la plus exacte et la plus précise* : l'expérience du terrain. Capable d'enregistrer, puis de restituer et transmettre un point de vue, la photographie nous met d'abord en relation avec la mémoire de ce que vécurent les auteurs des images. Dès lors qu'ils ont été capables de trouver la forme pertinente pour que nous ressentions ce qu'ils veulent partager avec nous, les photographes nous laissent percevoir que ce que nous regardons n'existe plus. Cette mémoire, *par nature*, impose de manière diffuse un sentiment de temps qui se croisent, se chevauchent, s'imbriquent, opèrent en oubliant le rythme de l'horloge un balancement entre un avant et l'instant non de la prise de vue mais de mon regard en action. Je regarde une photographie et lui confère du présent et, implicitement, je sais qu'elle me renvoie au passé.

A l'aune de l'histoire, le siège de Sarajevo c'était hier, c'était il y a très peu de temps, cet épisode tragique fait partie de notre histoire. De notre histoire en partie déjà gommée de la plupart des mémoires de nos contemporains. Et pourtant, il suffit que des images et quelques mots viennent frapper nos yeux pour que, étrange processus, nous réactivions des images d'hier. L'émotion d'aujourd'hui face à des ciels, des arbres, des paysages, des visages dont on nous dit qu'ils ont été vus en Bosnie-Herzégovine aujourd'hui fait œuvre de mémoire. Simplement parce que le propos n'est pas de décrire, de démontrer, de donner à comprendre, d'expliquer. Mais simplement d'inscrire au fond de nos yeux des visions rencontrées, entrevues puis organisées, des évocations dont les teintes, dans leur subtilité musicale, imposent une temporalité qui nous arrête net alors que tout, autour de nous, s'agite et disparaît.

Des images fixes mais traversées de vibrations qui viennent nourrir la mémoire. Elles sont elles-mêmes une nouvelle mémoire, d'aujourd'hui, alors que ce qu'elles nous donnent à voir n'est déjà plus. Hier, aujourd'hui, demain peut-être coagulés en un seul instant de regards partagés.

Christian Caujolle est une figure emblématique dans le monde de la photographie. Critique, directeur artistique et curateur de nombreux festivals, il est aussi l'un des fondateurs de l'Agence VU' à Paris.

2/3 Silhouettes dénudées I, II. Srebrenica, mars 2013

4/5 Silhouettes dénudées III, IV. Srebrenica, mars 2013

9 Ibro, 22 ans. Près de Srebrenica, mars 2013

10/11 La nuit tombe sur les collines boisées entourant Srebrenica. Bosnie orientale, mars 2013

12/13 Au col, ancien point stratégique, sur la route qui mène de Sarajevo à Goražde. Bosnie orientale, mars 2015

15 Le rôle des forces de l'ONU durant le conflit (1992-1995) reste très controversé pour la population locale. Zenica, mars 2013

16/17 La fine couche de neige laisse entrevoir la présence d'un sentier forestier. On ne peut s'empêcher de penser aux colonnes de fuyards qui les empruntèrent en tentant d'échapper aux forces serbes lors des événements de juillet 1995. Srebrenica, mars 2013

19/20 Pendant la guerre, cette région abritait le QG du Général Ratko Mladić. Han Pijesak, mars 2013

21 Sur le chemin du retour. Près de Šipovo, mars 2015

23 Meša, 23 ans. Srebrenica, mars 2013

24/25 Kolakovići comptait 271 habitants en 1991. Aujourd'hui, ils ne sont plus que 21. Bosnie orientale, mars 2015

27 Le temps a passé et pourtant personne n'est revenu. Près de Srebrenica, mars 2013

29 Salim, 23 ans. Brakovci, mars 2013

31 En prévision des hivers longs et rigoureux, matelas et couvertures sont soigneusement empilés. Brakovci, mars 2013

32/33 A perte de vue, des collines boisées. Près de la moitié du pays est recouvert d'épaisses forêts. Bosnie orientale, mars 2013

34 Mythes et légendes demeurent ancrés dans l'esprit de la population rurale. Il arrive que l'emplacement d'une fosse commune soit, durant la nuit, révélé aux habitants par de mystérieux chuchotements. Près de Pale, mars 2015

35 Deux décennies se sont écoulées depuis la fin du conflit mais des milliers de personnes sont toujours recherchées par leurs familles. Près de Srebrenica, mars 2013

37/38 Il aura fallu près de dix ans pour que les habitants de Brakovci regagnent leur petit village. La région de Srebrenica fait désormais partie de la Republika Srpska. Bosnie orientale, mars 2013

39 Des maisons dévastées côtoient de nouvelles habitations. Sarajevo, mars 2015

41 Samra, 23 ans. Tuzla, mars 2015

42/43 Des nuages menaçants. Une nuée d'oiseaux prend son envol. Sarajevo, mars 2015

45 Anida, 18 ans. Travnik, avril 2014

46 Graffitis sur les murs d'une salle de classe. Dans la cour, un haut grillage sépare les élèves bosniaques des élèves croates. Travnik, avril 2014

47 Adis, 28 ans. Tuzla, novembre 2013

49 Bois de chauffage collecté et lesté dans la neige. Kupres, mars 2015

50/51 Affiche religieuse à l'entrée de la ville. "J'ai tout fait pour vous, j'ai souffert, j'ai été crucifié et je suis mort sur la croix, pourquoi me maudissez-vous ?" Novi Travnik, mars 2013

53 Scène hivernale sur les rives du lac Klinje. Gacko, mars 2015

54/55 La ville de Gacko sous la neige. Bosnie orientale, mars 2015

57 Il fait froid et tout n'est que mélancolie. Près de Trnovo, mars 2015

58/59 Un panneau commémore la construction du chemin de fer Brčko-Banovići sous le régime de Tito en 1946. Živinice, mars 2015

61 Emil, 32 ans. Banovići, mars 2015

63/64 Petite ville minière au crépuscule. Banovići, mars 2015

65 Poussière de charbon recouvrant le sol. Bien que les mines de fer, de cuivre et de lignite aient fait la fierté du pays sous Tito, elles n'ont qu'une importance limitée dans l'économie actuelle. Banovići, mars 2015

66 Dans une chambre de l'Hôtel Internacional. Zenica, mars 2015

67 Elma, 23 ans. Tešanj, mars à 2015

69 L'absence de perspectives d'avenir pousse de nombreux jeunes à quitter leur pays et à repartir à zéro à l'étranger. Živinice, mars 2015

70 Au cœur de la forêt I. Han Pijesak, mars 2014

71 Au cœur de la forêt II. Han Pijesak, mars 2014

72/73 Au cœur de la forêt III. Han Pijesak, mars 2014

75 Azra, 25 ans. Osmaci, mars 2015

77 Des brindilles percent les dernières neiges. Kupres, mars 2015

79 Dans l'immensité silencieuse des plaines qui furent le théâtre de violents combats. Kupres, mars 2015

80/81 Chevaux sauvages sur le plateau montagneux de Livno. Remplacés par les machines agricoles dans les années 70, ils ont été relâchés dans la nature par les villageois. Près de Livno, mars 2015

83 Après l'hiver. Près de Livno, mars 2015

84+89 Au sud du pays s'étendent des paysages sauvages de maquis. Sud de la Bosnie, mars 2013

85/88 La présence de mines

antipersonnel anéantit la beauté des paysages, les rendant inaccessibles. Près de Trebinje, mars 2013

91 De nombreux pays musulmans financent la construction de nouvelles mosquées. Turbe, avril 2014

92 Les usines métallurgiques sont l'héritage de l'ère précédente : sous Tito, elles furent largement implantées dans toute la Yougoslavie. Lukavac. mars 2013

93 Selon l'interprétation des rêves dans la tradition des Balkans, rêver d'oiseaux signifie que l'on va bientôt recevoir des nouvelles. Près de Travnik, avril 2014

94/95 Le pays ne s'est toujours pas remis des séquelles de la guerre dévastatrice des années 1990. Vitkovići, mars 2015

96/97 Construction d'une église orthodoxe et de nouveaux immeubles en plein centre-ville. Pale, mars 2015

99 Ahmo, 20 ans. Srebrenica, mars 2013

101 Portrait géant du général Ratko Mladić peint sur la façade d'un bâtiment. Considéré comme un héros par certains, Mladić est actuellement jugé pour crimes de guerre devant le Tribunal pénal international pour l'ex-Yougoslavie (TPIY) à La Haye, Pays-Bas. Gacko, novembre 2013

103 Bojan, 30 ans. Banja Luka, novembre 2013

104/5 Travnik au crépuscule. Bosnie centrale, avril 2014

106 Elma 20 ans. Tuzla, mars 2015

107 Appartenance ethnique et orientation religieuse sont des paramètres que subit la jeunesse bosnienne qui est soumise à une énorme pression sociale. Zenica, mars 2015

108+113 Les débris accrochés aux branches rappellent le niveau atteint par la rivière Bosna lors des inondations qui frappèrent le pays au printemps 2015. Maglaj, mars 2015

109/12 Tout autour des arbres dénudés étirent leurs branches. Près de Srebrenica, mars 2013

115 Un paquet de cigarettes Drina portant une notice d'avertissement en trois langues. Depuis le conflit, la langue serbo-croate est divisée en bosnien, croate et serbe. Travnik, octobre 2014

117 Des branches flottent dans les eaux profondes de la Drina. Celle-ci marque une grande partie de la frontière entre la Bosnie et la Serbie. Près de Goražde, novembre 2013

118/19 Un nouveau jour se lève sur les rives de la Drina. Goražde, novembre 2013

120/21 La ville de Zenica connue pour ses industries de charbon et d'acier. Zenica, avril 2014

123 Nedim, 28 ans. Près de Srebrenica, mars 2013

125 Monument commémorant la bataille de Sutjeska qui eut lieu durant la Seconde Guerre mondiale. De nombreux Bosniens sont des nostalgiques du règne de Tito. Tjentište, novembre 2013

126 La ville de Hong Kong imprimée sur une bâche, ou le rêve d'une meilleure situation économique. Sarajevo, novembre 2013

127 Eldar, 26 ans. Tuzla, mars 2015

129 *Madame Vigée-Lebrun et sa fille*. Imprimée sur une boîte de chocolat, l'illustration a été soigneusement découpée. Srebrenik, novembre 2013

130/31 Paysage urbain du sommet de la tour Awaz, le plus haut bâtiment du pays. Sarajevo, novembre 2013

137 Nature morte avec pomme, oranges et grenade. Mostar, novembre 2013

133/34 En octobre 2013, l'un des plus grands charniers de la guerre de Bosnie a été découvert par l'ICMP (Commission internationale des personnes disparues) près du village de Tomašica. En novembre 2013, 430 dépouilles ont été exhumées. Bosnie occidentale, novembre 2013

135/36 Ce paysage innocent est perturbé par le bruit incessant des pelles mécaniques. Derrière nous, s'étend la fosse commune. Près de Tomašica, novembre 2013

139 Jasmina, 32 ans. Tuzla, novembre 2013

140 Promenade nocturne. Mostar, novembre 2014

141 "Quand vous subissez une répression politique, le seul endroit qu'il vous reste est la sphère privée. Les gens ne se sentent pas à l'aise dans les espaces publics. Ils demeurent reclus chez eux, vivant côte à côte." - Selma, 31 ans. Tuzla, octobre 2013

143 Rupture. Mostar, novembre 2014

145 Anita, 22 ans. Mostar, novembre 2013

146 Arbre en fleurs dans la vallée de la Neretva. Près de Mostar, mars 2013

Stéphanie Borcard et **Nicolas Métraux** sont deux photographes suisses basés à Bangkok, Thaïlande. Leurs projets personnels sont souvent influencés à la fois par leurs voyages et par la relation entre l'individu et la société. Ils sont guidés par le désir de mieux comprendre le monde et par l'interrogation permanente à laquelle ils le soumettent.

Ces photographies sont le résultat de quatre séjours en Bosnie-Herzégovine entre les printemps 2013 et 2015. Les images ont été prises dans tout le pays dans des espaces aussi vastes qu'exigus. *Grey Skies Black Birds* n'aurait jamais vu le jour si, lors d'un après-midi d'hiver froid et humide comme la Suisse les connaît si bien, un inconnu, dans un café, n'avait pas engagé la conversation.

Merci Šaban de nous avoir invités à découvrir ton pays.

First published in an edition of 1000 copies
in 2015 by
GOST Books
8a West Smithfield
London EC1A 9JR
info@gostbooks.com
gostbooks.com

GOST Books was founded in 2012 by
Stuart Smith and Gordon MacDonald
to publish photography and visual art
driven by ideas and critical excellence.
For more information about this book
please visit the GOST Books website.

Printed in Italy by EBS
ISBN 978-1-910401-05-7

A GOST Books Production

British Library cataloguing-in-publication
data. A catalogue record of this book is
available from the British Library.

GOST